Growing Up with Bakers Corner

Mary Elizabeth Wilson
A Hamilton County, Indiana, Life

Edited by

Carol Lee Stewart Longenecker
and
Ellen D. Swain

Senior Editor Nancy Niblack Baxter

Hawthorne Publishing
Carmel, Indiana

ISBN: 978-0-9841456-3-8 Softcover
978-0-9841456-4-5 Hardcover

Unless otherwise noted, all photographs are from the collection of Mary Elizabeth Wilson Stewart Robbins.

We'd like to thank all the people who made this book possible, especially Mary Elizabeth Robbins's children, Eugene Stewart, Mary Lee Jones, and Margaret Ann Musgrove. Real appreciation is due Nancy and Art Baxter of Hawthorne Publishing who edited, designed, and produced this book. We also thank all who encouraged this effort, with special thanks to Brenda Bush and Jim and Donna Pickett at the Sheridan Historical Society.

The cover of this book and section page designs were by Glendale, California, book illustrator Wilson Swain, who is also a great-nephew of Mary Elizabeth Robbins. To him we owe real appreciation.

The map of Hamilton County in 1922 in the front cover design is courtesy of the Indiana Historical Society.

Published in the United States by
Hawthorne Publishing
15601 Oak Road
Carmel, Indiana 46033
317-867-5183
www.hawthornepub.com

Table of Contents

Introduction

A word from the editors of this book...

From Carol Longenecker. . .

I'm sure many people shaped and formed who I am today. But the one who probably had the most influence on my life was my grandmother, Mary Elizabeth Wilson Stewart Robbins. She was my mentor and friend. I miss sitting at her feet and listening, just absorbing her wisdom. My "Grandma Who Lived in the New House," as I so aptly called her because she and Grandpa built a new house when I was rather young, was an amazing woman. I don't know how she did so much in a day's time. Up early in the morning, she would start preparations for that day's dinner, make plans for the day, spend some quiet time reading her Bible and in prayer, then begin breakfast, while everyone else slept on. She was always ready to take food to a family in crisis or reach out to a neighbor having a rough time. She always shared large bouquets of flowers from her garden at church on Sunday, on graves at the cemeteries, and with neighbors and family. She taught a children's Sunday school class and was church secretary for years. She taught kindness and generosity through her actions as well as through her words.

While peeling potatoes or snipping beans in her chair or playing Chinese checkers or dominoes, Grandma would tell us stories of years gone by so that we would remember our family and heritage and learn by them. I am privileged that I got to live a bit of that "long-ago" life. We picked black raspberries along the same split-rail log fence she had picked from as a child. Picking, shucking, and putting up corn was a neighborhood affair, with games in the evening when we were finished. Picnics and family reunions were special times to reacquaint ourselves with family. Grandma always had a reading or poem to give. Hers were always the best.

Family Christmas and Easter events were the best days of

the year at Grandma's. Grandma never put a limit on how much fudge or candy we ate on those two special days. When we arrived at her house, she always had her change purse full of nickels ready. She knew first thing we would want to go to Casey's store. Three nickels apiece—one for a candy bar, one for a Coke, and one for an ice cream bar. When Grandma would take us to town (Sheridan), Grandpa would sit in the car and talk to passers-by while we shopped for penny candy at the Ben Franklin store. She made our favorite foods: vegetable soup and black raspberry pie, hamburgers with toothpicks, rice with raisins and milk, cranberry salad, butterhorns, sorghum cookies, persimmon pudding, apple dumplings, cinnamon rolls, soda cake, and divinity fudge.

Meal times were such happy occasions. Everyone gathered around the table sharing their day and laughing together. Sometimes our stomachs ached from laughing so hard. Anyone there when it was time for a meal was welcome to join the family at the table. There were always people stopping in to visit, as Grandma's house was Grand Central Station. Everyone felt loved and safe there.

She passed on traditions to the next generations, such as the tables full of Christmas cookies she made with us grandchildren each year—cut-out sugar cookies intricately decorated with sugars and sprinkles. Then we divided them onto plates and delivered them to neighbors and family. I have continued this tradition with my children, who are also continuing it.

She left this world for a better one six days before her ninety-sixth birthday, with her hands lifted ready to meet the God she had so faithfully served so many years. Goodbye, Grandma. Thank you for teaching me to love the Lord and to love my neighbor. I love you.

Carol Lee (Stewart) Longenecker

From Ellen Swain. . .

I first became enchanted with Aunt Mary Elizabeth's stories at age eleven, when I asked her to answer a few questions about her mother, my great-grandmother. I remember well the day the large manila envelope arrived in the mail containing eight single-spaced typewritten pages detailing her mother's life. She was working on some other stories that I might like, she said, some written years ago and others just recently started. She'd send them to me if I wished. One by one they arrived by post: memories of raising chickens on the farm, celebrating Halloween, attending prohibition rallies, and making rag rug carpets. Each time a new story arrived I'd devour it, savoring every sentence. I was hooked, and so began our long-shared interest in the history of our family.

I particularly loved how Aunt Mary Elizabeth captured the lives of long-ago Hamilton County ancestors—tales passed down from her Aunt Louva and others about early Indiana days. She told of Grandmother Lydia Pickett, a staunch Quaker who smoked a clay pipe and practiced herbal medicine. And of Grandmother Ruth Wilson who packed up fresh meat and staples for her grandchildren's long wagon ride home in 1899, just as my own grandmother Wilson sent packages of leftovers home with us after weekend visits a century later. These names on a chart became real people with hopes, interests, personalities, and faults.

This book, compiled from more than 1,200 single-spaced typed pages of Aunt Mary Elizabeth's writings, celebrates a life that spanned the course of almost one hundred years (1907–2003) of Hamilton County history. Her times witnessed the impact of new technologies and innovations that transformed the countryside and the nation. We hope you will enjoy her piece of Hamilton County history as much as we have.

Ellen Diane Swain, granddaughter of John William Wilson, Mary Elizabeth's brother.

Part One

Early Childhood

Through the Little Room in Bakers Corner's Red Brick School

Do you remember, O cousin mine. . .

The memories of childhood—surely you have them, too?

The darning needle insects we found and tormented in the tops of the buggy and carriage in the old buggy shed? Going to the ditch, being careful a crawdad did not pinch our bare toes? He would "not let loose until it thundered."

The large, luscious dewberries that grew along the lane fence to the pasture field? The minnows that swam around our feet as we waded in the water of the ditch?

The leeches we pulled off our feet and legs after wading? The plank board bridge where we sat and fished with bent pins for hooks?

The doodlebugs in the lane and barn lot rolling along their perfectly round balls? When we came to their hole we would call down in it, "Doodlebug, doodlebug, come out," but I never saw one come out.

The "cherry dance" we made with a dandelion stem, a green cherry, and a pin? Uncle Clark pegging away, mending shoes?

Drinking water from a tin cup through a long leaf of the winter onions? Looking for wiggle-tails in the rain barrel in the corner of the house?

Counting wild white daisy petals?
"One I love, two I love, three I love I say,
Four I love with all my heart, and five I cast away.
Six she loves, seven he loves, eight they both love.
Nine he comes, ten they tarry,
Eleven they court, and twelve they marry."

When it became dark on a warm summer evening and we ran to catch the many lightning bugs that made the front yard a starry heaven? It was another time and place. Let me take you there again.

Early Childhood

I was born on a Friday night, August 16, 1907. I have been told that my grandmother Hodson missed prayer meeting that evening to be with my mother at my birth.

At the time of my birth, we lived in a little white house at the west end of Bakers Corner on the north side of the road, where my father was share farming for his uncle Harvey Pickett.

When I was three weeks old my parents moved from the little white house in Bakers Corner to a small piece of land, probably twenty acres, which they had bought. On it was a three-room house and a tiny barn, really just a shed, attached to a neighbor's barn that stood on the boundary line between the two plots of land. I am sure my father was very happy to own this tiny farm. He would be living almost across the road from his uncle Clark Wilson and his family. Some of Uncle Clark's children were only a few years younger than my father. He would also be living near the place he had spent so many happy years with his grandmother Wilson after his mother had died.

My parents moved the house to the northwest corner of their land, a location along what is now U.S. 31, then called the range line road, and about three-fourths of a mile north of the Cicero-Sheridan road, which was later called State Road 47, now 236th Street, near a small settlement called Pegville. This little village got its name from Clark Wilson's shoe repair shop, where he made shoes from leather and pegs.

An old smokehouse that they made into a kitchen was attached to our family's house as a porch. Later my father enlarged the porch, enclosed it, and made it into a dining room, to be used in the summertime only. Its boarded-up outside walls were never finished with lath and plaster and were never even painted.

Beside the kitchen door into the dining room was a ladder nailed flat to the wall. It was used to take glass fruit jars used for canning and other things up to be stored in the attic. One day my mother was sitting on the step in this doorway while I was nursing. One of the empty glass cans which had been taken up there had not been properly balanced. It fell, with its sharp top edge hitting my baby face on the cheek-bone just below my eye. I carried a scar there for many years. Finally the rim of my glasses and wrinkles hid it.

Among my earliest memories are those of my toys. I loved a teddy bear which I likely got for my first Christmas or birthday. I played with him like a doll and loved him like a doll. I was told, before I was old enough to remember, that Teddy met with a terrible accident. My father was playing with me and my Teddy, tossing Teddy in the air and catching him in our little old smokehouse kitchen, when my mother lifted one of the round lids on our old wood cook stove to put in the wood. Teddy fell in and got somewhat singed. It made no difference to me; he was still just as loveable, even though he didn't have much hair or fuzz.

Of course I had several dolls at that period about 1910, some beautiful, some plain, but all loved. I had several celluloid dolls about four or five inches long, dolls you could buy at a dime store for five or ten cents each. Mostly what I wanted with these dollies was to sew for them. I could get a doll dress out of such a small scrap of material.

I must have been a terrible nuisance to my mother. All during my childhood I loved to sew. Every time Mama tried to sew, I would beg her to let me sew the straight seams in the garment. I well remember the new sewing machine that arrived about my sixth birthday, bought to sew baby clothes for my brother John William, who was on the way. My father was so proud of this new sewing machine from Montgomery Ward ($14.50 according to an historic catalogue) that he hemmed some of John William's diapers on it.

My most wonderful doll was probably Rose-Ma-Belle. Her eyes were brown like mine and opened and closed. Her head was bisque, her body a shiny flesh-colored material similar to oilcloth, and her hip joints and knees would bend. I gave her a lovely French name because of a poem I had learned to recite at our Hodson reunion.

ROSE-MA-BELLE

Sometimes I wake in the deep, dark night,
And the thunder roars outside,
A spatter of rain puts out the stars,
And I cover up close and hide.
"You can't get me—oh, you can't get me,
Though you beat on the window pane,
But I wonder what—oh, I wonder what
I've left outside in the rain!"

Oh, Rose-Ma-Belle was the loveliest doll!
Her hair was as long as mine,
Her lashes were as gold as the jonquil buds,
And her eyes had the starriest shine!
She was dressed like a bride,
Though she hadn't a groom,
But that was a small affair;
She'd a dress as white as a lily in bloom
And a long white veil in her hair.

And I took her to sit in the orchard grass
For the birds and the bees to see,
And I showed her the hole where the Gooches live
In the side of the old plum tree.
Then Daddy honked in the lane outside—
(Oh, this is so hard to tell!)
And I laid her down—and I went for a ride—
My sweet little Rose-Ma-Belle!

And oh—and oh—in the deep, dark night
I woke, and I heard the rain!
Splash and patter and swish it fell
On the roof and the window pane.
So I snuggled down in my warm white bed
(For the rain just sang as it fell)

Then all of a sudden I raised my head
And I thought about Rose-Ma-Belle!

Out in the dark and pouring rain,
Lonely and dressed so thin!
And I ran and stood by the window pane
And howled till the folks came in.
And mother said to me: "Go and look
In your little wickery chair!"
And I pattered quick to the playroom door—
And Rose-Ma-Belle was there.

And I hugged my mother for bringing her in,
And I hugged my Rose-Ma-Belle,
And I hugged my daddy and all the rest,
And I laughed till my heart got well.
And always now in the deep dark night,
When it beats on the window pane
I cover up close and wonder what
I've left outside in the rain!

St. Nicholas Magazine for Children

I had what I thought was a very nice playhouse. I always liked a playhouse, and I'd scrubbed out an old double hog house where my mother had set hens earlier in the season, cleaning it in every way. In it I arranged a table and davenport that my father had made for me, a davenport large enough for two children to sit on. I padded the seat of it with straw and tacked over the straw some green-figured ingrain carpet and put in a little blue cupboard with two shelves and a door. On its shelves I set a few pieces of pretty broken dishes and on each shelf, and on the top of this cupboard was a pretty paper napkin with a red rose on it. I thought a lot of those napkins.

I was so often outdoors. From that early childhood period animals surrounded me on all the farmsteads of my youth. I remember Billy, my Billy! I claimed that goat although he had been bought for my little three-year-old brother John William as well as for me. Bought? I wonder, I wish I knew how much my father paid for him. Five dollars? Surely not, maybe three, or maybe just two! I wonder!

When I was eight we moved to the farm of my grandfather, John Hodson. It was located about three quarters of a mile south of Bakers Corner. My father was driving his first car, a Model T Ford between the years 1915 and 1918, and about that time he decided my brother and I could have a lot of fun with a billy goat. He could easily get a goat for us with that car.

My father knew Grandpa's large front barn lot would be a perfect place for kids to have fun with a goat. There was lots of room to play at Grandpa's farm. The front barn lot was a lovely grove of a few acres with all kinds of trees. At the front, next to the road, were several very large sturdy oak trees, and it was shady under them with not much grass growing. Large elm trees grew along the path to the big red barn, near the large tool shed. With a heavy hayrope my father had made a high swing for us up in a black walnut tree. There were two hickory trees in this lot, one a shellbark hickory, with nuts good to eat although rather small. The other hickory was a large tree with smooth bark and nuts that were very bitter, pig hickory nuts.

Besides other trees there was the large old linden tree, which stood where the drive from the second story of Grandpa's big, red bank barn curved. This tree marked the place where I was to lead the horse to pull up the big hay fork-loads they had in hay-making season, until the men hollered, "Whoa." I had to lead the horse and not ride it as most kids did because my father was afraid the hame string might break, throw me off and hurt me.

While the horse and I cooled and waited under the linden tree for the men to pull the empty hayfork back to the wagon to reload, I liked to look at the suede-finish, tan-colored hard berries that hung in clusters on that linden tree at hay-making time of year. I wondered about the narrow sheet of thin leaf material that followed the stem down to the berries. I still don't know their reason for growing like that.

Anyway, that area on Grandpa's farm was where my billy goat was going to go. My father and I went to the nearby town of Terhune to the home of a man named Quincy Miller. We bargained for, and we brought home, a full-grown, black-and-white spotted young billy. His large white spots were dotted with fine black specks like pepper, and he had slightly curved horns and a short bushy tail. My father fastened him securely to the floor in the back part of the car.

I was not very anxious to have a billy goat. I supposed I would be afraid of him. But I quickly found he was already tame, and soon we were friends. My father made a harness to fit Billy out of some old horse harness and a set of shafts that I could use to fasten him to the little wagon we already had. It did not take long with my father's help to get Billy trained to pull that little wagon, but only one of us children could ride at a time, because more was too large a load for Billy. My brother was not old enough to drive yet anyway. When he rode in the wagon, I walked along beside the wagon and drove.

I liked to ride along by myself. Billy was a good "balker;" some-times he was a good "driver," as we used to call the animals them-selves in those days. Although sometimes he would run, making it hard for me to keep up, I never did let him get away from me.

My cousin, Morris Foulke, lived in the first house north of us on the same side of the road. He was the only child in the family and a year younger than I. They lived with his grandfather, my uncle John Foulke. Uncle John had a light sorrel-colored driving horse that Mor-ris was allowed to ride. He would bring that horse over to our house quite often to play, riding him up and down the two or three cement steps at the front of Grandpa's yard next to the road.

Another cousin, Hazel Simmonds, lived between Morris's and our house on the west side of the road. She usually played with us, but she did not have a pet except for a dog. She also had a little wag-on, and sometimes Hazel and I would play with our wagons in the road between our houses, especially of an evening after supper until dark.

Our billy goat and Morris's horse could neither be worked to-gether nor played with together. So Morris begged his father to get him a goat, too. Then the fun really began. His goat was about the same size as ours but was brown with white spots. I secretly thought ours was the prettiest. Morris's father made a harness for his Billy, and also shafts for his little wagon. This way we could ride along side by side or one following the other.

By this time I had learned to love Billy dearly. I did not want a switch used on him although sometimes he was contrary and would not mind. Just a tap with the lines was all I would allow. I did not want him abused in any way, I loved him too much.

One day my father made a wagon tongue with a doubletree and two singletrees for our little wagon and showed me how to change from the shafts to the tongue. When we used the tongue we could hitch both billys to our wagon and two of us could ride at the same time in the same wagon: great fun. I could ride with my little brother, now, too. We also let Hazel have turns riding. Too bad no one had a camera, but very few people had one then.

There was so much room in Grandpa's large front barn lot, but the solid gravel road was easier pulling for the goats. We spent a lot of time riding on the road between our houses. You may say, "That was dangerous for children and goats to play in the road." Not in those days—a time of few automobiles, with one passing so seldom-ly. If there was one it was likely a Model T Ford chugging along at twenty or twenty-five miles an hour—some neighbor we knew—we had plenty of time to get out of the road before they reached us. I daresay there were more little wagon tracks on the road then than there were automobile tire tracks.

Roads were so dusty then. Our little steel-rimmed wagon wheel tracks were not very wide but showed very plainly in the dusty gravel road. It is true that if Billy turned too short and dumped us out, we got dirtier in the dusty road than we would have in the grassy barn lot. That made no difference to us.

Time went on, a year or two passed, and Grandpa died in October 1917. About a year after Grandpa's death, his farm was sold to my uncle Ernest. We bought a farm about two miles away and moved to it. This stopped all of our fun together with our goats.

We moved to our own farm the last of August 1918. It was a hot, dry, sunny day, just before school began, the day my father decided to move Billy to the new house. He loaded the wagon flatbed with a variety of farm tools and "this and that." I wanted him to put

Billy upon the wagon bed and haul him, but my father said it would not hurt him to walk behind the wagon and tied him to a brace under the back end of the wagon bed. This just about broke my heart. I thought he was being mean to Billy.

My father fixed a place for me to sit at the back of the wagon with my bare feet dangling as we rode along in the hot sunshine. Billy trotted along behind us, getting hot and panting. How sorry I was for him every minute of the way. Again I begged my father to put him up in the wagon, but he said that would be foolish; it would not hurt Billy to walk. Although I felt so very sorry for Billy, my father was right; it didn't hurt that goat at all to walk the two miles.

After we moved I missed Morris and his goat and did not play with Billy as often. Also I was getting older and my play time was changing. And there was not as much room there for Billy as there had been at Grandpa's large farm, so he got into more mischief. He would climb a fence post brace and go wherever he pleased. He liked to eat the tender new leaves off sprouts, vegetables, and flowers. He enjoyed climbing all over the farm tools, and if anything was loose he would knock it off and it would be lost. He chewed holes in feed sacks or maybe took a notion to chew a sock off the clothesline or holes in the bottom of a pant leg. He would get into all manner of things that my father did not want bothered. So poor Billy was accused of everything wrong that happened, even if he was not guilty.

I knew my father wanted me to sell Billy because he caused so much trouble, but I was not willing to part with him. His antics grew progressively worse. The goat began to like to climb over the hood of our Model T touring car. Wherever he stepped his hooves scratched the shiny surface, whether it was the hood or fender. He was making the car look rough and tough.

The thing that aggravated my father most was when Billy got onto the car top and danced a jig on his hind legs, looking down at my father as if to say, "Just look at me." My father knew he was punching holes in the car top with every dancing step. He threw a stick at him and made him get down, but the damage was already done. The top was full of tiny pin holes, causing it to leak. The cars in those days were not made with hard tops but were similar to convertibles. The cloth covering the top was not very strong, with just a thin rubberized coating. My father knew it would take a new top cover to fix the damage that goat had done. When this happened, he was ready to sell Billy right that very minute.

But I still loved Billy and did not give in to the idea of selling him. I loved to lay my head on his and hold his horns with my hands and feel the jarring as he chewed his cud. He would chew it for a little bit then swallow it, belch and bring up a fresh cud and start chewing again. While chewing he worked his lower jaw sidewise and back. It was so interesting.

Well! I was not that willing to part with our Billy, but the moment finally came. I guess I left the playhouse door unfastened and Billy got in. He chewed up my favorite paper napkins. That upset me. I knew everyone thought I should get rid of Billy; they could not understand why I was unwilling to let him go when he was doing so much damage. Now I was beginning to understand. I knew my father was at the house and it would make him very happy if I let Billy go. Finally I went to the house and told my father that he could sell Billy. He was happy and went straight to the telephone and called a trucker to take him the next day to the Indianapolis stockyards. So, it was, "Goodbye, Billy," but I still loved him and always remembered Billy, my Billy!

Grandpa Hodson

Mostly as a child I remember the people I loved. As I have said we came to live with Grandpa Hodson, near Bakers Corner, when I was eight. We had moved into his large ten-room house to live with, and care for him a few days after my eighth birthday.

Grandma Hodson had died and left him alone just three years earlier. My uncle Ernest, aunt Lizzie, and cousin Margaret had lived with him after that. My father had been farming for himself, his small farm of twenty acres, with a team of horses. He also rented some fields of a neighbor whom I called "Grandpa Hiatt." This he did along with tuning pianos and giving stringed instrument lessons, in classes, once or twice each week in the evenings. Along with making brooms, this is how he made a living.

Since Uncle Ernest desired to move to a farm that he had recently purchased, it was arranged that my father would rent Grandpa's farm of one hundred and ninety acres. We would move the two miles to Grandpa's, and he would live with us.

The house being large, Grandpa told us he would keep three rooms for himself. The rest we furnished, except the far east room upstairs, which was kept for storage.

Grandpa lived mostly in our part, except for sleeping in the downstairs bedroom quarters in his white, enameled iron half-bed. His large southwest bedroom upstairs was furnished with his best bedroom suite, and he was privileged to have company overnight if he desired.

Grandpa also had his own living room, which he used only when he had his friends or relatives over or there was a family gathering when the whole downstairs was used. In the summertime it was open for Grandpa to use, and both outside doors were kept open.

His living room was the large south front room. It was furnished with his own rug and furniture, including a dark green crushed velvet sofa with a raised head, the high end being to the west, sitting along the north wall. Above that sofa hung a large old picture of three young women, "Faith, Hope and Charity."

I can remember going to Grandpa's while Grandma yet lived and sitting on the floor on a flowered rug in front of the green sofa and looking in their large Sears Roebuck catalog at the old-time farm tools, furniture, and clothing.

Along the west wall of that living room between the front window and front glassless door hung a large mirror with a wide bronze frame. White cotton Nottingham lace curtains hung at the window. No one ever heard of any color window blinds except dark green, and these were always drawn halfway down.

In front of the mirror was a large Morris chair, upholstered with black leather. The back would let down almost flat like a bed. I liked to sit in it although I was always afraid it would tip backwards with me. It had quite a habit of doing that with wiggly children. I don't think grownups had any trouble.

While I sat in the Morris chair in Grandpa's living room, I liked to look at the postcard album that lay on a small stand in front of the window. It had a hard cover and its inside pages were black with two short slits for each of the four corners of the post-cards. I eventually came to have some of the postcards that were sent to me from Grandpa and Grandma when I was quite small. On them Grandma always said, "Be a good girl and love Jesus."

In the southwest corner of Grandpa's living room, sitting catty-cornered, was a secretary desk. On the left side of it, from top to bottom were bookshelves behind a rounded glass door. On the right side at the bottom were two shelves behind a wooden door, and just above the door was a drawer. Above the drawer was another wooden door, hinged at the bottom and leaning back at the top so it could be let down to be used as a desk. Behind it were a few pigeonholes for important papers and stationery. Also among the pigeonholes was a tiny drawer for holding pencils, pen holders, pen points, erasers and such. There was always a bottle of ink in this area.

In the corner in front of the secretary was a rocking chair. Between the two windows on the south wall the chimney stood, built inside the room. A corner shelf stood on each side of the chimney. On the west one resided a stuffed fox squirrel sitting up on his hind legs, holding a nut between his two front paws. On the east shelf sat a large stuffed barn owl. These two things always fascinated me. I would study the owl and imagine I could see Grandpa catching him in his big red bank barn.

An old gas pipe was still fastened to the chimney. One end went down under the house through a small round hole in the floor, the remains of the gas-burning era from 1880s till 1900. At one time, when Grandpa's children were at home, there had been a gas jet fastened to the top end of this pipe. When it was lit it made a nice flickering light, lighting the whole room. Grandpa burned natural gas for lights and possibly cooking and heating, which would have been possible because gas was so cheap. My uncle Ernest, Mama's brother, said that when he was growing up he never had to cut or chop firewood.

Grandpa likely bought his gas from the Bakers Corner Gas Company. I don't believe there was ever a gas well on Grandpa's farm. I can remember my mother speaking of the gas jet lights in her father's house, how she enjoyed them, and how sorry they were when the gas wells burned out in Indiana. The burning gas in the jets, however, was hard on books, whose pages in that house were crumbly. It also tarnished silver very fast.

Grandpa's living room stove was a Florence Hot Blast, which really was a good heater. This stove was not used unless there was company, and it was not taken down in the summertime, as were the other stoves in the house.

A door along the north wall of the living room at the foot of the green sofa opened into the stairway. I always supposed this was the door through which my parents came into the living room at their wedding.

Our living room was the large north front room. Both Grandpa's and our living rooms had doors opening onto the front porch; also each had a door into the dining room. The stairs went up between the two front rooms.

We all used the dining room as our living room in the winter, because during chilly or cold weather it was heated by burning wood in a wood saver stove, which was very common then. Grandpa's big base burner kept the dining room, Grandpa's bedroom, which was north of the dining room, and the kitchen very comfortable even during the coldest weather. Also an open register in the ceiling above the base burner kept one large room over it upstairs warm. A wood and coal cook stove helped in the kitchen.

We all loved and respected Grandpa greatly.

I can see him in my mind's eye to this day. In the wintertime Grandpa wore gray felt boots, even in the house, about one-half inch thick, reaching almost to his knees, and made of warm wool. When he went outside he wore one-buckle rubber, waterproof "arctics" or overshoes over the felt boots. When Grandpa was in the house, the arctics sat in the southeast corner of the dining room between the old fashioned built-in press and the outside door. My brother, who was two years old when we moved there with Grandpa, loved to plod around in the house in Grandpa's big arctics. In the same corner was also Grandpa's knotty cedar-colored cane which he always used when he was outside but did not need in the house.

Grandpa and Grandma had raised a family of six children, two sons and four daughters. I am sure they were a lively bunch. One girl, Florence, had died when she was eleven months old.

Grandma had sugar diabetes and was unable to work much. There was always a hired girl there when I came to visit, before the years when she was gone and we lived with Grandpa. Before they had the hired girl, Grandpa would get up early, go to the barn, do his chores, and then go back to the house hoping that Grandma would be up, but she would not be. He would have to help there in the kitchen before he could go to the field.

Grandma would rise from bed so late on Sunday mornings that she could hardly get started to church on time, so Grandpa would get moving early and start walking ahead. After he had gone she would tell the children to hurry up now and get ready so they could beat him to church. They were driving a horse hitched to a carriage, and two could play at that game of "me first" because she did not always stop to pick him up.

My cousin told a story about a tiny graphophone Grandpa bought. The bottom part was a small square box with a small colored horn. It played cylinder-shaped records. The grandchildren played "Red-Wing" on it until they almost wore out the record.

Red Wing

There once was an Indian maid
A shy little prairie maid
Who sang a lay, a love song gay
As on the plain she'd while away the day
She loved a warrior bold
This shy little maid of old
But brave and gay he rode one day
To battle far away.
Chorus: Now, the moon shines tonight on pretty Red Wing
The breeze is sighing, the night bird's crying
For afar 'neath his star her brave is sleeping
While Red Wing's weeping her heart away.

My older cousin Gladys, the daughter of Mama's sister Anna loved to tell stories about our grandpa. Grandpa owned thirty acres across the road from his barn that he kept in permanent bluegrass pasture. It had been in bluegrass since Gladys could remember and was never plowed up until Uncle Ernest bought the farm. Grandpa had inherited the thirty acres from his father.

One time Gladys and Mary, another cousin, were there when Grandpa took the cows across the road to pasture. The bull got after the girls, or at least they thought he was heading in their direction. They ran and climbed up on a shed roof. Frightened Mary was shaking so much she almost fell off the roof.

It seemed like there were minor catastrophes waiting around every corner as Gladys told it. One wonderful day, the day after Christmas, the ground was covered with deep snow and the sun was shining brightly. Gladys had stayed overnight at Grandpa's following the Christmas dinner on Christmas Day. Grandpa had put straw in the bottom of the bobsled and hitched the horses to it. Everyone there piled in on the nice clean straw, wrapping themselves in bed comforters.

Grandpa headed the team of horses toward Aunt Myrtie's near Westfield. Going was good until they reached the Lindley Hill. This hill was a dangerous place a mile or two north of Westfield, at the north edge of what was called the Great Dismal Swamp, right along the range line road just south of the Lafayette road, today State Road 38. This was before the road was cemented, and the hill had not yet been cut down and was long and very steep. The bobsled slid to one side of the road, then to the other. It was all Grandpa could do to keep it off the horses' heels. If it had hit them they would likely have run away, possibly injuring those in the sled. Everyone looked from one side to the other, very much frightened, but they reached Aunt Myrtie's in fine shape. Trips could often be hazardous, and we always remember danger.

But the memories of that older generation of the 1890s and turn of the century were also mellow. My cousin remembered when my mother Minnie and her brother Ernest were still at home. One special time, Uncle Ernest had a red sweater with white turtleneck and white cuffs. He looked very nice, tall with dark curly hair, wearing the red sweater. He was going to see his best girl, Lizzie, in the sparkling black buggy with yellow wheels. He drove a high-stepping horse named Pearl, a beautiful picture for all who saw it.

The family's life centered around the church at Bakers Corner, called from its earliest days the Liberty Wesleyan Methodist Church. If they ran out of things to argue about among the relatives, they could argue about the church. At one time Grandma Hodson and Aunt Clara Pickett and others did a lot of talking about getting an organ for the church. Until that time, there had not been a musical instrument in the old Bakers Corner church. Some people at that time thought the devil was in musical instruments. Grandma Hodson was one who argued to keep it out of the church; Aunt Clara was determined to have an organ. She went to town, bought one, and had it delivered to the church. There was no more talk about it after that and it was always used.

Mostly it was the "small stuff" that made the days pass, so Gladys said. One day Grandma was going to make one of her boys a pair of pants. She spread the material on the kitchen table over the oilcloth cover and placed the pattern over the material. When she got them all cut out and picked up the pieces, she had also cut a pair of pants out of the oilcloth.

Having a large family to raise took lots of food. In those days, farmers raised almost all of their food. Grandpa especially liked fruit and believed in having plenty of it. North of the house was a large apple orchard. Along the rail fence on the west side of the orchard was an early red June apple tree with rather small fruit. These apples, ripening very early, had dark red skin and very white, crisp meat. Next to the early tree was the creamy white maiden blush with its pink blushing cheeked fruit. Maiden blushes were good summer cooking apples, also good to just pick up and eat raw. These were followed by the juicy wealthys and the sweet, small-fruited rambows which were a greenish color with some red stripes, mostly on one side. They were a favorite to eat raw.

A little later came the luscious eating apple called grimes golden, a very popular variety at that time, and the winter apples, which were stored in wooden crates in the big cellar under the two large front rooms. The dirt floor of the cellar was damp and cool enough to keep the apples well all winter.

Once in a while during the winter there came an apple-sorting day. Some weren't keeping well and had to be thrown away. Always at butchering time in the winter the apples would be sorted so the good part of the partly rotten ones could be used in making mince meat. There were not many worms and insects, like now. The fruit trees never needed spraying, yet they yielded bushels of good fruit and they did seem to keep well in that cool cellar.

The wooden-slat apple crates were stored along the east, inside wall north of the cellar door, which opened into the cellar way from the open back porch. The crates stored there and elsewhere were many and in the fall were filled with winter keeping apples, such as the pippins and ben davis varieties.

Grandpa had one tree that bore two kinds of apples, grafted that way. One side was white pippin, the other side I believe was bellflower. Another apple which was a very good keeper and did not ripen in the cellar until very late winter, almost spring, was called york imperial. It grew in a funny shape, like it had been squashed sideways.

In the fall while it was still warm weather, the apples would be gathered for cider to replenish the vinegar supply. A team of horses was hitched to the wagon and taken to the orchard. Everyone helped pick up the good apples off the ground where they had fallen, dead ripe. The team was driven from one tree to another until all the good apples had been picked up or until the wagon bed was full. Milk cans, eight-gallon ones, were placed on top of the apples, and the load was taken three-quarters of a mile to Bakers Corner to Warren Pickett's cider press.

There was one apple tree called Wolf River that I especially remember standing near the middle of Grandpa's large apple orchard. The fruit on this tree was very large, the largest apples I have ever seen, and very dark red. They were not good keepers with many of them rotting on the ground before time to pick up apples for cider.

The fresh sweet cider was brought home in the milk cans, some of it to be kept in the cool cellar to preserve it as long as possible before it got bitey and fermented. The rest of it was taken to the cellar and poured into the large oak vinegar barrels. Two or three of these were stored along the west wall of Grandpa's cellar. The vinegar barrels had wooden spigots in their tops, so that when the barrels were laid on their side, the spigot could be used to draw vinegar out of the barrel.

They left one barrel that already had some vinegar in it, not adding fresh cider because that would spoil the vinegar for their present use. But in the others the vinegar mother, a thick ropy substance, was left in the barrels, aiding the cider in turning to vinegar quicker. By the time the cucumbers and beets were ready to pickle the next year, the vinegar would be ready to use.

Grandpa grew more than just apples for his family. A long narrow lot in front of the apple orchard, next to the road, had a row of cherry trees yielding gallons of beautiful plump red cherries each year for pies and preserves. There were also red plum trees and pear trees in this lot, a row of gooseberries and another of currant bushes, and a quince bush.

In the large garden behind the house, a grape arbor ran full length from east to west, each year providing a bountiful harvest of sweet purple grapes and a few white ones. There were also blackberry and black raspberry bushes, and a few hop vines so Grandma could make her own yeast for making light bread.

At the west end of Grandpa's garden were a large asparagus patch, horseradish and rhubarb, and several persimmon trees, which provided enough persimmons for several families for the puddings they loved.

After Grandpa's children were grown, married, and had families, he was glad to have them come home and gather great supplies of fruit and berries to feed their families during the winter months with all kinds of pies, jellies, jams, butters, and preserves. He was proud to be able to furnish so much for his children and grandchildren.

Besides enjoying the abundance of fruits, berries, grapes, and garden vegetables he grew, Grandpa was a great lover of flowers. He tended a small flower garden fenced off along the east side of the yard along the west side of the woodhouse. It extended west to the walk from the back porch at the kitchen door to the yard gate at the drive, with a small gate at the southwest corner to keep out a stray chicken or his curious, thoughtless grandchildren.

Black-speckled orange tiger lilies grew alongside the woodshed, while blue and red morning glories covered the north fence. Each spring he set out his assortment of dahlia bulbs which had been dug up in the fall and stored in the cellar during the winter months. The dahlia I liked best was a yellow quill type, a little larger than the pom-poms of later days.

An enormous old-fashioned purple lilac bush, like that the early settlers took west on the covered wagon trains, was in his garden. A large snowball bush, a deutzia bush, and other hardy shrubs and flowers bordered his yard. A cream-colored iris remains today where it was when Grandpa lived and tended it.

I remember well the dark red, velvety, almost black roses that flanked the path to the outdoor toilet. In a wooden tub grew a pink oleander bush, a tender plant, unable to survive northern winters. It took two strong men to carry the oleander to the cellar each fall and back up each spring.

Besides cows, hogs, and horses which all farmers had, Grandpa always kept sheep. He needed them to keep down weeds and grass in his large apple orchard and woodsy front barn lot. At night they stayed in a small barn we called the sheep shed, to prevent them from being killed or frightened by wandering dogs.

Grandpa hated weeds, especially burdock. He could be seen quite often on a summer day cutting burdock in the shade in the orchard, hog lot, or some other place on the farm. He liked his farm to look neat and kept the ten-room white house and the large red bank barn well painted.

While we were there he still had a white work horse called Bird, which my father used some for the farm work. Grandpa also had a small sorrel driving horse, not much larger than a pony, named Dolly. He was always pleased when Mama drove Dolly to town, but Dolly got so old and skinny Mama was ashamed to drive her. Grandpa could not see how distressed Dolly looked, and kept insisting that

Mama drive her. So one fall day after the days had become much shorter, Mama drove Dolly to Sheridan much against her will. Evening came and Mama did not come home. My father began to be worried. He was going to start out on the hunt for her as soon as he finished his chores. Before he had them quite finished, Mama came slowly driving up the lane in the dark.

She was not in a very good humor because she said she had been terribly embarrassed. While driving on the way home old Dolly had fallen down. The poor old thing was hardly able to pull the buggy. Finally a man Mama knew came along and unhitched Dolly from the buggy, got her up, and hitched her up again so they could come on home. Mama was so embarrassed she said she would never drive old Dolly again. My father took Dolly across the road and turned her loose in the thirty-acre field of bluegrass. She did not live long but fell down and died of old age at the back side of the field.

Grandpa raised his family on maple syrup for their pancakes and fried mush. On his farm was a large woods of thirty-five acres, which had never been cleared, and in it were many large sugar maple trees, which provided the syrup for those breakfast treats. After Grandpa got older and was unable to care for the sugar camp, he let two or three of the men in the family run it.

My father never made maple syrup alone; it was a job for two men. While we lived there, my father would open the sugar camp the middle or latter part of February when the sap began to run in the large maple trees.

I would go with him with Fred and Coalie hitched to the mud-boat or bob-sled. The boat was loaded with wooden and galvanized buckets and spiles, which were the spigots the sap ran down into the buckets. As I remember, some of the old wooden buckets had belonged to Grandpa's father, Uri Hodson.

With his brace and bit, my father would drill a small hole in the side of the tree trunk about three feet above the ground. This hole did not go deep into the tree, just through the bark and deep enough to hold the spile which he drove into the hole. The spile had a ridge on it that showed how far it was to go into the tree. Then he hung a bucket onto the spile.

The sweet sugar water began to seep out of the tree, run slowly down to the end of the spile, and drip into the bucket. On he would go, hanging the buckets until fifty or more trees were tapped. Sap needed to be gathered, a task that began every day early in the morning. Even then some of the buckets would be overflowing.

The sap was gathered into two barrels on the mudboat or bobsled, depending upon how much snow was on the ground. The horses knew to follow the driver or dray from tree to tree without being driven. All my father had to say to them was "get-up" and "whoa," once in a while "gee" or "haw." The clear sweet sugar water splashed as it rode along.

The camp was a boarded-up shack in the woods, with the east side left open for the steam to escape, roofed so the rain and snow would not fall into the metal vats.

During the heavy part of the season, the barrels when full were taken to the sap cooking camp and emptied, and the gathering of sap resumed until sufficient sap had been collected.

In the northwest corner of this shack was a heavy, long, steel cooking vat. It was probably six feet long and three or more feet wide. It was not very deep, maybe eight inches. This vat was based on a brick foundation, making it around thirty inches above the ground floor. The south end of this foundation was left open for the fire. The vat was divided into three or four square inch openings, allowing the sugar water to flow from one section to the next. The sugar water was poured into the back or north section. The fire under the front section caused evaporation, and the water gradually flowed to the front section. This process was continued all day or until the sugar water was all gone. When it was cooked down as thick as it was wanted, it was dipped into milk cans and taken home to be cleared on the kitchen cook stove.

Clearing was done by putting the boiled syrup in the scoured clean wash boiler and heating it on the kitchen range. An egg was broken and dropped into the syrup. The sediments in the syrup would then come to the top and be skimmed off with the egg, leaving the syrup nice and clear. It was sealed in fruit jars while hot and stored in the cellar with the supply of other home-canned goods.

Sometimes some friends or young people would come to the sugar camp in the evening, maybe bring their musical instruments and have a joyful evening. Mama would bake potatoes and apples in the coals and ashes at the front of the furnace and boil eggs in the boiling syrup. She would take bread, butter, and other things for the supper.

After about three weeks of maple syrup making, the buckets and spiles would be gathered into the mud boat again to be cleaned, and the vats would also be scoured. All would be stored in the loft of Grandpa's buggy shed until needed the next spring.

One of the fun things in maple syrup season was making maple sugar. Mama would boil some of the syrup down in a kettle on the stove until it sugared, then mold it into cakes in muffin tins. It was better than any candy you could buy but very rich and sweet. When making maple sugar, instead of molding it in muffin tins, some people would pour it in small quantities on the snow, making small cakes. The snow hardened it at once.

The old timers made their own sugar for use and cooking in this way. I do not know if Grandpa and Grandma ever did use the sugar much themselves or if they bought their sugar at the store. After Grandma developed sugar diabetes she could not use any sugar but was allowed honey in its place. Although they used a large quantity of honey, I do not remember Grandpa ever keeping bees.

Grandpa was just as neat about his person as he was about his farm and house. As I remember, Grandpa Hodson was rather tall, not much under six feet. He was of slender build, brown eyes, and plenty of gray hair and gray beard, which he kept neatly trimmed.

When he needed a haircut, my father, who was good at barbering, always cut it, as he did for several of our neighbors. In the summertime this job was done on the long back side porch. Grandpa sat on the kitchen stool with a large cloth around his neck to keep the hair from falling down his neck. He wore his hair parted on the side with a regular shingle hair cut.

There was more to cutting Grandpa's hair than just shingling the hair on his head. His beard always needed trimming at the same time. He never wore a long shaggy irregular beard but kept it rather short and neatly trimmed. There was an odd thing about Grandpa's beard. One side of it grew faster than the other. By the time it needed trimming the difference showed very plainly.

One time when his children were young, Grandpa went to town and had his beard shaved off. On his way home he stopped at his father's. Aunt Anna was just a little girl and she was visiting there. She could tell who he was in spite of his being clean shaven at that moment. When they went home Grandma and his other children did not know him. Aunt Anna gave him away when she went to him and climbed upon his lap. Grandpa was pretty fastidious about his fingernails and toenails, too. When Grandpa trimmed his toenails, he used a big file like we use to sharpen a hoe.

Reunions were exciting days for Grandpa. How he loved seeing folk he had not seen for a long time, probably not since the year before. This family gathering included more people than just his children and their families; cousins and distant relatives attended. He loved the afternoon programs of speeches and songs, and the big dinner, but visiting meant more to him than anything else. He always loved to visit, and although he had his special friends, he loved to talk and joke with everyone.

Grandpa loved Christmas. He loved to give good gifts to his children and grandchildren. He and Grandma gave a small child's rocking chair to each grandchild for their first Christmas. One Christmas he gave each of his children a set of Rogers silver tableware. Another time he gave each of his daughters a cane-bottom rocking sewing chair. One time he gave his daughters a fancy basket with a handle.

One year before Grandma died, my grandparents gave me a smooth china-headed doll with printed blond hair for Christmas. Grandma had made the body of muslin, stuffed it with cotton, and made a pink-and-white, fine-checked calico dress. I called her Marie.

Grandpa loved to play jokes. One Christmas at his house, all of his children with their families were there. He had brought a tall evergreen tree from the woods, tall enough to reach the high ten-foot ceiling in the north front room. It was lighted with different colored twisted candles.

All of his sixteen grandchildren were happy. Not so his children.

Everyone had received a nice gift from Grandpa except his six children, who had received nothing at all. All of his children had noticed they were left out but said nothing. Grandpa acted very normal as if that was all.

Finally Aunt Mima, my mother's sister, could stand it no longer and spoke to him pretty crossly and cuttingly about it. She really told him off. Her brothers and sisters were embarrassed that she would speak to him like that. Grandpa was unperturbed, as they say, "getting a kick" out of it, but did not show it.

When he thought she had said enough, he reached into his shirt pocket and pulled out a one hundred dollar bill and gave it to her. Of course he had one for each of his other children, too.

As the years went along, Grandpa slowed down. He also became partially blind. I do not know what caused his blindness, maybe cataracts. He could see well enough to get around in the house, yard, and lots, but he was unable to read. My mother read to him his letters, the newspaper, and the Bible. It was quite a handicap for him. Reading would have been a wonderful pastime for him after he became unable to work.

I remember after we moved there he was still able to see to pick the wild black raspberries that grew along the rail fences along the lanes and the woods on his farm. I would go with him on a bright sunny July day to gather them. We usually brought home enough for a few pies, and sometimes Mama would make some tasty black raspberry jelly with them.

Although he could not see well, he still had a desire to work, especially wanting to help during the heavy farming season. He would go to the barn and throw manure out of the horse stables. But I can remember he rested a lot. Through the summer months he kept a bright-colored striped hammock on the front porch, the head fastened to the south post, the foot to the house. There he rested and relaxed many hours in the shade. It was a relaxing place for me when Grandpa was not using it, although I got spilled out of it quite often.

In nice weather I liked to ride to Sunday school and church on Sunday mornings with Grandpa in his buggy behind Old Dolly. I didn't mind being behind her. I thought Grandpa's buggy was prettier than most because it had yellow wheels.

I also liked to sit with him during preaching service in the old Bakers Corner church. His particular pew was along the south wall near a window, and in the summertime with the window open we could hear the songbirds singing their merry tunes and the droning of the bees as they gathered nectar for their winter supply of food. The southern breeze cooled by the shade of the large maple trees was pleasant. In the winter it was still comfortable. His pew was close to the south heating stove, making it a cozy place to sit on a cold winter Sunday morning. He also had his special place to sit in the new church, which was the second row at the front at the far east side.

Grandpa had been a faithful churchgoer most of his life. He had a birthright membership in the Quaker church because at the time of his birth both his father and mother were members of that denomination.

Grandma had left the Quakers and joined the Wesleyan Methodist Church at Bakers Corner in 1871, soon after its organization. But Grandpa remained a Quaker until January 1900, when he was converted in a revival meeting at Bakers Corner conducted by Reverend C. S. Smith. He joined the church at that time.

That old wooden church had been his home. Now he was older, and a new church was being built—just as he was going out. The new brick Wesleyan Methodist Church at Bakers Corner was dedicated May 6, 1917. The cornerstone laying service had been in 1916.

The basement had been finished first. The auditorium and Sunday school rooms upstairs were to be finished during the winter months in time for the dedication in May. It was decided to sell the old church building and move the worship services and Sunday school classes into the basement of the new church in the fall of 1916 and continue there until the upstairs was finished to move into in the spring.

By the fall of 1916, then, the building had been enclosed and roofed. Sadly, Grandpa was able to enjoy worshipping in the new sanctuary only a few months after it was dedicated. He passed away after a relatively short illness that fall on October 2, 1917. He loved the church and all it stood for and so it was right that his funeral was the first funeral held in the new church.

His last illness remains vivid in my mind. Children in their first decade remember death that way. Grandpa had not been well for a year or more before his death. It was the middle part of September 1917; I had started school and was by this time in the fourth grade at the Bakers Corner two-room schoolhouse, to which I walked three fourths mile each day. Madge Lindley was my teacher that year.

Grandpa was so ill he was bedfast and was getting worse each day. He needed constant care. My mother did all she could for him. His other children, my mother's brothers and sisters and in-laws, came and helped. But he needed a nurse.

A trained nurse by the name of Carrie Cox was hired to care for him. She ate with us and had her few hours off to sleep during the day when the family could sit by his bedside and care for him. His tall-headed wooden bed had been set up in the north front room which was our living room, and he lay in it very ill for several days. I remember so well how still and solemn it was around our house, everyone wearing a long sad face, with the white-clothed nurse slipping so quietly around. Grandpa was truly very ill and I knew it.

Each evening as soon as I had walked home from school, the nurse said to me, "Take your little brother down in the barn lot where your grandpa can't hear him." I guess it was a hard job for her to keep him quiet during the day while I was at school. Sometimes it was a task for me too, and I would rather do something else.

By this time it was bright autumn weather. There was much fun that could be had in Grandpa's beautiful front barn lot. The hickory nuts in their cracked or open outer covers, the black walnuts in balls of spongy bright green, and the pig hickory nuts whose inside kernel was bitter and would pucker your mouth like a green persimmon, were falling among the rustle of swirling, early falling leaves.

Under the shellbark hickory were two rocks of fair size, which we used to crack the hickory nuts. We would place a hickory nut on its flat side on the top of the larger rock, then hit the nut with the other rock to crack it, sometimes smashing them until there was not much goodie left. Of course there was a lot of waste, but who cared then about wasting part of a hickory nut? Perhaps they were not cured yet, but we did not know the difference; we liked them and spent much of our time under the shellbark hickory nut tree.

There were things I could do to keep John William out of trouble besides opening nuts and snacking on them. He loved to swing in the hayrope swing that our father had put up for us in the tall black walnut tree. You could swing so high towards the clouds in it. It had been left up for us from the Hodson reunion. I liked to sit in the swing, twist the rope tight, then whirl round and round as the rope unwound. When the rope was all untwisted I would be so dizzy I could neither stand nor walk, and said I was drunk. This I would do sometimes when John William was playing around by himself.

Such beautiful weather, such a beautiful time of year, harvest time, but Grandpa was inside and sick. Everyone went around their duties with gloomy faces. My mother and father never smiled. I was sent to school day after day wondering if Grandpa would still be with us when I reached home that evening.

There came a day when he was not there; he had left this old world and gone to a better place. When I came home from school, how sad everyone was. I had been told my grandpa had died before I left the school building. I can plainly remember walking slowly across our front yard carrying my dinner bucket, through the fallen leaves with many questions in my mind, that evening of October 2, 1917.

The funeral, of course, would be in the church he had come to love so much. In those days the lids of the caskets were opened full length, not hinged to the casket. The lid had to be taken off by an undertaker standing at each end, lifting it off and placing it on the floor behind the casket. At Grandpa's funeral one of the undertakers dropped his end of the black lid, making a terrible noise. It was so unexpected that everyone jumped, and one of my cousins, George Baker, who was eleven years old at that time, was so frightened he jumped up to run out of the church. Someone caught him by the arm and made him sit down again.

My mother never got over the embarrassment of that funeral. She felt that the undertaker was very careless and should not have dropped the lid. A few days after Grandpa's funeral, his children all gathered at our house to divide his personal belongings, just his small things. In the middle of the floor in his downstairs bedroom, they made a pile of things to be disposed of. I was only ten years old and was around, in and out, keeping an eye on things, as children sometimes do.

In this pile were a few things that I wanted. No one cared if I had them; no one else wanted them. I took some items, among them a match holder. This item was clear glass and shaped like a bunch of grapes. One side of the leaf had been broken off, which was probably the reason for its being in the pile of unwanted articles. It did not matter to me that it was broken. I thought it was pretty. I prized it and wanted to keep it near me and put it on the wall with matches in it, where it has hung all these years.

During the last year we lived on Grandpa's farm, my parents sold their little farm with the little house and new barn. They then bought a seventy-acre farm from my father's cousin Alvin Foulke, a farm which was only about one-half mile from their first one, about one and a quarter miles northeast of Bakers Corner.

I was excited again when my parents were talking of buying the Alvin Foulke farm because I would again be living near my favorite cousin, whose name was Ruby, and I was resigned to moving away from my friends at Grandpa's place anyway. I had loved to play and spend much time in Grandpa's big woods, and now my father told me there was a woods on this place with other woods joined to it and a creek running through it. I knew I could have a lot of fun in and along a creek. So we said goodbye to Grandpa's and moved on.

The Big Snows

When I was quite small, in horse and buggy days before the new brick church was built, we were attending the old white-frame Wesleyan Methodist Church in Bakers Corner. During the two or three weeks of revival meetings in the winter, the weather was usually cold with lots of snow. We usually attended every night. These revivals stood in my memory as cold, cold events.

Sometimes my father hitched his team of farm horses to the bobsled, and put fresh straw in it along with several horse blankets and bed comforters. On our way to church several neighbors along the way would pile in and go with us.

Sometimes he used the Klondike, which was like a big box on wheels with a sliding door on each side and a glass window in each door and one in front. It was quite a cozy place in which to ride through rain or snowstorms and cold weather.

Other times we went to revivals at night in the wintertime in our buggy. Ours was a low phaeton buggy, with good side curtains and a storm front made of a heavy material similar to oilcloth with isinglass windows. This buggy was not as warm as the Klondike. In both the Klondike and buggy we had to wrap up warm and use horse blankets and old bed comforters over our laps.

My mother made a pretty face cover for me out of cream-colored, soft wool cloth, embroidering a shell design around its edge. When the weather was cold she tied this over my mouth to keep me from breathing in the cold air.

The horse blankets were a necessity, at least my father thought so for horses as well as people. He was good to his animals. Horse blankets were made of very heavy woven blanket material, mostly cotton with woolen thread interwoven through it. They were shaped to fit over the horse's back and part of its neck with straps to fasten it on the horse if the weather was windy. It was put on the animal as soon as we arrived at church and taken off before we started home. Sometimes a thief would steal a horse blanket off a horse while the owner was in the church service. It really happened quite often. Although I was very small I will always remember my father saying he thought one of the cruelest things a man could do to an animal was to steal a blanket off a horse and leave the poor thing to suffer in the cold.

It seems these revivals were always happening in the coldest weather. One of those winters there was a great revival meeting at the Methodist church at Sheridan, with the evangelist a noted man by the name of Reverend Bulgin. I remember well he had his own song books that the people bought and used. Their covers were red, white, and blue striped and I held onto mine as a keepsake.

We had attended a few services that year when there came a

very heavy snow, several inches. It was a real blizzard, and a very strong wind formed drifts several feet high. We could walk to school over the fence tops on the crusted white drifts. During this particular snowstorm my father and our neighbor, Otto (Doc) Cain, decided to take the Model T and attend the Bulgin revival at Sheridan. Doc lived in the first house south of us. No one in the rest of our two families wanted to brave the storm.

Although it was stormy and cold when the two men left home, they did not know it would worsen so soon. It was in the days before radios or televisions, and people were not sure of weather conditions ahead.

During the time of the service that night the weather became much worse, with even heavier snow and stronger wind. When the two men came out of the church building they realized it would be a problem to get home.

My father's Model T could not have been very old. I am sure it was in good shape because he always kept it that way. The cars in those days were not closed, though the isinglass window side curtains did do a lot to keep the snow, wind, and cold out. Besides not being closed, none of the cars had heaters in them.

My father and Doc managed to get the car started and crept their way through deep snow drifts and freezing weather until they reached an area about one-fourth mile north of home. There on a little rise they and the car bumped up against a solid drift about as high as the hood over the engine of the car. The car chugged and was done.

Doc and my father abandoned the car and faced the storm and cold, walking the rest of the way to our house. At home the welcoming room was nice and warm with the base burner spreading its golden glow. But Doc was not as strong and hearty as my father and was almost frozen by the time they reached our house. He could not talk. A little farther and he would have died. My parents worked with him, rubbing, walking, and exercising him. He finally came through it and was all right.

The next morning my father took his shovel and went to dig out his Ford. To his surprise the wind had changed direction and had blown the snowdrift completely away from the car. The Model T was sitting on top of the little knoll all by itself without a flake of snow around it. It started and he drove it home.

When I was around nine or ten years old, living at Grandpa Hodson's, I was at the right age to enjoy a good big snow storm. My fingers and toes always got very cold when I played in the snow, but otherwise I kept pretty warm and played outside in spite of cold fingers and toes. I never did get frost bitten.

When the big snow came with the blizzardly wind, it formed a very high drift, higher than the fence around Grandpa's small flower garden in the corner of our side yard, between the house and the drive. My father shoveled a narrow path from the back porch to the yard gate through the high drift to the drive. Then several feet of the drive had to be shoveled. It was fun for me to run down the path and on through the drive because I was tall enough to see over the high snowbanks at the side of the path.

Snow had drifted up into an enormous hill in Grandpa's flower garden. I got a good idea. I got lots of ideas when I was that age, some good, some bad. Some I tried, some I did not, but that big snowdrift was just sitting there out of the way being wasted, and it was a big temptation to me.

I got a shovel and worked my way into Grandpa's flower garden. In the summertime I was not allowed in there, but now, with all the snow, what harm could I do? I began digging and digging, stopping now and then to warm up and eat. Finally after hours and hours of work I accomplished my idea. I had dug out underneath the thick top crust of the large snowdrift and made a cave. It was like I thought an Eskimo igloo would be inside, and I believed it would be great fun to stoop and go through the opening into the cozy little white room. Of course it was not very big, but when company, especially cousins and neighbor children came, the little snow hut was where we played.

These cold days we all ate like horses. In my mind's eye I can still see my aunt Louva making dumplings and putting them in an enormous kettle of potato soup, enough to fill the stomachs of eleven hungry people at her home that night, including her own seven children, and me. She rolled her dumpling dough into a big circle on the end of the eating table. When she had it as thin as she wanted it, she sliced it across with a sharp knife into strips an inch or barely a little wider. She did not cut or break the strips in two but with one hand scooped up, right through the middle, a handful of the strips and sprinkled them into the boiling soup, while stirring all the time with the other hand, using a long-handled spoon.

My! How good that soup was on a cold winter evening.

On this particular evening I'm remembering at my aunt Louva Baker's, there had been a big drifting snow. We older children had great plans. As soon as supper was finished and the dishes cleared away, we bundled up well in our warm winter wraps and went to Aunt Louva's next farm neighbor's, taking sleds, scoop shovels, and dishpans.

There were four children around our age living there. They took what they had and we all went to a large hill behind their house. It was a lovely, bright moonlit night, and the snow was several inches deep and crusted over hard, making easy sledding. Did we have fun? Great fun. An evening we would never forget.

I'd loved sledding since I was little. I had started winter sports early. When I was around three or four years old my father made a sled for me for a Christmas gift, the only sled I ever had.

He took some pieces of strap iron to Warren Pickett's machine shop, where the sorghum factory stood for many years at Bakers Corner. Using Warren's equipment, forge, anvil, hammers, tongs, and whatever else was needed, he heated the iron strips red hot and pounded and shaped two of them into sled runners. He made some braces of the same material and attached them too, making the runners very strong.

For the top of the sled he used some pieces of wide lumber, sawed them to the right size and bolted the runner and top pieces together, making a strong solid sled. It never was painted. Soon after my father had given it to me on Christmas morning, he took me and the sled to a grove where he later made a park. There were some hills there.

It was wonderful, great fun for me to slide down the crusted white snow. I was still quite small, and pulling the sled back up the hill was quite a task for me until I was older. My father would walk down the hill and bring the sled back up so I could take another slide. By the time we sledded at Aunt Louva's neighbor's, I could easily pull the sled up the hill, over and over. Happy days! Happy winter days!

Homemade Carpets

My father's making that sled was really not that unusual. So much, really everything, was made at home. I remember my mother tearing, cutting, and sewing carpet rags when I was very small. She used only the good part of old clothing, sheets, pillow cases and such. If the piece had faded she dyed it with Putnam dye, boiling the material and dye in a wash boiler over the old cast iron cook stove, a process which made a bright, fast color. She liked to use bright shades that had not faded among the colors, and rejected white because it showed soil so easily.

When she had all the material of colors wanted, Mama began cutting and tearing the pieces into narrow strips, one inch to one and one-fourth inches, depending on the thickness of the material. When the strips of one color were all torn, she sewed the ends together, laying both pieces flat and lapping them enough to hold when sewn.

When the strips of one color were all sewed together, she rolled them into balls. Some balls were large, some small, depending on the amount of like material she had, and some multiple balls were made. These gaily colored balls were lots of fun for a little girl to play with, roll around on the floor, and stack in piles to see how high she could build them before they would fall.

Although I was very small, I can still remember going in the old phaeton buggy with boxes and cloth bags of pretty colored carpet rag balls settled all around us. We were taking them to a weaver, I believe near Hortonville, for him to make into a new wall-to-wall rag carpet for our sitting room. The expert weaver knew exactly how to mix the colors and the right color carpet chain to use to make a beautiful carpet. I believe the finished carpet was thirty-six inches wide.

After waiting days, seemingly weeks, we returned to the weaver's house to bring home the large rolls of brand new rag carpet. It was all so exciting. Mama sewed the long strips of carpet together to make it fit our sitting room.

Then came the day to lay the new carpet. All the furniture had to be carried out of the room; then my father brought in fresh straw from the straw stack in an old sheet and spread it thinly and evenly on the bare, freshly scrubbed or mopped and dried wooden floor. Then very carefully, not to disturb the straw, the new carpet was spread over the straw.

The quarter round at the bottom of the baseboard had been removed on one of the longer sides of the room. The edge of the carpet was tacked closely along the baseboard. Then it was stretched to the opposite side of the room. In order to get it stretched very tight, one or more persons put on rubber overshoes and stomped around, pushing the carpet with each stomp toward the opposite wall. While they stood holding the carpet in place, someone would put in a few carpet tacks to hold it in place. Then the one with the overshoes would go back to the other side of the room and pull the rug a little tighter. The tacks would then be pulled and tacked in again to take up the slack.

This stomp and tack process would be done several times until everyone was satisfied the rug was tight enough. At that point the far side would be tacked very closely, followed by each of the other sides. Finally the quarter round was put back in place and we were ready to bring the furniture back into the room.

It was always fun to rearrange the furniture. Usually the carpet rags were prepared in the wintertime when the womenfolk had more time for that kind of work. Then, too, it was nice to have the new carpet ready to put down in the spring or summer when everyone did a gigantic job of house cleaning.

That spring housecleaning was something to behold. We would wait to clean the living room until the weather was warm enough to put away the old, black wood or coal heating stove until the days began to turn chilly in the fall. It would be hid away and covered over for the summer.

My! How nice the room was with that beautiful, bright, clean carpet we'd just laid. Maybe new wallpaper, all the woodwork and windows shiny clean, the lace curtains freshly washed, starched, and stretched. It smelled so good that we wanted to stay in that room all of the time.

But by the next spring the new carpet and the straw underneath would be full of dust. No one had electricity, and therefore no vacuum sweepers. At least once a week that carpet had to be swept with a broom, and how the dust did fly by the time the rug had been down a year. If it was not too dirty it would be hung over the clothesline in one piece and the dust beat out of it with a hand carpet beater. Usually it had to be washed. Again all the furniture was removed. The floor seams and each strip were washed separately in the old Rocky-by washer and hung over the clothesline to dry.

When the cleaned carpet was put back down on the floor it would be reversed, with the bright unworn bottom side up. All of this was lots of work for the grownups, but for a little girl like me all the commotion and the pretty clean rooms was almost as much fun as Christmas.

Keeping the Sabbath

I remember one Sunday afternoon when I was visiting with my cousin Margaret. I was around eight years old; she was three years younger than I. We were playing upstairs trying to sew, as children can, a doll dress. Aunt Lizzie, Margaret's mother came up, I suppose to see what we were doing. When she saw that we were trying to sew she said, "Don't you know this is Sunday and it is wrong to sew on Sunday?" I knew that my mother did not sew on Sunday, but I thought we were only playing and that would not count. From that day until this I have not sewn on Sunday, neither have I crocheted, quilted, embroidered, or done any kind of fancy work on the Sabbath day. It goes back to this:

Exodus 20:8
Remember the Sabbath day to keep it holy
Six days shalt thou labour, and do all thy work:
But the seventh day is the Sabbath of the Lord thy God: in it thou shalt not

do any work, thou, nor thy son, nor thy daughter, thy manservant, nor thy maidser-
vant, nor thy cattle, nor thy stranger that is within thy gates:

When I was a little girl I was always taught to obey that commandment from the Bible. My parents were very strict about working or doing business on Sunday. And yet the regular farm chores, which included milking the cows and caring for the animals, were always done on Sunday. Also my mother cooked on Sunday the food she could not prepare on Saturday. We had our own way of keeping the Sabbath that we felt was right and important in the sight of God.

My father did not sell milk on Sunday. It was an item of business that he did not consider necessary. His uncle John Pickett was our milk hauler, and neither did he run his milk route on Sunday, because he thought it was unnecessary labor. Other milk routes ran on Sunday. Those farmers on Uncle John's route who wanted their milk to go in on Sunday took it themselves.

If my father and Uncle John thought the weather was cool enough, the eight-gallon can of milk was cooled in a tub of cold water direct from the well, at the windmill, then taken to the cellar until Monday morning, then sent to Sheridan on the route.

When the weather was too warm to keep Saturday evening's and Sunday morning's milk we made other use of it. Quite often on Saturday evening my father would go to Sheridan to the Pulliam ice cream plant and get a twenty-five or thirty-pound block of ice and we made our gallon and a half freezer of ice cream. Usually some neighbor or friends brought their freezer and we had wonderful times together.

The milk that was not used for ice cream was used in other ways. The cream was skimmed off, soured, and churned into butter. The skimmed milk was made into cottage cheese. We lived well on our Saturday evening milk in the summertime.

If my father lost some milk over the weekend it did not worry him. The pigs and chickens did well on it on Monday morning and he felt that he was honoring God by not selling it on Sunday.

All my life I haven't bought things–for instance gasoline–on Sunday unless it is really necessary, as in taking the ox out of the ditch, as

Jesus says. We have aimed to be sure our gas tank is full on Saturday evening in case we want to use the car on Sunday.

I sometimes wonder about eating Sunday dinner at a restaurant, which we seldom do. We are causing someone to work on Sunday—we are buying—it is business—is it right? It is something to think about.

My Other Grandparents

I've spoken of my mother's father, Grandpa John Hodson. Of course I had two sets of grandparents. My father's father, Dr. William Wilson, practiced medicine for many years in the small village of Scipio in Jennings County, Indiana. He had his office in one of the rooms of his home. He had lived in and practiced medicine in other towns, one of them Adams, where my father had been a boy. These were the days when doctors made house calls, and the first several years of his practice those calls were made by horse and buggy.

Grandpa Wilson was a jolly, joking man, six feet and three or four inches tall. At one time he weighed over three hundred pounds. He knew this extra weight was not healthy so he reduced to the size he thought he should be.

Grandpa was a handsome-looking man. His third wife, Sallie, my step-grandmother, whom we considered our grandmother, was a jolly person, too. She told my father and his brother, Uncle Clyde, who were each six feet tall, "You boys are stately and handsome, but you will never come up to your father."

Everyone who knew Grandpa and Grandma Wilson liked both of them. They had some hobbies, especially flowers and chickens. Their flowers were many, mostly hardy, some from many other countries. Like my other grandpa, the Wilsons had a few exotic flowers in tubs and buckets that were carried into the house or cellar before the cold weather of winter came. Grandma Sallie made preserves from the fruit of their fig tree, which stood in the corner of their living room by the window during the winter months. One winter, before I was eight years old, they sent us a large one-and-one-half-pound ponderosa lemon that they had grown in their living room.

Grandpa and Grandma Wilson had two enemies: cats and English sparrows. They did not like these creatures because they were destructive to songbirds, of which they had many. I have seen Grandpa Wilson sit on their side porch with his rifle in his hand for an hour. If an English sparrow showed up it did not last long, because Grandpa was a crack shot. If a cat showed up Grandma took care of him. She allowed him to stay only a few days. If he did not move on she gave him a feast the likes of which he never wanted again, because in it was a dose of strychnine, which soon took care of him. I went with her one day to feed a big old stray cat and that was the menu.

Their chickens were white wyandottes. Grandpa Wilson sent through the mail and bought eggs for these birds to set from pedigreed stock, then advertised them as "Wilson's Wonderful White Wyandottes." He was very proud of his chickens and sold eggs for setting purposes, shipping some quite a distance, advertising his chickens and eggs through the newspapers and by mailing literature.

Grandpa and Grandma had purchased some of these pedigreed white wyandotte chickens, twelve hens, and one rooster from a place in Hope, Indiana. They were so proud of them, they marked each with a W. W. under its wing. One morning Grandpa went to the barn to feed his horse and discovered the prized chickens were not there.

There were only two stores in this little town that would buy chickens, and Grandpa was well acquainted with both of the storekeepers. There at one of these stores he found his chickens. The W. W. marked under their wings proved they were William Wilson's. Furthermore, the storekeeper knew the old fellow there in town who had brought them in. Grandpa got the chickens back. I do not remember what happened to the old man, probably nothing. Grandpa knew him and he knew Grandpa, and I am sure Grandpa would not have pressed charges against him. Still, Grandpa was quite disapproving. I have heard Grandpa say, "I would rather spend the rest of my life in jail than to take something which does not belong to me."

Hens and Chickens

Grandpa Wilson at Scipio was only one of thousands of Indiana farmers raising chickens in the early days of the century. Every farm and most of the people in small towns and villages kept chickens. They raised pullets for laying purposes and young roosters to fry or sell. The pullets laid eggs all winter long. Chickens were about the most important animal on a farm, producing several kinds of wonderful food.

I grew very experienced in taking care of chickens. It was one of my jobs growing up on the farm. I was particularly interested in the hens. I gathered eggs all winter long. In the spring some of the hens would quit laying and want to set. They would stay on the nest all the time except when they got off to get something to eat and drink. Then they would walk around with their feathers ruffled and make a clucking, scolding sound. They would want to eat and make a nest after they had laid eggs all winter and spring, and had their layings out. But we needed them to lay more eggs. If we did not want to set them we put them in a pen or cage where there were no nests and gave them plenty of water and shelled corn. We left them there for two or three weeks to "break them up," which meant to keep them off a nest until they did not want to set any more.

Usually if an old hen wanted to set and you bothered her, she would get mean and peck your hands and arms. Her bill was sharp, and it would really hurt if she pecked hard, maybe even bring blood or make a blue bruised spot.

Sometimes every evening as we gathered eggs, if we did not want to take time to put a hen in the "breaking-up pen," we would pick her up by the feathers on her back or by the tail and give her a toss. She would not like this and would ruffle her feathers, squall, and make clucking noises, and sometimes come at you and flog at your legs. As soon as you left and let her alone, the hen would crawl back on the nest and be there the next evening when you gathered eggs. This determined chicken would want to set for two, three, or four weeks if you did not put her in the breaking-up pen.

There were not many hatcheries around when I was young.

Most people set eggs and hatched their own chickens. If you did not have roosters or you wanted to hatch a different breed of chicken, you would buy a setting of eggs of a friend or neighbor who had the kind you wanted. That was how Grandpa Wilson made some money on his hobby.

I well remember people coming to our house to buy setting eggs. They usually brought a kettle or basket with a soft cloth in it in which to carry the eggs home. Maybe they would want only one or two settings, with fifteen hen eggs considered to be a setting. My mother always picked out eggs as nearly perfect as possible to sell for setting or to set for herself. It was not good to hatch a thin-shelled egg or one that was irregular in shape, had a ridge on it, or showed rough places on the shells.

We expected to get at least one hundred new chickens from these settings, but hoped to get two hundred to three hundred baby chicks. We set the hens in the spring, a few maybe as early as the latter part of March if we wanted fried chicken early. We would never have thought of buying a chicken to fry or even stew or bake from the grocery store, that was just unthought of by the farmer. We always thought we should have chickens large enough to fry by July 4th, that and fresh cabbage from our garden. Cabbage is something else a farmer would never buy at the grocery store. It seems the chickens we used to raise, dress, and fry tasted better than the ones we buy at the stores nowadays. They were fresh, not frozen, and had been raised on an open range, not in a small cage.

Before we set the hens in the spring, the setting house had to be cleaned out. The old straw was carried outside and burned. For the nests, we usually used wooden orange crates in the setting house, taken out and held over the fire and smoked long enough to kill any chicken lice that might be harboring in them. Then new straw was placed in the nests and on the floor.

Then the fifteen nearly perfect eggs were placed in each nest. Usually early in the spring, only one, two, or three hens were set. Then in two or three weeks we liked to set several at one time, maybe ten, twelve, or fifteen hens at one time. Before the hens that we wanted to set were placed on the nests, each hen had to be dusted well with louse powder. We had to be sure to dust under each hen's wings and behind and to rub the powder into the feathers as well.

Usually we did not get a 100 per cent hatch. When we did we were really happy.

There were hazards to the hatching process. In those days in the spring many times a farmer would decide to clear a little patch of ground (woods). To do this the farmer would cut down the trees then cut them up into fence posts and firewood. In the early days they split fence rails out of the suitable trees. Whenever they cleared, they usually blasted the stumps out with dynamite, and if the blasting was very close it would affect the hatching of the eggs. Or if a thunderstorm came up and was close enough to jar the earth, sometimes the eggs would not hatch. The jarring killed the chicks in the shell.

When the hens were setting, they had to be tended every day. Feed and fresh water needed to be kept before them all of the time. We fed setting hens ear corn. If you did not have a setting house or setting room in the hen house, you had to put a board over the hen weighted down so she could not get off the nest or some other hen could not get on the nest with hen number one and lay fresh eggs in with the setting eggs. We always marked a pencil mark all around the setting eggs so if this did happen we would know the fresh eggs.

Sometimes a setting hen would break one of her eggs in the nest or use the nest for a toilet. What a disgusting mess. Then we would take out a pan of lukewarm water and a soft cloth and wash the eggs that were left and dirty, take out the dirty straw, and replace it with clean.

When it came near the end of the setting period, we would pick up one of the eggs, put it to our ear and listen. You could hear the little chick inside cheep or hear the shell begin to crack. What a pleasing sound. A day or two before they hatched they would pip the shell with the little light-colored pipper on the top of their beak, a pipper they soon lost. If you watched you could see them break the shell a little more, then a little more. Finally it would break all the way around the middle, the short way. The little weak, wet chick would get his head out and wiggle and wiggle until out came a wing, then another. When he had struggled long enough out came his feet, and the shell would fall off on each side of him.

This hatching process took quite a while, perhaps a few hours. We would go out several times a day and bring the new baby chicks in as soon as they hatched because sometimes if they were left in the nest the old hen would get her foot on their necks and they would die.

What a pleasure to lift an old setting hen off her nest some morning and see a nest full of fluffy baby chicks all dried off and chirping merrily, ready to take into the house in your apron and place in an old nickel basket or pasteboard box. We'd wrap them in a piece of warm woolen blanket and put them behind the stove to keep them warm for a day or two until all had hatched.

Maybe after a while one would chirp, loud and lonely. He would be out from under the cover, away from the rest of them and cold. How happy he was when placed back under the blanket with the others where it was cozy and warm.

When all the eggs had hatched, chicks did not always all come out of each shell. If the eggs were rotten we tossed them out into the field. We were ready to put the mother hen with her babies in a coop that we had worked hard to prepare.

A few days before time for the chicks to hatch, we cleaned and repaired the coops, scrubbed them with lye water, and allowed them to dry thoroughly. Then we placed a little clean straw in the coop.

After the chicks hatched in the nest, we'd soon see them out and walking around. They had to listen carefully for the hen. If a crow or chicken hawk came flying overhead, she gave a warning sound for the babies to get under her wings for protection. Hawks and crows loved to carry them away to eat and feed their young. If we heard the hen's excited warning clucks, we ran out to scare the crows and hawks away, screaming at them, clapping our hands loudly and flying our aprons in the air. It was a terrible feeling when one of us would get out too late and see a crow flying though the air with one of our baby chicks in his claws. Many baby chicks were taken that way.

We could always make a scarecrow, a common sight in the country. Made by nailing together two pieces of wood to form a cross about the size of a grown person, they worked fairly well. Old clothes and an old hat were placed on the wood pieces so it resembled a person. Some people stuffed old garments with straw and used them as scarecrows. These dummies did work to frighten birds; on wash day when the clothes were blowing and drying on the line the crows did not bother as much.

As long as the mother hen was cooped up, she could do nothing except give her warning. If she were out of the coop running free, she would fight a crow and sometimes save the young ones. When the mother hens were turned out together they sometimes fought each other. But the worst in the fighting line were the roosters. Sometimes they would fight each other until their combs were bloody.

Each spring threatening crows nested when the corn was coming up. When the corn began to come through the ground and until it was a few inches high, the crows would ruin lots of it along the fences next to the woods. They pulled up a shoot of corn and ate the seed grain. If their eggs had been laid or the baby crows had hatched, my father would take his double-barreled shotgun and go to the woods.

He had been watching all spring as he farmed near the different woods to see where the crows were building their nests. He knew exactly where to go to find them. Maybe the eggs had not hatched yet, and the mother crow was on her nest; maybe some had already hatched but were not ready yet to leave their nests. He would blast their nests and bring home some dead parent crows, then he would fasten them to the top of a pole high above the fence, letting them hang in the wind for days. This also was a help to keep away the crows, besides the young he killed and the eggs he destroyed; that helped to make fewer crows. He went to several different woods, his own and those that joined our property in search of the crows.

While the baby chicks were still in our house, we would take the cover off them and set them in a light place, in the sun if we could, and put a little fine sand on the paper in the basket for them. They liked to pick at it. This way they would get fine sand into their craws and gizzards to help digest their food when they began to eat.

We used to start them off with a little rolled oats mixed with some finely cracked corn and wheat. Or we could buy baby chick feed, which was a mixture of finely cracked grains and seeds. When they were a little older they were put on coarser cracked corn morning and evening. We made a round pen, six, eight, or ten feet across, using a few feet of old wire fence, which was a fine pen where the young chickens would not be disturbed by the hens and roosters. This was placed on a patch of bare ground and the cracked corn scattered by hand in the pen.

By this time they were starting to grow feathers and were large enough to run around and scratch and catch bugs and worms for part of their diet. In later years we began to feed them a mash of properly balanced feeds in feeders. They grew fast. Near July 4th we began to hope some of them would weigh at least two and a half pounds so we could feast on fried chicken that day. We felt it was a waste to eat them any smaller.

There came a time when most farmers' wives began to raise their young chickens in brooder houses and to feed the properly balanced mash in feeders. For the brooder they usually wanted around two hundred and fifty or three hundred baby chicks of the same age to start with, bought from a reliable hatchery.

In this later period of my life, jumping ahead a bit, we had a round brooder, which was fine because the baby chicks could not get far from the heat. In the middle of the more usual square or rectangular-shaped houses was a small oil or coal brooder stove with a large metal cover all the way around it, under which the chicks could keep warm. The feeders and watering fountains were placed out toward the side. Straw was on the floor; it had to be kept away from the stove. Once in a while a brooder house would burn, and that was a real loss for sure to lose the building, the chickens, and all the equipment. The feeders and water fountains needed to be kept filled at all times.

So many things endangered the brood. Sometimes baby chicks were lost because the burners went out and they got chilled, causing them to get pneumonia or some to pile up and smother the rest. Many chickens were lost because of poultry disease.

Once in a while young chickens would get "gapes," a disease caused by the gapeworm. I don't believe I ever had more than one or two get this ailment. They would stand around and "gape," or sort of choke, every few minutes. They could not eat or breathe and would soon die. Aunt Mima had so much trouble with them among her chickens. She would get a long hair from the horse's tail or mane, loop it, and run the loop down the chicken's throat and pull out the gapeworm that was causing the problem. Then the chicken would be all right.

One of the dreaded diseases among chickens, very hard to control, was coccidicosis, a living parasite in the intestines. Most people lost some young chickens with it. Or chickens could get cholera. This affected their bowels, making them terribly messy and dirty behind.

Lice were very hard on both hens and young chickens. The young ones raised in a brooder house were never bothered much with lice unless the sparrows brought them in after the chickens were older and the brooder house door was left open most of the time.

When the chicks were mothered by hens, farmers had louse problems. After the chicks had been put out with their mother for a while, we had to grease them by taking a small can lid with lard into the coop before we turned the young ones out for the day. Each one had to be treated separately. We rubbed a small amount on the chick's head around its eyes, ears, and beak, under each wing, and on its behind. Lice have to have some moisture, and the grease kept them from getting into these favorite spots. Then the mother had to be taken care of with either grease or dusting powder. When you raised the hen's wing and saw some lice run, you felt sorry for her and her young ones and were glad you were doing something to relieve them. If the weather was rainy or the dew still on, the small chicks could not be turned out until it dried off as long as they were greasy.

When lice got a head start in the hen house, we had to clean out all the straw from the nests and the floor and burn it outside. We'd take out the nests and smoke them and paint the roosts with used tractor oil. If lice were on the rafters, we sprayed them with disinfectant. It was necessary to catch each hen and rooster and powder each one separately with lice powder.

Roop was a disease among the hens and roosters, one I never did see among the young ones. Roop caused sores on their heads, which became swollen and full of pus. The chickens' eyes would be so infected they could not see. Even their combs would get sores on them. We used permanganate of potash in their drinking water, which was supposed to help them. I am not sure it did; it seemed to me they usually died.

Then there were chicken thieves. We were always afraid to leave home at night for fear of these varmints, human as well as animal. The human ones even slipped into the brooder and hen house at night and took chickens while the farmer was sleeping or in his house in the evening listening to the radio. Almost every newspaper told of chickens being taken, especially in the fall when the young ones were ready for market. They were more likely to steal heavy breeds than the lighter-weight leghorns.

Some neighbor women had what they called incubators in which to set the eggs to hatch their chicks. These incubators came in different sizes, from fifty eggs to four hundred or more. They opened on each side with drawers that pulled out. The eggs were set to hatch in trays in these drawers. Across the front was clear glass where you could see the eggs. The incubator was heated to "just warm" with kerosene lamps, to a temperature that had to be kept regular and even. There also had to be a certain amount of moisture in the incubator or the eggs would not hatch. Also, if the lamp went out for too long a time, long enough for the eggs to get chilled, they would not hatch. The worst problem came if the lamp caused a fire and burned down a building.

The eggs in the incubator needed to be turned every day by rotating the trays. The eggs under the setting hen had to be turned, too, but it was done naturally by the hen herself. After the hen eggs had been setting for three weeks in the incubator, they began to hatch. This was the interesting time, as we watched them through the glass front of the incubator. At first you saw a few eggs pipped, then more and more. Finally there was an incubator full of fluffy little cheeping baby chicks. It was not a fast process, but it was satisfying.

If a farmer wanted to sell his eggs to a hatchery, such as McDonald's Hatchery at Sheridan, he needed to abide by specifications. His flock of chickens had to be thoroughbreds. No other chickens could be kept there, not even the pretty little bantam hens. The roosters had to come from some other flock. The hatchery furnished egg cases in which to keep the eggs, which were to be delivered to them on each Saturday. The eggs had to be gathered several times each day in cold weather to keep them from getting chilled and kept about room temperature until delivered. Also the cases were to be tilted from side to side every day or two to turn the eggs.

When we lived at Grandpa Hodson's farm and after moving, when I was eleven years old, Mama raised Rhode Island red chickens, the kind she was raising when she began selling eggs to McDonald's Hatchery.

Later the hatchery offered an extra bonus for eggs from white leghorn hens if the farmer would keep black minorca roosters. The chickens hatched from this combination were austra-whites, good layers like the leghorns but a much heavier chicken. They were white with once in a while a black feather scattered over them.

Determined hens had a way of "stealing out" their nests, to take them to a haymow, under a cow manger, and even in the fence corners under a bunch of weeds, or other out-of-the-way places. If we did not happen to come across this hidden nest, after a while that hen would start setting. Then in three weeks she would surprise us by bringing out a group of tiny fluffy baby chicks. She was so proud and dared anyone to come near them. If it was very late in the season, a neighbor would likely say, "You're going to have to knit leggings for them this winter or they will freeze." If they were not too late we were rather happy to have them for late fryers. Most of the time we let the old hideaway hen go loose and take care of her babies as she pleased. If there were several of the little ones we might prepare her a coop and put her in it with them safe from the rats at night.

Most people used nest eggs to guide the laying hen to a nest. They thought if a hen saw an egg in a nest, she was more likely to get into the nest instead of laying it on the floor of the hen house or just any place outside on the ground, like a duck. The nest eggs were usually made of white, smooth, heavy glass with a rough spot on the small end, bought in a variety store or a hardware store. The last few I saw were made of wood and painted a light cream color, but the popular ones were made of glass. It seemed the hen could not tell the difference between one and the real egg.

It paid to cull the hens once in a while and get rid of the non-layers, especially in the fall to make room in the hen house for the young pullets coming on. My father was a good hand at culling them. If its eyes were dull and its comb pale, he did not keep a chicken. Then he measured between their bones in the back, and if he could not lay two or three fingers between those bones, it would be quite a while before they would be laying again and it would not pay to keep them so long. The old hens that were kept were banded with red or blue leg bands. By the next fall we could tell which were the older hens by the color of the coil band on each leg.

Eventually it was time to sell the young roosters. They had grown and would still be roosting in the coops or on the ground beside the coop because there was not room for all of them after they were larger. If they had been raised in the brooder house, they were likely still roosting there. But some were rather wild and had taken to roosting in the trees. You could only catch them at night. It took two or three people to catch and carry these roosters, and you could not catch them on a moonlit night. We did not have electricity so someone had to carry a kerosene lantern.

We would sort all the young roosters from the pullets, then put back a few to save to eat. The rest would all be sold. My, how those chickens would squawk when they were caught. We felt like everyone in the country round about could hear them.

When our young roosters were ready to sell in the fall and the non-laying hens had been culled out of the flock, Russell Pickett, the chicken buyer, was called to come after them. Russell, a first cousin of my father, had a chicken business in Bakers Corner that he later moved to Sheridan and Noblesville. Either he would come or send some of his help. They always brought their scales and hung them up in the hen house. They used lengths of lamp wick to tie the chickens' legs together, tying one leg of each chicken, weighing a large bunch at a time. To watch them catch the chickens looked so easy, I guess it was because they were used to it.

We were always happy when they were sold and we had the check in our hands, because we were afraid of their being stolen. The chicken money was used to get special things we needed, such as winter clothing for the children, maybe a little Christmas out of it, or something very much needed for the house.

Some women could not stand to kill a chicken to dress and eat and would have their husbands do the job for them. Some would tie their feet together, hang them from the clothesline, and with a sharp knife cut their heads off and let them hang, flop, and bleed while hanging there. I've seen many a person take the chicken's head in his or her hand and swing the chicken round and round until the head was wrung off and the body went flopping and bleeding away. My mother and I would lay the chicken's head on the ground, holding tight to its feet. We'd place a broom handle across its neck, stand one foot on each side of the head, and pull hard until the head came off and we'd give the body a toss, letting it lay until it quit flopping and kicking. The next step was putting it in scalding water to loosen the feathers. If you did not watch, the cats would start chewing on the chicken's neck while you were gone to get the scalding water. Sometimes the cats would drag the head away.

The first time Aunt Lizzie tried to kill a chicken to cook, she tried the broom method I always used. She could not stand to look when she pulled. She closed her eyes and pulled hard and gave what she thought was the head a toss. When she opened her eyes, there went the chicken strutting away, making a great noise and looking at her as if to say, "What do you think you are doing?" The last time Aunt Lizzie tried to kill a chicken, she tied his legs together to a persimmon limb. She tried to cut his head off with a sharp knife. The knife slipped and cut her wrist very badly. It took several stitches to sew it together.

My sister-in-law Roberta used a rifle and shot the chicken in the head when she wanted one to eat. They were living on Uncle Ernest Hodson's farm when she took her rifle out and aimed at one and shot. Two other chickens happened to be in line. The bullet went through the heads of the front two and into the head of the third one. She had three chickens to dress instead of one.

How many eggs and chickens would a farm person eat in a lifetime? A lot! They were the standby of every farm. Here's a story about egg eating. My father for many years did custom baling, and the balers in those days were stationary. They could not be pulled over a field while the men were working. The separate engine and baler were pulled from place to place with a team of horses, and the engine which was placed a few feet from the baler ran the baler with a wide belt. As far back as I can remember we had a team of black work horses named Fred and Coalie. The hay and straw they baled were in a stack or had to be forked out of a mow with pitchforks.

On this particular day they were baling out of a hay-mow. Along with others there was a young man named Carol Beard helping my father, they called him "Bunk." Some of the help found a hen's nest in the mow with about a dozen eggs in it. The baler had a big cooling tank on it, and the water in that tank got boiling hot. So the boys decided they would boil the eggs to go along with the dinner they had brought from home. When lunch time came the eggs were ready to eat. They were eating and enjoying them along with their other food when Bunk opened one that had a chick in it almost ready to hatch. It almost turned their stomachs, and they could eat no more that day.

My father loved people, especially children, most of all his own. When I was small he sang songs to me and recited short poems. "Ten Little Chickens" is one of them. It is a good one to say to tiny tots, counting their toes as you count off the little chickens. It goes like this:

Ten Little Chickens

Ten little chickens all in a line
Crow caught one, then there were nine.
Nine little chickens stayed out too late
Croup got one, then there were eight.
Eight little chickens left out of eleven
Weasel got one, then there were seven.
Seven little chickens, in an awful fix
Mink got one, then there were six.

Six little chickens before a bee hive

Bee stung one, then there were five.
Five little chickens on the barn floor
Rat got one, then there were four.
Four little chickens under a tree
Hawk got one, then there were three.
Three little chickens all wet with dew
One caught cold, then there were two.
Two little chickens see how they run
One got lost, then there was one.
One little chicken left all alone.
Cat caught one, then there were none.

Butchering

If you do not count horses, cows and pigs were the next most important animals on the farms of my childhood. After all, they could be eaten, like chickens. When I was growing up and for several years after that, the farmers did their own butchering of hogs and cows. Usually two or three neighbors would go in together and butcher one or two hogs for each family. Someone had a large iron or copper kettle in which to heat the water to scald the hogs. These kettles, which held twenty or thirty gallons of water, were heated outside with corn cobs, burnable scraps, and pieces of wood.

The farmer would get up very early on butchering day to light the fires that had been laid the evening before under the large kettle. The neighbors would arrive; the hogs would be shot or their throats cut. When the water was hot enough to scald the hog to loosen its hair and make it easier to scrape off, the hog was put into a barrel with a tripod over it. By using a block and tackle on the tripod, the men could raise and lower the animal as many times as needed into the scalding water. After it was out of the barrel, the hog was kept hanging so the hair could be scraped off the skin.

The butchering process always took place when I was in school. No one ever wanted to butcher on Saturday, one reason being that Sunday followed Saturday and because this was too big a job to finish in one day, these farm families wouldn't do this work on the Sabbath. The second day jobs such as sugar curing the hams and shoulders or sometimes a piece of side had to be completed. I can remember walking home from Bakers Corner School, when we lived at Grandpa Hodson's place on a butchering day. What a mess the kitchen was: tubs, dishpans, buckets, and other large containers filled with freshly butchered pork.

Sometimes my mother would slice the fresh side meat, fry it, and place it in a small earthen jar, pouring hot fresh grease from the frying over it to cover it two or three inches or more. In this way the meat kept for several weeks, maybe until warm weather. We called it "fried down side meat." We liked it.

The liver we preferred fresh and never tried to preserve it to use later. There was always too much of it for us to use, so we divided it with neighbors and friends while it was good. We liked beef liver much better than pork liver. Mama soaked the brains overnight in strong salt water, then for breakfast the next morning beat eggs with the brains and fried them.

The two small tenderloins, which some people called "catfish," we thought were the favorite meat in a hog. When they were sliced, pounded, floured, and fried just right they were really delicious. They were always used soon because everyone was anxious for them.

Some of the meat was canned with grease over it. All pork, beef, and chicken were canned by using the cold pack method, boiling the filled, sealed cans for three or four hours in water. How well I liked canned sausage! I liked to open a can of sausage, take out two or three pieces, scrape the grease off them, and make a cold sandwich using only pickles for extra flavor.

To sugar cure the hams and shoulders, a mixture of salt, pepper, and sometimes a very tiny bit of saltpeter was used. My mother's recipe was as follows:

For one joint of a 200 pound hog:

1 pint salt	*2 tablespoons black pepper*
¼ teaspoon red pepper	*3 tablespoons brown sugar*

Mix well and rub over whole joint of ham or shoulder. Rub it well into the joint at the bone. There is a hole that can be found on the side that goes to the bone; this hole must be filled. The excess of the mixture should be piled on the side opposite the skin side. Each joint is to be wrapped in several thicknesses of newspaper then in a large square of muslin, usually a large feed sack, sewed up tight. The joints are left laying on a table for two or three days, with the hole side up and the skin side down, to take salt. After these few days the joints should be hung in the smokehouse with the bone end down so they will drain well.

In a few weeks, what a wonderful breakfast: sliced home-cured ham with fried eggs, brown ham gravy, and puffy homemade biscuits.

Some farmers had smokehouses where they smoked the hams and shoulders. The pieces of uncured pork had to be salted and given enough time "to take," as they called it, before being smoked. Sometimes they smoked the sugar-cured ones, too.

Then there were the ribs and backbones. We really liked them while they were fresh, too. We could not and did not want to eat it all fresh; we wanted to feel we were well prepared with meat supply for several months. We usually canned the ribs, but there was so much bone in the backbones that it did not seem wise to try to can them. If the weather was freezing cold, they were hung from the rafters in the smoke house and kept frozen until needed. No one in the country had electricity, therefore no deep-freezers. We had never heard of them.

The tenderloins could be cut in two ways, depending on the preference of each family. Some families would rather have pork chops than backbones and tenderloins. Either way they could be canned. Sometimes the pork chops or tenderloins were fried down and covered with hot lard like the side meat and sausage. If the weather stayed cold sometimes they were kept frozen until used.

The head was hard to clean and no one liked to do it. Some folks would rather throw it away than clean it. My folks would rather clean it, although they did not like the job, because there was quite a bit of good lean meat on it. After it was skinned and properly cleaned it was cooked until tender. The meat was then picked off the bones and used for different recipes.

Sometimes my mother used it in a recipe called headcheese. The headcheese was made using the head meat with some of the pork shank and broth, creating a jelled loaf. It was sliced and used cold in sandwiches, very delicious. Another recipe was called scrapple; in this the meat was chopped or torn up fine and cooked with a small amount of broth thickened with corn meal, then allowed to cool and set. Then the scrapple was sliced and fried. It was very tasty. Some salt was added in each recipe.

I liked and remembered best the mincemeat made from the hog's head. Sometimes my mother made it from the neck meat of beef, but I liked it made from pork better. After the meat had been cooked until tender, it was torn into bits. Added to the bits were some cubed raw apples, and my mother usually added home-canned cherries and home-canned currents or gooseberries, and always lots of raisins. Added to this was plenty of sugar and vinegar and spices. Everyone was fond of mincemeat pies.

The lard was not usually rendered until the second day. Each piece of meat had the excess fat trimmed off, and the fat cut into small pieces was put together into a large, thoroughly cleaned kettle. The cooking crew built a fire and cooked the fat until they determined it was done. Someone experienced always seemed to know when it was just right. If the lard was not cooked long enough, it would not keep. In a few months you would find a jar or can of spoiled lard.

The "done" contents of the kettle were then dipped into a lard press where the crank was turned to press the hot lard out of the meat. The hot lard was poured into large earthen jars or six-gallon metal lard cans with tight fitting lids, where it was stored until needed.

After the lard had been pressed out of the fat meat, what was left was a crispy product called cracklings, which were fun and tasty to nibble and piece on. We liked to cut the soft part off and put a cupful of this in corn bread or biscuit dough. Hot biscuits with cracklings and syrup on top are delicious. When my youngest brother Myron, born in 1919, was in grade school, through the winter months he usually had a crackling or two in his pocket, even at school.

As I have said earlier, when I was eleven years old we moved to a farm that my father had bought from his cousin, Alvin Foulke. Our closest neighbors were Charlie and Sallie Pierce, and their daughters, Lottie, who was about seven years older than I, and Violet, who was three years younger than I. Violet and I were good close friends as long as she lived.

Charlie and Sallie had a custom butchering shop. Their close neighbor, Erdie Spear, always helped them. It was Erdie who always knew when the fat in the kettle was done. Through the butchering season they butchered from twenty to twenty-five hogs per day.

My family never butchered at home after we moved to the Foulke farm. My father would help Charlie enough to pay for the butchering, either with butchering itself, or more likely with some other farm job. Sallie cleaned the entrails, and stuffed the sausage, and if anyone wanted the hams and shoulders sugar cured she did that. Charlie and Erdie did everything else.

Everyone could take home their cracklings. Later the butcher shops were not allowed to let folks have their cracklings because the government decided that they were not pure enough. But the stores are allowed to sell pigskins, which are not nearly as good as old-fashioned home-butchered cracklings.

We had never bothered to stuff the sausage into a casing until we began having our hogs butchered at Charlie's. Sallie stuffed so much sausage she did not mind it and wanted to stuff ours. From then on our sausage was stuffed, not canned.

That custom butchering shop was helpful. When Mama wanted to sugar cure our hams and shoulders she would take brown sugar, salt, and pepper with the meat cloths to the butcher shop and cure and wrap the hams there where there was plenty of room.

Each year after the butchering season my mother and Sallie made homemade lye soap in the lard-rendering kettle. I never did know their recipe, but they knew exactly how to mix and cook the ingredients just right for making a very good laundry and dishwashing soap. They sometimes added oil of sassafras to perfume their soap.

They put water in the large kettle with all the cracklings that had not been used, grease saved through the year from different meats they had cooked, and lye. I never did work with them and do not know the process, but when it was cooked to the right stage it was left to set in the kettle until it hardened. A few days later Sallie and Mama cut the soap out in irregular pieces and placed the pieces on a board to dry. When dried the new soap was put into a pasteboard box and kept in the smoke house until used.

Mama had a small gray enameled pan that she used to melt the soap with a little water to make liquid soap to use in the washing machine. We also used it for dishes. I did not like it for dishes but it was great for the laundry.

My parents and Charlie and Sallie Pierce were good neighbors and very good friends. They did many work jobs together for many years. It made the work go faster and was companionable.

Nuts

In the fall at school a child like me could tell who had been gathering black walnuts by their stained, black hands. Sometimes some of the girls had a little stain on their hands, but they were more careful than the boys. The spongy, juicy, bright green hull turns black, shrinks, and gets hard, and it is hard to get the hull off if the walnuts are allowed to lie many days after falling from the tree. One way to get that outer shell off is to run it through a hand-turned corn sheller. But my father would rather we did not use the sheller for that purpose because it took a long time to get the black bits of the hull out so there would be none on the corn.

Later some people placed the walnuts in their driveways and ran back and forth over them in the car to get the soft hull off. Another way was to pound these things off with a hammer or a wooden mallet. Boys usually stomped them out with the heel of their shoe, then picked them out with their fingers. After the spongy green hull was removed, the nuts needed to be spread out to dry. Many people spread them on the hen house roof or the roof of some other low building.

Up the road a short distance north of the schoolhouse was a thick woods on the west side of the road, on Uncle Harvey Pickett's farm. One bright, sunny fall afternoon our teacher took all the children in her room nut hunting. I was probably in the first grade. In this woods, I suppose like all other woods around, were black walnut and hickory nut trees but what I remember was the hazelnut thicket. I liked the fat, round, sweet goodies inside their thin shells. These nuts are mostly called filberts now. That is the only time in all my years that I can remember gathering hazelnuts. There were only a few of these wonderful trees in our Bakers Corner area.

Mail at Bakers Corner

We were such a close-knit community. I remember my mother telling about going after the mail at Bakers Corner when she was a girl. She would have been able to pick it up for all the neighbors. As she walked along the muddy dirt roads, in places the mud holes reached from a rail fence along one side of the road to the one on the other side. She would climb up and walk on the fence to get past the mud hole. But she was glad to deliver to each of the nearby folks.

There never was a rural route to deliver mail from Bakers Corner. The little post office, about the size of a dresser sat in the corner of the Charles B. "C. B." Jones store. Everyone in the community round about walked, rode horseback, or went in wagons to get their mail. When one person went after their mail, they usually brought the mail to the folks along their road. Sometimes folks did not get their mail for several days.

A post office was first established at Bakers Corner in Hamilton County on February 7, 1873, while the village was still called Englewood. Since there was another Englewood in Indiana, with a post office already established under that name, this village had to have a new name.

It was changed to Baker's Corner. It carried this name for twenty years. The postal department decided the apostrophe was too much of a nuisance. It was dropped February 20, 1894. The post office then operated under the name Bakers Corner.

In 1893 C. B. built a new brick store building, and it was the last place the post office occupied in Bakers Corner. That little dresser-size post office with a number of pigeonholes behind glass stood in the front corner to the west, to your right as you entered the front door of the store.

A star route came from the post office at Cicero to the post office at Sheridan and back every day. A horse-drawn vehicle, like a Klondike, stopped, leaving mail and picking up mail at Bakers Corner.

On December 31, 1900, the little post office left Bakers Corner. The mail then was delivered to everyone from the Sheridan post office on a rural route. It was called rural free delivery or R.F.D., and was delivered in horse-drawn vehicles.

The postmasters at Bakers Corner were as follows:

Phelps, Eli N.	2-7-1873
Baker, William H.	10-23-1874
Jessup, Elihu	2-17-1876
Baker, Anthony	11-20-1878
Martin, Benton P.	11-2-1883
Cross, David	1-25-1886
Stanley, Embree A.	3-16-1887
Jones, Charles B. (C. B.)	1-22-1889

The Store at Bakers Corner

Smack-dab in the heart of the town was the C. B. Jones Store which housed the post office and much more. In 1893 C. B. Jones built the two-story, red-brick store we all knew and loved, on the southwest corner of the crossroads. In its glory days the store had a pleasant feeling inside. To the left was a candy case and a counter; behind that were shelves with Quaker Oats and Aunt Jemima Pancake Mix and other items like that. The clerk could reach these items by using two tall ladders, which were on rollers and reached to the shelves near the ceiling. To the right was the "liar's bench," where old-timers competed with each other to tell tall stories. A stove warmed the store in the cool seasons. Steps at the back went up to another level, where a piano stood against the wall.

The store was a real community center where people came for food, clothing, and anything else you could want. In the early days it offered a huckster service that ran routes through the week, so those wagons were nearby, parked in the big barn behind the store. There was a period of time, too, when folks gathered at the store on Saturday evenings near that piano for music and visiting, along with buying their week's supply of groceries. At noon some of the farmers around the countryside would loaf at the store, talking and eating their meals together.

When our older children were small, the grocery store at Bakers Corner had a Halloween get-together for the neighboring community. Folks from all directions came in after dark. Some were masked; others were not. There would be music. Sometimes my father and Oren Kelly would furnish guitar music. My father played the Spanish guitar and Oren the Hawaiian guitar. Casey would treat everyone with cider and doughnuts.

After C. B.'s death in 1921, D. C. Sowers and Wayvern "Casey" Jones bought the place and operated it until about 1928 when Casey purchased the full share. Casey's store was a familiar landmark until 1978, when he closed the business and retired. The building was demolished in 1992.

The Telephone Exchange

Thank goodness for that telephone exchange established in the C. B. Jones store, which was the center of most of the talking in the town. The telephone tied the Bakers Corner area together even better than the mail did. We could sure communicate with each other, and we did!

My cousin Ruby, only one year older than I, could say, "Halla" (as it was pronounced) as well as her older sisters, who were the regular operators in the telephone office. She could place the plugs where they belonged and push the levers, which rang one long, two shorts, or three shorts or two longs or one long, one short, or any other combination of longs and shorts that might be called.

Some of the rings I can still remember—my grandpa Hodson's ring was one long and one short on line eight. Aunt Myrtie Coffin's was one long and one short on line thirteen. After we moved to the

Alvin Foulke farm, our ring was three shorts on line twenty-three, and Uncle Clark Wilson's ring was five shorts, but I do not remember their line number. If we wanted to call the Bakers Corner store we said, "Twenty, please."

The plugs connected two lines, one coming in, the other going out. The regular operator put through the not-too-frequent long-distance calls.

The party lines usually had several families on a line, and the lines were busy much of the time. If you wanted to use the party line and it was busy, you just waited. Maybe you grew impatient. If it was an emergency, you asked for the line, and most folks gave it up pleasantly. Maybe a couple of women were visiting and grew huffy; sometimes this was one of the trials of the day.

There was much eavesdropping on party lines. It was one way of finding out what was going on in the neighborhood and learning all the neighborhood gossip.

No matter how many there were on one line, everyone's ring went into every home. When the telephone started ringing, we had to listen and count the rings to see if it was for us.

If my mother wanted to talk to her father, Grandpa, he was also on the Bakers Corner line, so she would turn the crank on the old wall phone, making one short ring which was for the operator, who we usually called "Central." She then put the receiver to her ear, and when Central answered, she told her Grandpa's ring. Then the operator rang his number for her.

If she wanted to call someone else whose number she did not know, she hunted their number in the phone book. Maybe if she was in a hurry she would call for them by name.

The exchange was located above the C. B. Jones store, that tall brick building at the southwest corner of the crossroads. In order to reach it, you had to climb the long, iron framed stairs on the outside, on the west side of the building. We climbed these shaky stairs once each month to pay our two or three dollar telephone bill.

It did not cost extra to talk to someone on Cicero, Westfield, Carmel, Arcadia, or Ekin. We paid twenty-five cents each month for service to Sheridan. Other places around were long distance, costing ten or fifteen cents for a short talk.

If a fire truck went by or we saw smoke in the sky in the daytime or the sky lit up at night, we knew to "Call Central; she will know what it is." If there was sickness in the neighborhood, "Call Central; see if she knows how (so and so) is." Central usually knew the answer to all of these questions.

Whoever Central was closed the switchboard at nine o'clock at night. We were not supposed to call anyone after nine p.m. unless it was an emergency. On Sunday mornings the board was closed from nine until after church services were over. There was no need to call during that time because the operator was not there. It was closed to give her an opportunity to go to church, and she went.

I remember well when Uncle Clark Wilson's girls worked there. On Sunday morning the carriage load of the family went on to West Grove Church near Deming, but the buggy went to the Bakers Corner telephone office to get whatever Wilson girl was working there, then take her to Sunday school and church services. Then after the services were over, they would bring her back to the telephone office. The office was open on Sunday afternoon, although it was not a very busy place then.

Central carried her lunch and other meals from home. There was a half bed in the switch-board room where the girls slept if they were on night duty. There were two operators who took turns with night and day hours. Ruby and I enjoyed spending a night once in a while with one of her sisters in the telephone office, but I don't know how we all three slept in the little half bed.

This telephone office was a very important part of Bakers Corner from the year 1901 until 1955, when we changed the old wall crank telephone to the new dial system. The dial telephone was installed in our house on January 7, 1955 but was not hooked up ready to use. We were not able to use it until April 30, 1955. At that time we were changed from a private line on the Bakers Corner exchange to a party line on the Sheridan exchange. Our number changed from 12 to Pleasant 8-5208.

The Red Brick Bakers Corner School: The Little Room

I suppose the real "built" center of life in Bakers Corner along with the church and store was the schoolhouse. I started school in first grade in the two-room brick schoolhouse at the crossroads. The first, second, third, and fourth grades were in the east room with a lady teacher. The fifth, sixth, seventh, and eighth grades were in the west room. The east room was called the "Little Room" and the west room the "Big Room" because of the size of the pupils, not the room size.

I was six years old when I started school, living with my parents on the east side of the range line road about three-fourths of a mile north of its intersection with the Cicero-Sheridan Road.

The land on the east side of the range line road was Jackson Township, but Bakers Corner was in Adams Township. My parents desired for me to start school outside our actual territory, in Bakers Corner. Since we did not live in the same township as the school my father went to the township trustee and asked to have me transferred to the Bakers Corner School. This is where my cousins who lived across the road in Adams Township attended. I could walk the one and one-fourth mile with a group of children. On the other hand, if I attended Johnson School in our township I would have to walk one and three-fourth miles, half of the way by myself.

The Bakers Corner school building had a separate entrance for each of its two rooms. Along the outside wall of each entrance were hooks upon which to hang coats and other wraps. The girls hung theirs on the south side of the window and the boys on the north. Below these hooks were benches where lunch pails, baskets, or boxes were kept. Overshoes and boots were also kept under this bench.

The belfry was over the entrance rooms, and the bell rope hung down into the Big Room entrance. The Big Room teacher, who was always a man until the last few years of school there, was the bell ringer. There was one large window in each entrance, a door between the enrance rooms and a cement platform in front of the schoolhouse doors.

Before the old slate roof was covered in the 1950s, the date 1889 showed very plainly on the dark gray roof in lighter gray shingles. This marked the year the brick school house had been built.

The large windows—two on each end of the building, four on the south side and two on the north, one on each side of the entrance—were covered on the outside with framed, heavy wire netting. I don't believe that netting would keep out a burglar, but it must have been to protect the window glass from a stray ball. No curtains covered the windows, but there were window shades controlled by a heavy cotton cord.

A first bell and a last bell signaled the opening of school in the morning and noon break. The first bell, which rang five minutes before time for school to take up, was a warning to drop your games and get ready to come inside for classes to start. In nice weather when the children could play outside, at the sound of the first bell they were supposed to line up in front of the door, ready to march in when the last bell rang and the teacher gave the sign. When the last bell rang it was time to get into the seats and be ready to start classes. At each morning and afternoon recess there was only one bell. It meant to get into your seat now, ready for class or study.

The school took up of a morning at fifteen minutes until nine; two fifteen-minute recesses broke the routine, the morning one at 10:10, the afternoon one at 2:10. At noon there was an hour for lunch and play, from twelve until one o'clock. The children who lived in Bakers Corner went home for their lunches. The others brought food in various kinds of containers, the most common one a shiny, round tin pail with a tightly fitted lid and a bail (handle) with which to carry it. Some brought their lunch in tin half-gallon molasses buckets.

In the fall and spring in nice weather the children ate their lunches under the shade of the large maple and tulip poplar trees. Sometimes we would swap an article of food in our lunch for something in a friend's lunch. We would all like to have swapped with Josephine Poore once in a while. Her father worked for C. B. Jones grocery until he built his own little grocery store on the range line road and drove a huckster wagon out from it. We did not realize how much better our home-grown and butchered ham, sausage, and tenderloin was than the store bologna that was in her sandwiches. Neither did we realize the difference between our home-baked cookies, pies, and cakes, and her store-bought baked goods.

We did not have running water in the building. The water for the school was furnished by the C. B. Jones grocery store, the only store in the little village, with a fresh pail being carried inside every day by one of the older boys. In warm weather another fresh pail came in at noon. It sat on a kitchen cabinet in the Big Room with a dipper in it, and everyone refreshed himself with a drink from the same dipper. A wash pan sat beside the water bucket.

Later we became more sanitary. The water bucket and dipper were replaced with a covered tank that held two or three buckets of water with a faucet on the side. A tin cup for everyone to drink from sat beside it. If you did not want to drink from the same tin everyone else used, you could furnish your own. Not many did. At recess and noon you could get a drink at the water hydrant in the yard.

Each room was heated with stoves just alike, large pot-bellied cast-iron stoves with black sheet metal jackets around them to help circulate the heat. The older boys were to keep the coal buckets filled. The stoves were very efficient, except in zero weather, when the rooms stayed chilly in spite of the bucketsful of coal that were fed into them. On these very cold days we were allowed to move our seats and sit close to the stove to study. Our faces would get very hot while our toes were almost frozen. One person could not sit there all of the time, everyone took turns. We did not recite sitting around the stove.

The janitor, always someone who lived near the schoolhouse, built a fire in the big stoves each morning through the winter months and stoked it in the evening to hold overnight. Sometimes this man came to sweep and dust in the evening before all the children were gone from the building. Each summer the building had a thorough cleaning, repairs were made, if there was any painting needed it was done, and the floors were freshly oiled and disinfected. How I hated the smell of the fresh disinfectant when school started in the fall or when we returned after the Christmas holiday.

The schoolyard was a pasture during the summer vacation months, which helped to keep the grass down. It was probably mowed just before school started in the fall.

Some pupils would sometimes misbehave very badly and need to be punished. In the Little Room, having to stand in the corner facing the wall was a popular punishment. Sometimes the teacher sent someone out into the hall for a while. One of my Little Room teachers had a habit of striking misbehaving fingers with the sharp edge of a ruler, a very painful way of learning a lesson.

One time when I was in the third or fourth grade, John Pickett was due for a whipping with a paddle. I do not remember what he had done; he was always full of life and mischief. The teacher placed a straight chair in front of our class. She took her paddle in her hand and sat down on the chair, then called John up to the front. He knew what was coming and had prepared for it. He went up very willingly. After the teacher had him lie on his stomach across her knees, John turned his face toward us with a grin and a wink. Up went her paddle; it came down with a terrible loud explosive noise. John had put an electric light bulb in the hip pocket of his trousers.

John Pickett made the first radio I ever listened to. I did not hear anything but squeaks and grinding noises and whistles on that crystal radio that time, but sometimes you could hear stations pretty well over it. John was a very smart, inventive boy. Our neighborhood often wondered what he would have invented had he lived. Poor John! He was killed on the road from Sheridan to Noblesville when it was still a gravel road. We lost him that day in a motorcycle accident when he was only sixteen years old.

One winter evening when I was six years old and in the first grade, I went with my parents to visit across the road from our house at my father's uncle Clark Wilson's. Usually when we went over there for an evening there was lots of music, guitar, mandolin, pump organ, banjo, fiddle, and French harp. While Aunt Jane and my mother visited beside the glow of the base burner, and Uncle Clark and my father and the older young people played music, we smaller children played games and romped about. No one seemed to care how rowdy or loud we became. Maybe they could not hear us above the sound of the music.

We played mostly in the large, long dining room. A big dishpan or two filled with popcorn and another with a variety of apples and pears satisfied our hunger. What pure fun everyone had by the light of kerosene lamps and by the warmth from the coal stoves.

One of these evenings was not quite as much fun as usual, especially for me. Ruby and I had been having so much fun sliding off of the davenport arm in the middle room, an area between the dining room where the music was and the front living room where our mothers were visiting.

Instead of sliding off the rounded front of the arm of the davenport, as I had been doing, I fell off the side onto the floor, feeling intense pain. Doctor Clark Newby was called out from Sheridan. I am not sure if he had an automobile by that time or if he drove out to Uncle Clark's in a buggy. I know he came to the house, which was the custom at that time. He said my arm was broken at the elbow and bound it up in a splint with plaster of Paris. After a few weeks it had healed, and I was using the arm with the splint so much it was not doing any good by the time it was removed. I did not need it any longer. That arm has never bothered me since.

There were always accidents at school, too, or sickness. One time during warm weather Lowell Ross got a bad nosebleed. The teacher put cold wet packs on the back of his neck, using cold water; no one had ice then. Another time Maurice Carr was very sick to his stomach. He was outside vomiting, and several of the children were standing around feeling sorry for him. Why did our teacher allow them to watch? Why didn't she send them away? It turned out he had diphtheria, but fortunately no one else took it.

Especially during winter months each year, colds and flu caused many absences. The latter part of the winter and toward spring, other diseases common to children that are prevented now by vaccination took their toll. Whooping cough came early after Christmas. I remember one year in the Big Room when so many had the whooping cough at the same time, everyone who had never had it took it then. When they all got started coughing, it was so noisy the teacher would dismiss class until it quieted down. Also the children could not recite while coughing so hard. Sometimes a child would run outside, coughing so hard they threw up. I didn't go through the school-time epidemic because I had whooping cough the summer before I started school.

A little later came the epidemic of mumps. Children could not come to school with mumps and were required to be quiet, or the illness might become severe. Toward the end of school each year came measles, quite a serious disease, sometimes affecting the eyes. The patient had to stay in a darkened room and in bed for several days.

Most of the children came to school after two or three days with chicken pox. Usually that sickness did not cause you to feel ill, but sometimes the itchy sores left small scars. Other diseases such as scarlet fever, smallpox, and diphtheria were not common by the time I was in grade school, but had been terrible in my parents' and grandparents' generations.

When the weather was rainy, very snowy, or extremely cold, my father or one of the neighbors picked up the neighborhood children and took them to school and brought them home in the evening. A few parents had cars, but my grade school time was still horse and buggy days, the days before many Model Ts. Some parents had buggies or carriages with side curtains, which did a pretty good job of protecting and keeping us dry.

When the snow was deep, the roads were not cleared of the snow. Most people used sleighs, bobsleds, Klondikes, or mud boats, all drawn by a horse or a team of horses. Many used sleigh bells on their horses, and as they slipped along over the snow the buggies with the bells made a merry, happy jingle that carried across the crusted snow.

During the winter, sometimes there would come a big rain before a hard freeze. A patch of ice would freeze around the southeast corner of the schoolhouse, and a large one would appear in the front yard. Some of the children would bring ice skates and skate during noon and recesses. A boy named Lawrence Ross brought double-runner ice skates, the only ones I have ever seen. He would let the other children wear them. They were the only skates I ever learned to stand up on.

During cold spells there was always a large pond of ice in the field east of the schoolhouse on the north side of the road, and we often walked to it to skate during the noon hour. When the first bell rang we had to hurry back to make it before the last bell. There were also many snowball fights, of course, during the snowy winter months.

At noontime all through the school year children of all sizes played games in the schoolyard. When blackman was played by all sizes together, it seemed unfair to the little ones. Other games were tag, leap frog, old witch, and all kinds of ball, then fox and geese when snow lay on the ground. In the spring, as soon as the weather gave us spring fever, the boys played marbles and the girls jumped rope, lining up for our turn to see who could jump the highest number of times without missing.

On cold or bad weather days we ate our lunch and played indoors, games such as cross questions and crooked answers. On the blackboard we played Jack, Go to the mill, and tic-tac-toe. Or we just talked, sometimes with the boys teasing the girls.

Once in a while a parent would visit school. This was exciting, especially if it was yours. If a small child who was not yet old enough to go to school happened to come to visit for a day, all of the girls wanted to have a turn letting him sit with her.

We also had visiting day once each year. School would be closed for one whole day, during which time we were each supposed to visit some other school. I can remember visiting Johnson School, the one I had been supposed to attend, which was about one and three-fourths miles away. It had only one room with one teacher in charge of all eight grades. I walked there with my neighborhood friend Violet Pierce. I knew several of the children who attended there.

When I started school at Bakers Corner, Bert Eudaly was teaching in the Big Room. By the time I was ready for the fifth grade, Jesse Hodson was teaching in that room. My first-grade teacher was Fern Branson, whom I liked very much. The next year another lady named Madge taught in the Little Room. We children in the room did not like her. I don't think she liked us. She was a very nervous person, and some of the parents complained to the trustee about her, enough that she did not get to teach at Bakers Corner the next year. A Miss Alberta Trueblood, whom we all liked very much, taught my third year.

During the summer months between my third and fourth grades, Miss Madge decided she wanted to teach again at Bakers Corner. She went around to the parents to get them to sign a petition to get her back. I did not want my parents to sign it, and I never did know if they signed it. The day she came to our house for that purpose I did not want to see her and ran to Grandpa's big barn to hide until she was gone.

She promised the parents if they would let her come back she would be good to the children. Evidently enough parents signed it to get her reinstated as teacher again the year I was in the fourth grade. She kept her word and was good to us. I learned to like her and I believe all the other children did, too. She became a wonderful teacher, one of the best, later teaching at Sheridan awhile and then at a large school toward the northern part of the state.

As far as studies went, in the first grade we spent much time playing. The teacher would place on each desk a handful of brightly colored pegs: red, green, yellow, purple, blue, and orange. They were about an inch long, one-quarter-inch square and pointed on one end. We could make anything we chose with them. She also gave us sewing cards and a darning needle threaded with a cheery colored yarn. If we followed the holes in the card correctly we made a picture or a design with the yarn. She also had us rest for a short time by crossing our arms on our desk and putting our heads on our arms. If someone went to sleep during that time she would not awaken him or her until it was time to go home.

I can still remember some of the first grade and second grade teaching, as I learned to read and spell. Some of the words were divided into different families such as the "ing" family and the "at" family.

At the back of the Big Room were bookshelves running from floor to ceiling, from the south window to the corner. They were pretty well filled with books. Sometimes we would get some new books. I can't remember reading many of them, though.

Each morning we had opening exercises. Sometimes the fifteen minutes would be used by the teacher reading us a story or a chapter from a book, continuing other mornings until the book was finished. One time someone read the book *The Hoosier Schoolmaster* to us.

Some mornings we sang for opening exercises. A few times each year the Big Room invited the Little Room in to sing with them, perhaps to the organ, which stood in the Big Room. We all liked to sing together. Most of the songs we sang were old familiar songs such as "Tramp, Tramp, Tramp," "Sweet and Low," "Miss Jennie Jones," and "Juanita."

One round I especially remember, to the tune of "Row, Row, Row Your Boat." In the evening, near the close of school, this was a favorite:

Put away your books and papers, closing time has come
School is over, study ended, now we're going home
School's a very fine place to be, nothing like it for you and me.
But we turn our faces homeward right merrily.

So much for another school year.

Mary Elizabeth Wilson at age six months, 1908.

Uri Hodson (1811–1888), father of Mary Elizabeth's grandpa John Hodson, walked from Wilmington, Ohio, to Hamilton County, Indiana, to purchase land in 1833. In 1838 he settled three-quarters of a mile south of present day Bakers Corner.

John and Mary Elizabeth Bates Hodson, seen here at the time of their marriage in 1866.

Grandpa John Hodson as Mary Elizabeth remembered him in 1917.

C. B. JONES

OF ADAMS
TOWNSHIP

DEMOCRATIC
NOMINEE

FOR

COMMISSIONER
THIRD DISTRICT.

C. B. Jones (1867–1921), Bakers Corner entrepreneur and politician, built the red brick store on the crossroads in 1893. Jones was a Democrat who served as Hamilton County Commissioner and president of the First National Bank in Sheridan. (Evelyn Wilson)

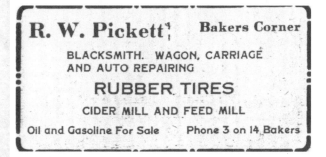

R. W. Pickett   **Bakers Corner**

BLACKSMITH. WAGON, CARRIAGE
AND AUTO REPAIRING

RUBBER TIRES

CIDER MILL AND FEED MILL

Oil and Gasoline For Sale   Phone 3 on 14 Bakers

Robert Warren Pickett (1872–1937) opened a blacksmith shop at Bakers Corner in 1892. This advertisement appeared in the Bakers Corner Wesleyan Methodist Church cookbook, about 1914.

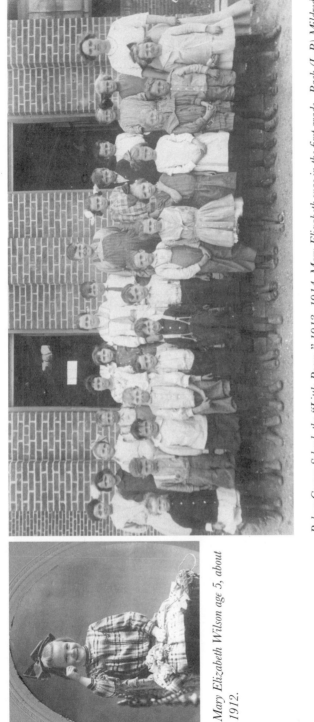

Mary Elizabeth Wilson age 5, about 1912.

Bakers Corner School, the "Little Room," 1913–1914. Mary Elizabeth was in the first grade. Back (L-R) Mildred Watson, Ruby Wilson, Weltha Johnson, Lester Carr, Helen Vogg, Ethel Beard, Lois Carr, Myron Cross, Leland Beard, Joyce Wise, George Baker, John Baldwin, Denzel Cross, Edith Gray and Fern Branson (teacher). Front (L-R) Doyle Gray, Forrest Taylor, Harold Noble, Doyle Bolen, Ardra Wise, John Pickett, Herman Wise, Maurice Carr, Viola Baldwin, Josephine Poore, Mary Elizabeth Wilson, Devvain Bolen, Lawrence Ross, Ruby Baker.

John Hodson residence, three-fourths of a mile south of the Bakers Corner crossroads, where Mary Elizabeth lived with her family from 1915-1918. This Indiana Centennial Farm stayed in the Hodson family for nearly seventeen decades. It still stands on Dunbar Road.

Mary Elizabeth and brother John William during the time their family lived at Grandpa Hodson's home, about 1916-17.

Jesse Havila Carson, known as "Brigg" or "Vila," ran a threshing operation in the area at the turn of the century. This photo was taken in 1909. Mary Elizabeth loved to sit along the roadside and watch them go by.

Mary Elizabeth's grandparents, Dr. William Wilson and his third wife Sallie, in the 1940s.

Grandpa Wilson's Wonderful White Wyandottes.

Dr. Wilson visits his prize-winning chickens. (Evelyn Wilson)

Bulgin revival songbook cover, 1917. (Evelyn Wilson)

Rev. E.J. Bulgin was a prominent evangelist who held revivals across the country. Mary Elizabeth's father Archie and Otto Cain were caught in a blizzard after attending his revival at the Methodist Church in Sheridan, about 1917.

Part Two

Back a Generation

Aunt Louva's Heavenly Summer

Do you remember, O cousin mine. . .

How we could hardly wait for the grapes to ripen? The ones that grew on the crossbars on the posts in the yard by Uncle Clark's shoe shop?

The tank room with Mary Jane's white iron bed with the patchwork quilt cover?

Aunt Jane moving her sewing machine onto the long rambling front porch, to sew where it was more comfortable during the hot weather?

Climbing the board fence, then on up the persimmon tree onto the woodshed roof where we well knew Uncle Clark did not want us to be? Or watching from the coal shed roof for Uncle Clark to come home from town?

After going barefoot all day, washing our feet at the iron sink in the kitchen, pumping water on them from the cistern with the pitcher pump? And sitting on a winter's night on the board seat behind the dining room stove?

When Uncle Clark brought home a pump organ, and we said goodbye to the old square piano? Or when Uncle Clark brought home two buttoned, genuine leather upholstered davenports, just alike and then two tapestry room-size rugs, just alike?

The earthen jars of cider apple butter, plum butter, pickles, and sauerkraut along the west wall in the back room or the pies on the pie rack in the tin-door safe in the back room?

How good cold biscuits and cider apple butter tasted to two hungry little girls when they went to the bottom part of Aunt Jane's cupboard? There was always some there and no one cared how many we ate.

Playing under Uncle Clark's dining table and under tents made of the dining chairs and Aunt Jane's bed comforters?

The call "Hoo-oo-ooo-oo-oo," belonging to Ruby and Mary Elizabeth and no one else? Or"Johnnie's Sorghum Cookies" Aunt Jane made by the jar full?

Aunt Louva Comes to Bakers Corner 1899

Let's go back a generation now, to the time when Grandpa Wilson was raising his own family, including my own father, Archie, in Adams, Indiana. I'd like to set a scene for you of an earlier Indiana, a scene that made life different for everyone in my family.

Grandpa Wilson as a medical doctor had his office uptown in that town in Decatur County in eastern Indiana. His home was not far from the office; there the family lived: my father, who was a freshman in high school; Uncle Clyde; Aunt Louva; and the children's stepmother, Grandpa Wilson's second wife, Hattie.

It was to the office in circa1899 that my father Archie went one night when he left the house. In the waiting room of this office was a solid walnut desk with a sloping table top and pigeon holes behind closed doors above. Here my father was sitting at this desk and penning a letter to his grandmother, Ruth Wilson, in Hamilton County, asking her if he could come to live with her and go to high school in Boxley. Things had not been going well with his stepmother Hattie.

Earlier that evening Hattie had cooked a nice roast and placed it on the table with a large butcher knife which Grandpa was to use to carve the roast. All were seated at the table when Hattie became angry at Grandpa. She grabbed the butcher knife and raised it high to bring it down through Grandpa's head. Of course Grandpa had his arms up trying to prevent her, and my father stood up, picked up a kitchen chair, and moved to hit her. Grandpa told him to put it down. Archie set the chair down and left the house while Uncle Clyde and Aunt Louva looked on nervously.

When the letter was finished and Grandpa came back into his office for "after supper" hours, my father told him he could not live in the home any longer because he was afraid he would kill Hattie. Grandpa read the letter to his own mother that Archie had written and decided it would be best for his son to go to this grandmother's in central Indiana.

He promised to give his son a horse to ride there, around seventy-five miles, if Archie's grandmother agreed to the visit. He also would give him a saddle. This horse had been a racehorse that had lost heart, a "shyer" and a "balker." But at least it would be available to get him to Hamilton County. And so they went on home that night.

My father's grandmother wrote back that she would be so happy to have him. He could help with the chores, which were getting hard for her as a widow to do anyway. So my father came to live with his grandmother Wilson and go to Boxley High School not far from Bakers Corner. After my father was with his grandmother awhile, he traded the balker horse for another he liked better.

When school was out or just a little before, he went back to Decatur County to his father's home to see if Uncle Clyde and Aunt Louva could go to Hamilton County too for the summer, Uncle Clyde to their grandmother Pickett's and Aunt Louva to their grandmother Wilson's with him. He drove his new horse, hitched to his grandmother's two-wheeled road cart. For the journey he was wearing an old straw hat of his grandfather's that had hung in the old house for years and blue denim coveralls and wampus (jacket). When he drove into Adams and stopped in the street in front of the house, he whistled. Aunt Louva came to the door. He had his head down a little, and she did not know him; still, she could not understand why the old hat looked so familiar. So she said, "Do you want to see the doctor?" He raised his head, looked at her, and said, "No, I want to see you." Of course then she recognized him.

Grandpa said Archie's brother and sister could both go. So, in a couple of weeks, my father returned to Adams after them in Uncle John Pickett's covered hack or spring wagon in which Uncle John hauled milk.

My father stayed over a couple of days. There were animals to transport back to Hamilton County. He and Uncle Clyde made a hog crate and put screen wire on some boxes in which to haul rabbits. Early the next morning they loaded a pig, a good-sized shoat Grandpa had taken in on a doctor bill and did not want to keep. He said for them to take it to their grandmother; she could fatten and butcher it or turn it out with the rest. Grandpa had five or six Belgian hares and he did not want to raise any more of these animals, so the boys put them into the screened boxes to take with them. They also loaded feed for the horse, rabbits, and pig.

For themselves they took some food that had been bought at the store: cheese, crackers, and bologna. A neighbor lady, Mrs. Small, had baked a large white coconut cake for them to eat on their way. After loading their suitcases and themselves they started on their merry way.

It was the spring of the year 1899. Goodbye to Hattie! And nothing could be more fun, going to Grandmother's for the summer and to be with Big Brother. If their father loved one of his children more than another (but of course he didn't), it would have been my father. But Aunt Louva and Uncle Clyde adored him so much themselves they wouldn't even have cared. They were free from trouble now and happy. It was heaven on earth. Before it became nearly dark they reached the home of friends at Clarksville, near Noblesville, the William Lehr family. They had all lived in Clarksville at one time. The Lehrs' son, Harry, was near my father's age, and another son, George, was near Aunt Louva's age. Here they put up for the night.

The next day, bidding the Lehrs goodbye, they were on their happy way again to their grandmother Wilson's and Uncle Clyde to his grandmother Pickett's for the summer.

Their grandfather, Howland Wilson, had died at the family homestead near Bakers Corner ten years before on August 20, 1889, at the age of sixty-three years. So Grandmother Ruth Wilson (my father's father's mother) was alone and delighted with the prospect of having her grandchildren with her.

To keep this former generation genealogy straight, my father Archie was born on December 1, 1882, to William Wilson and Susan Pickett. Archie, Clyde, and Louva's father William first met his wife Susan Margaret Pickett at a spelling bee or a box supper one night at Johnson Schoolhouse. She was a beautiful young girl with long black curls, a daughter of William and Lydia (Simcox) Pickett. This family lived one and one-half miles northwest of Bakers Corner on the farm where her father and mother settled soon after they came from Spiceland in Henry County, Indiana. My paternal grandmother, Archie, Clyde, and Louva's mother, Susan, was herself born on October 20, 1860, at this home place.

At the time she met Grandpa Wilson, she was engaged to marry a man whose last name was Edwards. When she met young William Wilson, he asked to take her home, and she let him do that. The next day she told her parents she was breaking her engagement. Her parents were very set on her marriage to Mr. Edwards and did everything possible to persuade her, but her heart was set, her mind made up. Her mother said, "There is just no way we can change Susie's mind."

She and William Wilson were married July 2, 1882. This happy marriage was ended when she died on November 2, 1891, with hasty consumption, which we now call tuberculosis, leaving young Doctor William L. Wilson with three children, Archie age nine, Clyde six, and Louva not yet four years old. In 1894 he married Hattie so his children would have a mother, and it was this woman who caused the trouble that sent the children all away for the summer. Hattie (Harriett Davidson) was one of the early women doctors in the state.

During the summer of 1899, while Aunt Louva was visiting her grandmother, she visited all of her aunts, uncles, and cousins, having all the fun imaginable. All her life she remembered the time as her heavenly summer and often told us tales of a time gone by even in my time. This included visiting Jimmy O'Rear, whose wife was her grandmother's niece. She spent one week with Uncle Enos Pickett's family. While there they had a wonderful picnic. She spent a week with her stepmother Hattie's sister, Anna Mitchner, and her family, who lived between Cicero and Noblesville. She enjoyed so much Anna's two little tots.

It was during her stay this summer with her Grandmother Wilson that Louva, as we will now call her, became acquainted and very fond of her lifelong friend, Nellie Carraway. Nellie lived with her father and mother, William (Bill) and Nettie Carraway, her sisters Tessie and Zonda, and her brother Fred in an old log house in the middle of the farm, a cabin where her grandfather and grandmother had raised their family and had left to live in their new house. Louva liked to wade back through the tall clover early so she could sit on the rail fence and visit with Nellie, her sisters, and her brother.

In the evening Louva liked to go after the two or three cows her grandmother kept for milk, cream, butter, and cottage cheese. Grandmother Wilson never sold any milk or cream; if there was more than they could use, it was fed to the pigs and chickens.

Sometimes during this summer Clyde would come from their other grandmother's to visit his grandmother Wilson, too. He enjoyed so much being with Louva and Archie. Sometimes Louva went back with him to their grandmother Pickett's for a few days. They usually walked from Grandmother Wilson's, west three-fourths of a mile to the range line road, then north a short distance to Uncle Clark Wilson's, then down their lane between that farm and Bill Myers's place, across the bridge over the ditch and on through Dan Mills's pasture field. Then they went on through Dan's lane, passing his barn and house, on the road to Grandmother Pickett's. All seemed easy and the weather was good.

In Dan's pasture field, however, was a large red bull. They were scared to death of him. Clyde would whisper to her, "Now keep quiet, don't let him hear you, and hurry," as Louva scurried along, and luckily not once did the old red bull pay any attention to them.

Louva's other nearby grandmother, Lydia (Simcox) Pickett, was a widow, too. Louva remembered when she had visited a few summers earlier that her grandmother's youngest son, Uncle John, and his wife, Pearl, with their small sons, Russell and Rolland, lived there with her. Uncle John placed two piano boxes together, making the children a playhouse. Aunt Pearl put straw on the floor and covered it with a piece of clean rag carpet. This made a nice place for the children to play with baby Rolland, who had not been walking long.

By this summer of 1899, Uncle John and his family had moved out, and their grandmother's daughter, who was Louva's Aunt Mary Simmonds and her family, were living there. This family consisted of Aunt Mary's husband Uncle Phillip, his father Grandpa Simmonds, and Uncle Phillip's son Frank with his tiny baby girl Olive, whose mother had died at her birth. They had just moved back from Michigan. Olive was so tiny when she was born her head would fit in a teacup. She was so small Aunt Mary held her on a bed pillow on the train all the way from Michigan. Louva loved her grandmother Pickett very much but would have been a little happier if there had not been quite so many grown-ups living there when she visited.

Across the road from Grandmother Pickett's, in the next two houses west, lived two of grandmother's other sons, Uncle Job and Uncle Will, with their families. Their children could come to their grandmother's to play. What a bunch of them when they all got together! Uncle Job had Laura, who was older and usually stayed at home to help her mother; and Lin, who was near Archie's age; Lula; Pearl; and Wesley, who came to play with their cousin. Vernon was too young to come. In Uncle Will's family Nellie, Lowell, and George were old enough to come. Mary was too small. Louva, Pearl, Nellie, and Uncle Enos's daughter Ethel, who did not get to come often, were very near the same age. How much fun they had, racing around the house like a bunch of wild Indians.

The children didn't stay for meals often. Along in the afternoon her Grandmother Pickett would come to the door and call to them in her Quaker way of speaking, "Don't thee all want something to eat?" Of course they always did; you can't play as they did and not get hungry. Her grandmother would get a loaf of her homemade salt-rising bread, always made just perfectly in large, almost square pans. She sliced it the long way, making very large slices. Then she went to the old brick and stone milkhouse for some of her sweet, home-churned butter and spread some on each slice. On top of this she spread each slice heavily with homemade cider apple butter. Each child held out both of his or her hands together, palms up, while she placed one of the large slices on each pair. Then they started eating at the middle of the edge next to them, eating through, making two slices. The large slices were a little awkward for them to handle, but how good they tasted.

Sometimes when Louva and Clyde were outside playing, their grandmother would come to the door and say, "Clydie come and rock Ollie; she's a-cryin'." Sometimes they thought tiny baby Ollie was a nuisance, but Clyde went willingly. Just as soon as she heard him, Olive would quit crying, seeming to know he was going to rock her.

Earlier, when Uncle John and Aunt Pearl lived with Grandmother Pickett, Uncle John made and fixed many things for the boys to play with, but Grandmother and Aunt Pearl did not do much for the girls.

When Aunt Mary and her family moved in, which was at this time, she thought the girls should have something, too. So she bought two dolls with china heads and painted faces and hair. They came undressed, so she made two sets of clothing for each doll, dresses made from calico scraps Grandmother had. She always sewed a lot and had plenty of quilt scraps. The doll clothes were made very well and finished nicely with tiny shirt buttons and hand worked button-holes, which were a little hard for little girls' fingers to button. She even made little sunbonnets for each doll.

In those days all of the women and girls wore sunbonnets, for it would be a shame to get a little tanned; their skin should be kept lily white. Louva's Aunt Mary thought it was a child's delight to change and rechange doll's clothing. Louva and her cousin Nellie played with the dolls more than the other girl cousins, happy to undress and dress these dolls and trade and mix their wardrobes.

Grandmother never allowed her grandchildren to go into her garden unless she was with them. It was a beautiful place, laid off in square patches, maybe a patch of onions and next to it a patch of pansies, and so on. There were narrow paths between these beds. She raised all sorts of vegetables, flowers, and herbs.

She needed many herbs because not only did she doctor her own family but for many years took care of many of the neighbors all around. She had a large medical book and an herb book, and she studied in these books almost all of her spare time.

All around this garden was a high fence with a closed gate. Although the children were not allowed to go into the garden, there was a nice place near it in which they could play. Behind the house was a clump of plum trees with many hollyhocks growing. They were allowed to pick and play with them. Louva and Nellie liked to make "hollyhock dolls" from the flowers.

They removed the stems of the blossoms and placed one on top of another until the doll was as tall as they wanted. They used another on top, leaving the green bottom for the head, another on top for a hat. They tied striped grass around the dolls' waists and hats.

This particular summer Uncle John and Aunt Pearl Pickett had four children: Russell, Rolland, Horace, and a new baby, Marie. Louva visited them, too, and she was so proud the first time she saw tiny baby Marie and held her.

Aunt Louva's own description of Grandmother Pickett's garden is very interesting:

Grandmother Pickett's garden was a large, long tract of ground that reached from the fence of her front yard to the public highway. At the southeast corner stood a huge walnut tree, just outside the garden fence, which afforded a cool shady place for little folks to play.

This garden was surrounded with a paling fence, which was almost covered with vines of various kinds; honeysuckle, morning glory, wild cucumber, pepper vines, with trumpet vines predominating.

Growing all around the inside were hardy flowers of every kind and color. Tulips; narcissus; iris; jonquils; peonies; hollyhocks; larkspur; ragged-robin; bleeding-hearts; columbine; oriental, red, yellow, and pompom poppies; many colored phlox; sweet williams; and magnificent chrysanthemums of all colors. Consequently, her garden was a riot of blooms from the first dainty snow drops and hyacinths of early spring until the last chrysanthemum before the freezing winter came.

Along the east side ran a long, tall trellis on which grew red, pink, and white rambler roses. When these were in bloom it was a beautiful sight to see. The rest of the garden was laid out in beds. I don't know who spaded these but they were undoubtedly spaded for I do not believe Grandmother would have allowed a horse and plow inside her garden. But it was she who tended it from spring to fall.

The mixing of flowers and vegetables made a pretty picture. Next to the radishes would be tall snapdragons, neighboring with the slim spikes of green onions. Four o'clocks were next to beans or peas and zinnias and marigolds were alongside the fat cabbage and the green and bright scarlet of tomatoes. It was a beautiful garden but the blossoms were seldom gathered except for sick people and funerals. Then she would gather the finest blossoms and take them to the suffering or bereaved to express the family's sincere sympathy.

I have never remembered a vase or a glass of flowers in Grandmother's house except during her sickness and death. They were to be enjoyed where they were growing as long as people were able to see them. However, we grandchildren were never allowed to enter that garden without her permission and only when she was with us and not allowed to pick the blossoms without her permission also, and the gate was always kept securely locked.

One cousin, a boy a little younger than myself grew resentful and decided to enter that garden by climbing the fence and fell and broke an arm. As we stood around in hushed awe we learned a valuable lesson in obedience.

Today the memory of Grandmother Pickett's garden stands out in my mind as a beautiful painting hung high above the reach of my desiring, childish hands.

After spending these wonderful days with Grandmother Pickett and her brother Clyde, Louva was happy to return to Grandmother Wilson's.

At the time of Louva's heavenly summer Grandmother Wilson had her own garden, too. It was located on the slope of ground at the west side of her house. The driveway into her place leading to her barn followed along the west side of her garden and was set apart from the field by a neat hand-split rail fence. Unlike Grandmother Pickett's garden, Grandmother Wilson's garden was a place where a little girl could play with kittens and dolls among the sweet williams, ragged-robbins, pinks, columbine, peonies, large-faced pansies, and vegetable plants. She could pick raspberries and swing on the big rope swing under the apple tree in the orchard.

Grandmother's son, Uncle Clark, lived about a mile west from her on the range line road. and he looked after the farming of her land. His oldest son, Theodore, did most of the work with the next son Fletcher helping. Archie was high school age and was busy helping around the house and barn and doing odd jobs. He also did some plowing and other jobs for Uncle Frank Baker, Grandmother's son-in-law, who lived across the road and just a little east of her.

Archie was inventive, always making or fixing something. That summer he made a barrel stave hammock, using the staves from an old barrel and heavy wire. He twisted the wire around the staves, making them stay side by side until it was long enough for a grown person to lie on. He fastened one end to a post at the west side of the little front porch. The other end he fastened to a large maple tree at the west side of the house, padding it with several thicknesses of clean rag carpet. Here his sister Louva spent many happy hours playing, swinging, and dreaming as little girls do.

Grandmother Wilson kept an old solid cherry bureau in an old house which stood just back of the new house, across a bridge plank porch. She and Grandfather had gone to housekeeping with the bureau when they were first married in Raleigh, North Carolina in 1846. This bureau stood just inside the door along the south wall west of the door. In a deep top drawer was Grandfather's bee equipment. Louva never bothered this drawer; she had probably been told not to. In the other drawers were dead people's clothing and some things the children had outgrown. Louva liked to play with these old clothes.

One day in this old house Louva took some of her outgrown gingham underwear from the bottom drawer of the old cherry bureau. Her everyday panties and pantywaists were made from gingham, her Sunday one being made of white muslin. She took safety pins and pinned some of the gingham ones together, then stuffed them with wool from some triangular shelves in the corner of this room. This wool had been sheared from her grandmother's sheep, and from these things she made herself a life-size doll. She dressed it in one of her outgrown dresses. All she needed now was a head. She showed it to her grandmother, who took a dipper gourd, covered it with white muslin, stuck the stem end into the body, and drew a face on the muslin. She took ink and dyed some of the wool black and sewed it onto the muslin for hair. Louva loved this homemade doll.

There was a family who lived on the Cicero-Sheridan road east of the range line road who had a grown sister named Rachel. Rachel was not normal because of a disease she had when she was very small. Her mind was like that of a five-year-old.

Rachel liked to spend a day now and then with the neighbors, and would sometimes come to stay with Grandmother Wilson. One particular day, soon after Louva and her grandmother had finished the doll, Rachel came to visit. She sat in a rocking chair and rocked the doll constantly, not even wanting to put it down to eat dinner.

Finally, Grandmother persuaded her to put the doll on the bed and eat her dinner. As soon as she had finished eating, she rocked the doll again all afternoon. Louva became anxious for her to leave. She wanted to rock it, too.

Louva enjoyed playing in the front room of this old house; here she spent many hours making bottle dolls. She took glass bottles, all sizes with cork stoppers. Using corn silks for their hair and braiding the hair, she put it on the women and girls. She made the large bottles into women and girls, gathering a piece of calico around their necks for dresses. The ink bottles were babies. Of course they had no faces. She played with them on one of the wooden tables her grandfather had made.

A piece of rag carpet was kept hanging over the doorway between the two downstairs rooms of the old house. In the back room of this old house Grandmother salted her meat. There was a small smokehouse behind the old house in the front barn lot. In this building she smoked hams after they had taken the salt and were well cured. To smoke the pork, she slowly burned bark, usually hickory, in an iron kettle on an earthen floor. The hams, shoulders, sides, and sausage of hogs were hung in this little building and smoked for several days.

A stairway in the house went almost straight up, very far between steps, from the southwest corner of the back room of the old house to the attic, where many antiques, even for that time, were kept. Among them was a plate warmer similar to our old kerosene ovens except the warming shelves were closer together. The warmer was to be set close in front of the fireplace to keep the plates heated so when they were ready to eat, the food would stay hot longer.

In the northeast corner of this front room of Grandmother's old house sat an old cook stove, a "Home Comfort." The Home Comfort cook stove was probably one of the first kinds of cook stoves ever made. Louva's grandmother was the first woman in this part of the country for miles around to have a cook stove; all the other women were still cooking over a fireplace when she went to housekeeping long before the Civil War. People swarmed in for many miles to see it and watch her cook on it—such a novelty. She had trouble getting her work done because of all the visitors. Of course she always invited them to stay and eat with them. Now the old stove was in the old house when Louva visited, a curiosity in the 1890s.

When the daughters, Aunt Mary Ellen and Aunt Adaline, were married, cook stoves and sewing machines were both very new. Grandfather bought one of each for each daughter. They thought they were set up in fine style.

Grandmother still heated her wash water in a copper-bottom wash boiler on this old cook stove. She did her wash in a wooden tub, rubbing the clothes on an old fashioned washboard with her hands. Beside the old Home Comfort cook stove sat a large heavy wooden table that Grandfather had made. Louva saw Grandmother empty her basket of laundry on the table and sort it there. She used homemade lye and homemade lye soap. After a little lye was put in the water in the boiler, when the water heated up, the rust and lime rose to the top of the water. After skimming this off with a gourd dipper Grandmother had nice soft water in which to do her wash. She would treat her water in this way if she did not have rain water on hand. Many homes had cisterns to catch rain water and hold it, but she did not.

This Wilson grandmother of Louva made her lye by placing a wooden barrel on a sloping wooden platform and filling it with wood ashes as she cleaned the ashes from her stoves. When the barrel was as full as she wanted it, she poured buckets of water in the barrel on top of the ashes. After placing an iron kettle below the sloping boards to catch the lye as it seeped from the barrel, she had to make sure no chickens got into the yard and drank from the kettle of lye.

She also made her own lye soap, which was used for laundry and dishes. It was made outdoors in a large iron kettle, using grease she boiled out of cracklings, and any grease that was left from everyday cooking. She knew just how much of her homemade lye to put into a kettle of grease and water to make soft, golden brown soap. When it had cooked enough to make a soft soap, it was cooled and dipped with a gourd dipper into a wooden barrel in which it was kept in the old house to be used as needed. A dish of this soft soap was kept on the cook table in the kitchen to use for washing dishes. Each summer she made enough to last a year. (This was the same process my mother used thirty years later.)

Sometimes Louva saw her make a supply of hominy. Grandmother had white field corn raised for hominy. She soaked the shelled white corn in lye water in a cast-iron boiler a number of hours until the skin came off the grains. Then she rinsed it in clear water until she was sure the lye was all out of it and cooked it a long time until tender. This process insured they had enough hominy to last for quite a while.

At a certain time of the year when the hops season arrived (and Grandmother knew when they were just right), she gathered hops and made enough yeast to last a year, with enough to give a new start to her neighbors. She knew just how to prepare the hops with cornmeal, salt, and potato water and whatever else it may have taken. When it was all prepared, cooked, or whatever had to be done, it was forced into a cake, pressed thin, and left to dry. Louva always thought it was funny that after it was finished it still showed her grandmother's finger and thumb prints. When it had thoroughly dried it was broken into pieces and hung in a cloth bag in the front room of the old house until needed.

None of Grandmother's family liked "light bread" very well. So if she made yeast bread it was usually near the end of the week when she thought she might have company. She usually made biscuits or corn bread for common use; everybody did.

There was very little light bread baked in Aunt Mary Ellen's house either. They too preferred the biscuits. Before this eldest daughter of Grandmother's was married, she said that when she got a home of her own there would be coffee and biscuits made and served three times a day. Louva observed that that had come to pass. Aunt Mary Ellen's husband, Uncle Frank, always arose first in the morning, built a fire in the cook stove, and put the coffee pot on filled with water. Then he went to the smokehouse, got out the meat, trimmed it, and brought it into the kitchen for breakfast. By that time Aunt Mary Ellen would be up and making the biscuits. Every morning they had meat, gravy, eggs, biscuits, and rice, and sometimes fried potatoes.

Louva noted another of the large heavy tables that Grandfather had made on the wooden porch between the house and the old house. There was no roof over this porch, and it was where Grandmother dried apples, apricots, and peaches in the fall. Sometimes when the weather permitted, they ate there; she was a great one to eat outside.

Uncle Frank and Aunt Mary Ellen had a daughter, Nora, who was a few years older than Louva. Louva went to Uncle Frank's to be with Nora and go places with her. One time they went in a buggy to a funeral at the Salem Methodist Church, which was about two miles northeast of where they lived. A neighbor woman took her several children in a carriage to the funeral, and coming home the carriage was in front of the buggy. One of the children in the carriage was dressed in a red-and-white striped outfit. He kept jumping in and out onto the fender of the carriage. All of this attracted the attention of an old red bull in Alfred Johnson's field, which had one of the first wire fences in this part of the country. The striped outfit and the noise had made the bull very angry, and he ran to the fence and gave a lunge to go over it but could not raise himself high enough. The fence caught him just under his front legs and there he was, unable to move. Uncle Frank went and helped Alfred get the bull off the fence.

People those days did not go to town often. Louva's grandmother had no horse or other means of transportation. There was a two-wheeled road cart kept in the barn that Archie, Louva's brother, used sometimes. Uncle Frank and Aunt Mary Ellen took Grandmother everywhere she wanted to go. Louva went to Sheridan two or three times with Nora but never just "into town" with her grandmother.

One day she went with Nora to get a new hat. Nora was rather stylish and particular about her clothing. She saw a broad-brimmed, white chiffon hat that she thought was just what she wanted except that it had blue flowers. She wanted pink flowers because her dress was pink, so she paid twenty-five cents to get the flowers changed.

Nora brought that hat home and decided the wire frame hurt her head. Aunt Mary Ellen said, "She ought to have thought about that before she brought it home."

Uncle Frank came into the house and, hearing the conversation, said, "Now, let me see it." He tried it on. Louva thought he was quite a sight with a long beard and a broad-brimmed white, frilly chiffon hat with pink flowers on his head! In a few days they made another trip to town to exchange the hat. This time she settled for a natural black sailor hat.

One day Louva was at Uncle Frank's when Nora said to her, "Let's go to Fin Couch's." Finley and Laura Couch and their family of one daughter and several sons lived in an old log house just west of Grandmother's. Louva loved to go there and play games with their children. They also enjoyed gathering around the parlor pump organ and singing. Sometimes brother Archie went with her there. He and the Couch boys were wonderful friends and played stringed musical instruments together. On this particular day Nora said, "I'm going to fix you up until they won't know you." She put some fancy grown-up clothes on her. Louva was tall for her age anyway, and she fastened her naturally curly black hair on top of her head, letting the tendrils of shorter hair at her temples and at the nape of her neck hang down prettily. (She had been wearing it in two braids that hung down her back.)

Next Nora put a hat on Louva and a veil over her face: the veil had dots on it, making it harder to see who she was. The Couch children saw them coming, ran into the house to their mother, and told her that Nora was coming with a strange lady. Nora introduced her as a friend who had come to visit her. Laura, Fin's wife, did not know Louva. Then Fin came in from the barn. When Nora introduced her to him, he removed his hat and bowed low to the "lady." Imagine his surprise when told who she was.

Uncle Tom, who was a brother of Grandfather Wilson, and his wife Aunt Ruth, who was a niece of Grandmother Ruth Wilson (two Ruths), had come in earlier days from North Carolina to Indiana on the same wagon train as Grandfather and Grandmother. Then they had come to live in Hamilton County, near Deming, three or four miles from Grandmother's, and were Quakers who had never been churched. They usually came to West Grove to Fifth Day (Thursday) meeting. In those days the Quakers did not say Sunday, Monday, Tuesday, etc. as we speak of the days of the week, but First Day, Second Day, Third Day, etc. This meeting was held in the forenoon. If the Spirit moved, the meeting might last quite a while; if the Spirit did not move, they sat awhile in Holy Quietness, and then everyone stood up, shook hands and went home.

Now, Louva saw, after these Fifth Day meetings, Uncle Tom and Aunt Ruth quite often came to see how Grandmother was getting along. There were not many other ways of contacting their relatives. Louva knew that on that day there was sure to be an especially good dinner, although her grandmother always set a good table.

Her grandmother looked for Tom and Ruth and usually cooked a one-pot meal, saying, "Ruth likes a one-kettle meal." Using the old, three-legged, black iron kettle, she would take off one of the cook stove lids. The kettle just fit to the rim, and she settled the kettle down in, next to the blaze. In the kettle she put potatoes, onions, turnips, and cabbage with a good sized piece of meat. She kept the vegetables separated in the kettle, and when she placed them on the table she put each kind in a separate dish. It tasted extra good to a hungry little girl. Sometimes on those days, when Louva's grandmother went to her storage cave for the vegetables, she brought fruit to make two pies, always two. Pies were something of a treat that she did not make often.

After one of these one-pot meals the broth was saved and cooled, most of the grease skimmed off, and a little cornmeal stirred into it, making a kind of gravy that they ate over hot biscuits for supper. Sometimes if there had been cornbread for dinner and enough was left for supper, they would crumble it into the leftover broth instead of making the gravy.

When Uncle Tom and Aunt Ruth arrived, she and Grandmother had fun exchanging greetings like this, "How is thee, Ruth?" And was answered, "I'm fine, how is thee, Ruth?"

Louva's grandmother bought the bulk of her groceries from a huckster wagon that passed twice a week, but there was no rural mail carrier. Someone had to go once in a while to Bakers Corner to the post office, which was in the C. B. Jones General Store. When one neighbor went after it they would bring it to their neighbors. Always whoever brought it to Louva's grandmother also brought mail to Uncle Frank and Aunt Mary Ellen Baker, Finley Couch's family, and Isaac and Mary Jane Trueblood and her mother, Aunt Hamie Williams. Sometimes Uncle Frank or Archie would jump on a horse and go after it, or maybe Archie would walk. If they saw Fin coming they were sure he had mail for them. It was not every day the mail was brought. Sometimes it would be several days before anyone got it.

Grandmother liked to get the mail as often as possible. She wrote lots of letters, and how she welcomed letters from North Carolina and Henry County, where they had first settled before coming to Hamilton County. She told Louva that during the Civil War it cost twenty-five cents to send a letter. In that time they did not have envelopes but folded the paper into an envelope and sealed it with a drop or two of hot sealing wax.

A few times that heavenly summer Louva walked that mile and a half for the mail. One very hot summer day when she walked for it, she got ready to wear what they called a sunshade. It was similar to a broad-brimmed hat, with a gathered crown. Hers was made of red calico and starched.

She had been playing with the old clothing in the cherry bureau in the old house and had found a cream-colored, sateen parasol that had belonged to her Aunt Adaline. When her grandmother asked her if she would walk to Bakers Corner for the mail, she said she would if she could carry that parasol. She was allowed to do that and also wore the red sunshade. She walked proudly and happily down the dusty dirt road carrying a nickel basket with a few eggs in it in one hand and the stylish old parasol in the other. Her grandmother usually liked to send a few eggs and pick up a few light weight things at the store when anyone went for the mail.

On her way back, Louva came to Uri Baker's first. Dian, his wife, gave her a couple of freshly baked cookies. She ate them on her way to Mary Jane's. The cookies along with the heat made her very thirsty. Mary Jane and Isaac drank water from a spring near the road in the northeast corner of the yard. There was no cold water at the house for Louva to drink. Just at that time Isaac came home with some good fresh cider from Uncle Clark's, up the road about a quarter of a mile. They gave her a good drink of cider, and she went on toward her grandmother's.

The cider had only made her thirstier. The next stop to deliver the mail was at Finley Couch's. Her father had always told her never to drink at Fin's because their well was a shallow-dug well. Typhoid fever was common in those days and much of it was caused from drinking water from wells not dug deep enough and so contaminated. So by the time she reached her grandmother's, she was very tired and thirsty, but she was so happy to have brought so much joy to their neighbors and her grandmother.

Until a few years before this summer Grandmother had canned mostly in tin cans with a few glass cans, sealing both kinds with sealing wax. One day in that earlier time, Hattie, Louva's stepmother, came to Grandmother's to can some fruit. The self-sealing cans were rather new then. She brought some to use for herself and some for Grandmother to try, who liked them so much, she said, "You never get too old to learn something new."

At the time of this heavenly summer in 1899, Louva was eleven years old. The Howland E. Wilson place, the home where she and Archie now were staying, was one of the very best and nicest in the country round about. It was trim and very well kept.

It had been too far from Adams in Decatur County for Louva's family to come often in a buggy to visit. This summer was so delightful to Louva because she was there all of the time. She would gladly have lived there if it had not been that she wanted to see her papa.

As this wonderful summer came to a close, Louva and Archie had a talk with their grandmother. They decided they would send three letters to the children's father. One would be from their grandmother, one from Archie, and one from Louva, each asking him if Louva could stay with her grandmother and go to school that winter. She could ride to Bakers Corner School with Archie as he drove the horse and buggy to high school at Boxley. They also asked if Clyde could stay with his grandmother Pickett and go to school from there.

When the answer came from the three letters, it was "no." He promised to buy his girl Louva a new bicycle, though, when she came home.

The day came; they had to return home to Adams to start school. Archie was taking them back. Grandmother boiled eggs and fried some of her home-cured ham. Louva always wondered just how she knew how many hogs to butcher, how much fruit to dry and can, how many vegetables to store in the storage cave each year; how much soap to make, how much jelly, preserves, and apple butter and such, but somehow there was always enough of everything.

Of course there was homemade bread to go with the ham. They washed lovely ripe tomatoes to take. Louva decided she would clean and wash a big onion. She put it in one of her grandmother's big deep coffee cups in water until they were ready to start to keep it cool.

So they were loaded and on their way. They stopped to tell Uncle Frank, Aunt Mary Ellen, and Nora goodbye. Then they saw their grandmother walking toward them. Louva had forgotten her onion. She ran to meet her grandmother to get it; then Grandmother came on to Uncle Frank's with her.

On the trip home the first day they reached the home of some people whose name was Coverdale who had been friends when the family lived east of Noblesville in Clarksville. They spent the night with the Coverdales and were on their way bright and early the next morning.

As they were nearing Morristown they met a country girl, barefoot, walking along with a basket of eggs. Archie decided he would have a little fun, so he said to her, "How far is it down the road about a mile?" The girl became flustered, no doubt wondering WHAT down the road, and finally answered, "I don't guess I know." After awhile they met another girl. This girl was all tidied up, her red hair slicked back and braided into pigtails, her freckled face aglow from a recent sudsing, her shoes shined and a clean, starched, plaid gingham dress on. Clyde thought he too would have some fun, so he asked her the same question. Right quickly she answered, in her saucy, sharp tongue, "None of your beesness."

It was getting near dark when they reached Adams. Neither their father nor stepmother was at home. Their father was at his office, and they had seen Hattie, their stepmother, uptown as they came through. They went into the house through the back door, then took their clothes and other things upstairs. When they came down they saw the supper dishes unwashed. Truly they were home to the same situation they had left. Clyde said he supposed they would have to wash the dishes yet that night, but they got to wait until morning.

Hattie saw them as they came through town, and soon came home. The children had not yet discovered the bicycle that had been promised. Hattie told Clyde to go to the dining room and bring it to Louva. Aunt Louva said she always felt rather conscience stricken about the bicycle. She felt her father should have bought two used ones, one for her and one for Clyde, instead of paying thirty-five dollars for a new one for her and none for Clyde. She was very generous letting Clyde ride hers because of this.

That bicycle was an "Ivanhoe," from one of the finest manufacturers, made partly of varnished wood and decorated with red and black stripes. Of course the frame and spokes were metal. It had a bell and a basket, the basket being needed to carry groceries. Townspeople went to town twice each day, in the morning for meat for the noon meal and in the afternoon for something for supper, since no one had a suitable place to keep food long. Now Louva or Clyde could bring things from the store with this bike.

Her father had bought the bicycle from Carl G. Fisher, the man who made the Five-Hundred Mile racetrack at Speedway. Fisher and his brother, just teenagers then, had started a small shop at Greensburg, and that is where her father had bought the bicycle.

One time later she rode her bicycle five miles to Greensburg to visit a friend. About one-fourth mile before she reached there, her pedals got so they would not work. She had to push it to the shop where her father had bought it. She then saw the young man Carl G. Fisher. They did not have the piece, so she had to leave it there until they could get it the next day. She stayed overnight with her friend, but what worried her most was that she had no way to get word to her father. The next morning he came hunting her. When the bike was ready they took it home in the buggy. She never rode that far again on her bicycle, but she was so very proud of it.

Sometime after her wonderful summer at her grandmother's, Aunt Louva may have been in high school when her teacher had each student in the class write a composition, each choosing his own subject. She chose to write about her summer with her grandmother.

The best of these were to be entered in a contest at the county seat, North Vernon. The best one of these, then, was to go to Indianapolis; the winner there would go on to enter a contest at the World's Fair at Jamestown, Virginia, that year. Aunt Louva's was chosen as the best at North Vernon and was sent on to Indianapolis. She never did know if it went on any further.

Two summers after Aunt Louva's "heavenly summer," her Grandmother Wilson broke her hip and went to live with her daughter and son-in-law, Aunt Mary Ellen and Uncle Frank Baker. She was never able to walk again. She left this world on March 13, 1902 at the age of seventy-seven years and was laid to rest beside her husband in the Cicero Cemetery at Cicero, Indiana.

For Louva, that time was the happiest time of her childhood in the late 1890s. She used to think if heaven would just be as nice as her grandmother's place, it would be wonderful.

Susan Pickett Wilson (1860–1891), mother of Archie, Clyde, and Louva Wilson.

Howland and Ruth Stanley Wilson, parents of William Wilson, were Quakers who traveled to Indiana from North Carolina in a wagon caravan about 1851.

William and Lydia Simcox Pickett, Susan Pickett Wilson's parents, were Quakers who came to Hamilton County in about 1850.

Dr. William Wilson (1860-1945) on a call.

Louva Wilson (1888-1976) as a toddler. (Max Benson)

Louva Wilson Baker 1913. (Kelei Baker Waltz)

Bakers Corner brick store built in 1893 on the southwest corner of the crossroads housed the post office. Louva went for Grandmother Wilson's mail at the store in 1899.

Advertisement printed on brown wrapping paper used by the store. (Evelyn Wilson)

C. B. JONES
DEALER IN
Dry Goods, Groceries,
Boots and Shoes, Hats, Caps,
CLOTHING and FURNISHINGS
Drugs and Medicines, Household Goods and Farm Fencing
ALL AT THE LOWEST PRICES
THE COUNTRY STORE
Bakers Corner, Ind.

Brothers Clyde (1885-1975) and Archie Wilson. (Evelyn Wilson)

Dr. William Wilson near the time of Louva's heavenly summer.

Archie L. Wilson (1882-1964), Mary Elizabeth's father, shown here as a teen.

West Grove Friends Meeting was located west of Deming on 226th street, a brief distance from U.S. 31. Many of Mary Elizabeth's relatives, including William and Lydia Pickett attended here. Mary Elizabeth's family attended West Grove during WWI because her parents felt the Bakers Corner Church was not taking a strong enough stand for peace.

Louva's family about 1914. In 1904 Louva married Bakers Corner native Alvin Baker and they became parents of seven children. The oldest three—George, Worth, and Susan—are shown here. From 1935-1938, Alvin Baker served as Hamilton County sheriff and Louva cooked meals for the prisoners. (Kelei Baker Waltz)

Louva Wilson Baker about 1970.

Part Three

Older Childhood through the Big Room and High School

Do you remember, O cousin mine. . .

The dandelion chains we wore around our necks? The whistles we made from dandelion stems and winter onion leaves? Sitting beside the road, blowing the fuzz off old mature dandelion blossoms?

Sitting high in the early apple tree in the south end of Uncle Clark's apple orchard, making apple-leaf hats? Making a blade of grass whistle between our thumbs?

Aunt Jane going along the road early in the morning, during spring and early summer, one of the girls with her, "Old Babe" hitched to the hack? Taking with her the wallpaper pasting board, stepladders, and other papering tools, going to some neighbor's house to put new wallpaper on their walls?

Mary Jane coming down the road just at dusk, a wool shawl around her shoulders, a hearing trumpet around her neck, a sprig of a bouquet in one hand, a half-gallon molasses bucket in the other? Bringing persimmons in the fall, taking home milk the next morning after spending the night?

The smell of the cave, the mixture of potatoes, apples, and pears? Taking the lantern at night and going to the cave for a dishpan of apples and pears to eat while sitting around the base burner at night?

The play garden in the corner of Uncle Clark's woods where we set out rag-weed plants pretending they were tomato plants, and plantain for lettuce?

When I was trying to learn to whistle at Uncle Clark's and the older girls told me to go home to learn? Or when the older girls made sorghum taffy and pulled it until it was light? It was so good!

"Sunny Park" where my father made a "Flying Jenny" and hung some high swings? And some boys changed the "S" to an "F," making it "Funny Park?" Hiding under the feather bed when it lightning-ed?

It has been said that people who have had happy childhoods remember them well, while those whose childhoods were not so pleasant may forget them.

Soda Cake

As I grew older, I began to assist in the cooking and other household chores. Almost every day we baked soda cake. How my father liked soda cake!

My mother would get up early with my father to start the farm day, at four o'clock if it was a day to plant or harvest a crop, or if he were going to do some custom baling for some farmer nearby. We lived on several different farms, but it didn't matter which one we were at a given year or week; life remained about the same each day.

When he went baling or wood-sawing with his buzz saw, he always took his noon lunch, and Mama always made soda cake for his lunch bucket.

She fried breakfast foods and made lunches while my father was doing the morning chores: milking, feeding hogs and other farm jobs. When my brothers got old enough they helped with the chores or the baling so she usually made fresh soda cake for them, too.

When they were to carry their lunch buckets, she baked the soda cake in muffin pans and called the little cakes "gem cakes." If it was to be eaten at home, Mama baked the bread in an iron skillet, and we ate it hot. She usually did not stir it up until everything else was about ready to place on the table, so it could bake while we ate and would be done when we were ready to eat it.

It was mixed in an aluminum kettle, and she never measured anything, she just put it in by guess, a cupful, a handful, or a pinch. It always turned out perfect. One day when I was planning to marry, I told my mother that I wanted her recipe for soda cake. She said she did not have one, she just put it together. I told her that on that day, before she "put it together;" we would measure each ingredient and I would write it down. This is the recipe as we wrote it down:

· *One Egg Soda Cake*

1 cup granulated sugar	*½ cup lard*
²/³ cup sour milk	*1 egg*
1 teaspoon soda	*vanilla*
flour to thicken to make a stiff batter, I use 1 ½ cups	

Mama's soda cake was a favorite with Reverend F. R. Eddy, pastor of the Bakers Corner Wesleyan Methodist Church. She always had one on hand when she knew he was coming. I believe he liked it as well as my father did and expected it every time he came. Mama made more soda cakes in the spring because eggs were so plentiful and cheap. Stewed rhubarb and soda cake eaten together are a special treat, and we had that often.

Not only my father and Reverend Eddy liked soda cake; everyone likes the staple that is also always a treat.

Sorghum and Cider

T-o-o-o T-o-o-o-o-o T-o-o-o T-o-o-o T-o-o.
(Six o'clock in the morning.)
Yip Yip Yap Yap, Bow Wow, Woof Woof, Bark Bark.

The Bakers Corner dog chorus cuts loose, sopranos, altos, bass, maybe a tenor or two. Their ears hurt. Chug, chug, here comes a pomace truck, a familiar sound. What's pomace? The residue left after making a vegetable or fruit product, the leftovers. The early morning air is crisp with a familiar fall fragrance. What does it all mean? Sorghum-making time.

Sorghum was part of our youth. It is an Indian-continent import used as a sweetener. Coming to America almost two hundred years ago, it took a long time to get to Bakers Corner. When it did, it really took hold.

I can remember when the sorghum business started in our little town, many years ago. Warren Pickett, the sorghum producer, originally had a blacksmith shop, a shop where the neighborhood could get blacksmithing work done, from shoeing a horse to getting a cooking kettle soldered or a broken farm tool welded. Warren could and did repair almost anything. How the sparks flew from the red hot piece of iron when he pounded it into shape on the anvil with his heavy blacksmith hammer!

Warren also had a large cider press, and the country round about still had many large apple orchards. My father would hitch our team of bay horses, Fred and Coalie, to the farm wagon, and we would go out to help pick up the apples in my grandpa Hodson's large orchard. There were many varieties, as I've described in an earlier chapter. Beside the early yellow transparent and mid-summer wealthys there were grimes goldens, baldwins, bellflowers, ben davises, sweet old fashioned rambows, the sheep-nosed pippens and the very large, dark red Wolf River apples which were usually part rotten. These were eating and keeping apples; not many of them went into cider. We took this wagon load of apples to Warren's cider press.

The sweet cider was brought home in eight-gallon milk cans, which were taken to the cellar by way of the outside stairs. There my mother dipped out some to can so we could have it to drink through the winter months, although during the canning process it lost some of its goodness. Some of it she cooked down to about one-third or one-half, thickening it with peeled quarters of raw apples. She then cooked it in the large kettle out of doors or in large dishpans in the oven until it thickened into cider apple butter. Cider apple butter did not require any sugar.

Enough of the fresh cider was kept out to drink for a few days. Without an electric refrigerator it did not stay fresh many days. It soon became bitey; it would even make one drunk before it made itself into vinegar. The rest of the cider was poured into the wooden vinegar barrels in the cellar.

Anyway, one day in about 1913, Warren Pickett, the blacksmith, got the idea of making sorghum, and he planted sorghum cane in his cornfield. During the summer months while it was growing he made a press to squeeze the juice out of the cane stalks in the fall when the stalks were ripe. He installed vats in which to cook the juice and also all other equipment he needed.

When fall came he started his new experiment, making sorghum. As the old saying goes, "practice makes perfect." He needed some practice. His first sorghum was strong and dark. A little neighbor boy, Harold Spear said, "It is the blackest burlasses you ever saw." It was black but not for long. He learned fast how to improve it.

Soon the neighbors began to plant a few rows of sorghum cane at the edge of their corn fields. When the time came in the fall they cut it by hand with a corn knife and hauled it to Bakers Corner on horse-drawn wagons. Some people stripped all the blades off before bringing the stalks in.

Inside the grade school, the brick schoolhouse at the corner of the crossroads, I could often see the wagonloads of cane lined up along the roadside beyond the schoolhouse, each waiting his turn at the mill. Some people brought eight-gallon milk cans, some earthen jars and other containers in which to take their sorghum home.

The line-up of wagons did not last many years. He found a quicker way to test and weigh the cane so they knew how much sorghum each wagonload would make. This way each customer could get his molasses immediately.

The sorghum kept improving and the gallons increasing as a few years passed. He began to use a little glucose with the juice, which improved both the taste and the looks of the molasses. Now the same mill, still producing in Bakers Corner, makes a beautiful autumn-gold color sorghum, which tastes wonderful.

The project continued to grow—times and things changed. Once the "pumeys" or leftover shavings and squeezed stalks, were hauled by truckloads to nearby fields, where they were dumped into piles and rows and burned. Being green they burned for days and weeks with the smoke settling over our little village in the evenings. There were no air-conditioners. Folks could hardly stand the heat with their windows closed, nor the smoke with the windows open.

Later a cattle herd was started. The "pumeys" then were packed onto a top-of-the-ground silo to feed to the cattle. This was profitable, less waste, and everyone was happy with cleaner air.

In 1937 Warren Pickett died in an automobile accident. His son Hollas "Hod," as we all called him, took over the farm and sorghum factory. He did much to improve the process and quality. He changed from cooking with coal to gas, put in stainless steel cooking vats, and installed a more powerful juice press. Also he added other improvements that lessened the labor, so fewer people could operate it. The Picketts came to raise many more acres of cane. Neighbors and people from long distances who at first brought in their custom cane have quit doing that and now buy their sorghum ready-made.

After many years, Hod also passed away. His two sons, Joe and Ronnie, carried on the business which was mostly a family project until Joe's death. Ronnie and his family have continued the family sorghum business, one of a few in America.

Thousands of gallons are made, labeled, and delivered to grocery stores for many miles around. Orders are filled for other states. I have been told it is the largest sorghum factory in the state of Indiana, probably in the United States.

We in Bakers Corner have believed it to be by far the best and enjoy the six-o'clock morning sorghum whistle. [Ed note: The factory burned down on July 24, 2009, and Bakers Corner and Indiana lost a venerable landmark.]

Salt Fish

Every time I fry fish, it brings back memories of long ago when I was growing up. My parents and two or three neighbor families would together order a keg or small barrel of salt fish, from a twenty-five-pound wooden bucket to a fifty-pound wooden keg, from Green Bay, Wisconsin. The size of keg ordered depended on the number of families ordering.

The barrel took several days to come. Then someone had to go to the train depot at Cicero to get it, usually my father. When he got home he would open the keg or bucket, removing the wooden top end. Then he weighed out each family's amount on the milk scales, covering them with enough salt brine to keep the fish fresh until warm weather in the spring.

The fish were herring, brought in from Lake Michigan to Green Bay, Wisconsin, where they were beheaded and the entrails were removed. Then they were packed in salt brine and shipped far and near.

During the winter months, we enjoyed fried salt fish with biscuits, butter and jelly or maple syrup if it was desired. Usually the fish and biscuits were all we wanted. We enjoyed these fish mainly for breakfast, seldom for any other meal.

The fish were always better when soaked in a large dishpan of fresh water overnight. The next morning we removed the backbone and all other bones, usually getting most or all of these troublesome things out.

During those years, during the Depression and for several years following, I made biscuits for breakfast every morning except Sunday mornings. Then we had toast with hot salted milk because there was no time to make biscuits and get to Sunday School on time.

I had learned to make very good hot biscuits with clabbered milk, baking powder, and Burlington flour, which we had traded our wheat for. I baked them in a coal-wood, Copper Clad kitchen range.

Cornmeal Mush

My mother made cornmeal mush once in a while for our supper, especially in the wintertime as early as I can remember. She would stir up a kettle of it and then I along with my father, mother, and two younger brothers, enjoyed a bowl of mush with some good farm cream and sugar on it, after the day's work was done and the evening farm chores were finished.

After everyone was filled, and as the leftover mush was still warm, soft, and pliable, it was placed in a loaf pan to let set to cool until morning. When morning came and it was firm, it was turned out onto a plate, wrong side up. Then Mama sliced it to the right thickness to fry in a little shortening. When it had fried to a light crispy brown on one side, it was turned and browned on the other side.

Eaten while it was hot with some home-churned butter and homemade maple syrup or sorghum, of which we always had plenty, it made a delicious winter breakfast.

It was so simple and so common but so satisfying.

May Day

My mother always said that May first, May Day, was the day to plant flower seeds. Usually the garden vegetable seeds had already been planted. She felt that by the time the tender little flower plants would get though the ground, the danger of frost would be past, and they would be safe.

May Day was always the first day we children could go barefooted. When my father was a little boy, he could hardly wait until the day so he could go without his shoes and socks. His father, the doctor, was strict with his children, not allowing them to go without their shoes and stockings even one day before May Day. He said when the first of May came they could go barefoot regardless of the weather, even if there was snow on the ground.

A girl named Dorothy McConnell invited me to a May Day party when I was a very small girl. She lived in a large house, second from the range line road on the Cicero-Sheridan road toward Bakers Corner. I was such a small girl, but I will never forget the Maypole. Dorothy's father and other relatives had put a tall pole in their large front yard. From the top of it hung streamers of rainbow colors of ribbon or crepe paper.

We children, all dressed in our "Sunday Best," each held to an end of one of these beautiful streamers and danced around the pole, a lovely sight. I do not know the object of this, whether it was a game with a prize at the end or just a dance for enjoyment, or if there was music with it.

Independence Day

In the country, holidays were large in families' lives. Food, fun, festivities, they all marked the passing year and got families together.

As all other holidays, July 4th always gave me an exhilarating feeling, a special thrill. Among my first recollections of this holiday are picnics, fireworks, and homemade ice cream with neighbors and friends.

I can remember times when I was quite small and we would go to the creek for a swim and a picnic on July 4th with Uncle Clark Wilson's family. My brother John William was just six years younger than I. I remember well the July 4th the summer he was one year old, in 1914.

That year, we and Uncle Clark's family went to a shallow place along Cicero Creek, south of Cicero, called Dewey's Ford. (This place later became the bottom of Morse Reservoir.) Although the water was more shallow there, it was deep enough to have a lot of fun.

Uncle Clark and Aunt Jane had seven children who were all older than I, DeSha, Fern, Capitola, Anna, John, Dortha, and Ruby. Ruby was only one year older than I, while DeSha, their oldest, was only around ten years younger than my parents.

Aunt Jane was always a good sport and a lot of fun, as was my father. Uncle Clark and my mother enjoyed themselves but were of a more quiet nature. But on the 4th, everyone was anxious to get started with the fun. So as early in the morning as possible, we loaded into our low, wide phaeton buggy with our picnic basket of food. We also took with us my baby brother's homemade slat playpen and a heavy comforter to place on the grass underneath it. With this John William would be more at home, he would not need to be held all the time, and he would not get as tired. Mama would put mosquito bar netting over him while he slept.

On this day, Uncle Clark's family came the seven or eight miles in their carriage and buggy. It was a beautiful day. Everyone put on old clothes to play or swim in the water. Few people had swimming suits then. Ruby and I went barefoot in the water. I believe our parents and perhaps some of Uncle Clark's older children wore old shoes into the water to protect their feet.

When noon came everyone was very hungry. Aunt Jane, Mama, and the older girls spread tablecloths on the ground and some old bedding on which to sit while we ate. They had prepared a delicious picnic lunch.

By July 4th we always looked forward to having our first fried chicken of the year. Also we hoped to have that head of cabbage in our garden, large and solid enough by the 4th of July to make some good, fresh cabbage slaw.

Our group of thirteen people could consume a large amount of fried chicken, potato salad, deviled eggs, slaw, bean salad, baked beans, macaroni and cheese, and homemade cakes and pies. Don't forget the homemade ice cream. My father and Uncle Clark were noted for eating large amounts of ice cream. Sometimes, especially at the threshing settling-up meetings, they ate their ice cream from gallon size stone crocks, for which they were much teased.

An hour or so after our bountiful picnic lunch, all were back into the water again. Neither Ruby nor I could swim. Aunt Jane, Ruby's mother, held us up by the backs of our dresses just barely high enough to keep our faces out of the water. She would tell us how to paddle, to throw our hands and feet, trying to teach us how to swim. Ruby could do pretty well, but I never did learn how to do it.

Then in a few hours it was time to go home. There were plenty of towels for drying. Everyone changed into dry clothes behind the bushes and we started home with adults and children tired but happy. All had enjoyed a wonderful day, a glorious 4th, the "End of a Perfect Day," as the popular song went.

Another happy place to spend an enjoyable July 4th when I was a child was at Bishop's Park, southwest of Arcadia. I thought there was no place as wonderful. I loved the big high swing that swung out over the hill for teenagers and the great flowing well where several could get a drink at the same time from the several holes along the long pipe, the high tank where watermelons were cooled, and the low cement tank where the cattle drank. The flow was heavy, making a large stream, and the water always cool and good tasting.

You always got your feet wet, sometimes the front of your clothing, when you went for a drink. Who cared? What fun! We all loved it. What if we were wet? Wasn't it a day to celebrate? July 4th, Independence Day.

There was a Slide-for-Life that went on a cable from a tall tree on top of the hill to another tree at the bottom of the hill for teenagers, not for children. So I never did ride on it because I was too young.

The thing I liked best was the light blue, painted homemade merry-go-round. It took a few people to push it to make it go around, although children could make it whirl. Sometimes it went really high if grown-ups were at the bars. There were several teeter-totters in that park also.

Near the middle of the park was a place for programs. The people sat on benches of heavy planks placed on large heavy pieces of stove wood upended, with the speaker standing in front on a small platform to deliver patriotic speeches, also many other kinds. During the fight for prohibition, "prohi" rallies were held there. My father used to sing in the Gideon Male Quartet at many of these rallies.

One of the large attractions for the children was a stand where we could buy cracker-jack with a prize in each box. For one penny we could also buy a stick of candy with a finger ring on it that displayed a colored set. Also for one cent we could buy a square stick of chewing gum. I still can remember the flavor of that stick. For a nickel we could buy a large ice cream cone, which we seldom had. That cone certainly tasted good to us on a hot summer's day. Our parents always gave us a few pennies or maybe a nickel to spend at the stand.

When I was a young teenager, Virgil Hammer was assistant pastor at the Bakers Corner Wesleyan Methodist Church. He practiced the children and teenagers on a flag drill in the basement of the church, that we presented at our Sunday School picnic at Bishop's Park on July 4th.

In those days I and most of the other young people liked to go to the fireworks at Sheridan. That was a special 4th of July in itself. If I remember rightly, fireworks were shot off where the park is now, but there was no park there then. It was called Compton's Woods. My folks usually took us early. We needed to wait for it to get dark; during the waiting time they would visit with neighbors and friends.

Ruby, my cousin, and I liked to go before dark because we could circulate and meet other young people. Some we knew but did not see often. Sometimes we would get acquainted with new young people. Some of the boys liked to tease the girls by throwing firecrackers so they would explode close to the girls' feet, causing jumping and squealing, just as the boys wanted.

Then there were the ice cream stands and snack counters where people were busy selling and buying refreshments. An ice cream cone was what we always wanted. There was only one dip, but, my what a dip, on a cone twice the size of later days. A cone cost only a nickel, but they were large enough to satisfy us. There was patriotic music by a band. Finally everyone settled down on folding chairs brought from home or on blankets, comforters, horse blankets or rugs spread on the ground.

Pretty soon it was dark enough for the fireworks to begin. Maybe the moon would come out bright enough we could even see each other. Even so the fireworks were bright enough to be beautiful against the dark sky.

The fireworks were very much as they have been for years, beautiful sprays in several colors, some of them resembling umbrellas as they came down. The big bright ones sounded like cannons when they burst and lit the ground below like close lightning. The half-hour of fireworks usually ended with ground displays, perhaps an American Beauty rose or the American flag, sometimes Niagara Falls, with a volley of cannon-ball noise bursting in the air. No one seemed to mind the mob of cars leaving, everyone wanting to get out of there at once as soon as the fireworks had ended.

When my two brothers were young and at home they sometimes shot carbide in cans instead of firecrackers. It was much cheaper and made just as much noise. Our father enjoyed shooting it with them. They put a small amount of carbide in a tin can with a hole in the bottom of it, added a little water, and put a tight lid on the can. When the water touched the carbide it formed a gas. They placed the can on its side and held it down solidly with one foot. When they lit a match and held it to the hole in the bottom of the can, the gas exploded and blew the lid off the can with a loud boom.

The Big Room: Grades 5–8

Summer holidays were over all too soon. It was a proud day when we returned from summer vacation and found ourselves in the Big Room. More things happened there than in the Little Room.

A music teacher, Mr. Charles Carter, lived in Arcadia, and traveled to teach in most of the schools in Adams and Jackson townships. He came to Bakers Corner only twice each month and spent some time in each room, and usually used his violin for teaching. We used small songbooks with short children's songs. The half-hour he spent with us was always a happy time.

Although we had a man teacher, we studied "domestic science," nowadays called home economics. The girls in the seventh and eighth grades took this subject and were graded on it. In the northwest corner of the Big Room stood a kitchen cabinet with a few cooking utensils and dishes in it. Beside it stood an old three-burner, short burner kerosene stove.

Once each semester these girls cooked a large kettle of soup beans, little white navy beans with plenty of soup. They cooked enough to serve the whole room their noon lunch. Each child brought his or her own bowl and spoon. We had to cook up a lot of beans to feed almost thirty people. Many things were brought from home, salt, pepper, vinegar some wanted in their beans. Each child was to bring two or three pennies so someone could go across the road and buy crackers to eat with the soup. One year we cooked beans enough to serve the Little Room their noon lunch as well as our own.

In these upper grades we did not have as many tests as they have in school today. We had to try to remember things we were taught until the big examinations, one at the end of each semester. Our first semester then ended at Christmas time when our week of Christmas holiday vacation started. It was rather hard on us to have our examination during the time we were practicing for our Christmas program and making other preparations for the Christmas season.

The examination questions were sent out by the trustee and had been made up by the state, and the teacher copied the questions on the blackboard. Usually we were to answer any six out of eight; in a few subjects eight out of ten. Geography was one of these subjects. I believe history was another.

We were given manuscripts of slick, lined white paper on which to write the answers in ink. Even the arithmetic problems were to be worked in ink by everyone down to third and fourth grades. We could use a sheet in the back to solve our problems, then copy them to the front.

We were required to use pen holders with scratchy metal pen points, dipping the point into a bottle of ink for every one, two, or three words, a very messy way to write, especially for children. The ink bottle was kept in a hole in the top right-hand corner of our desk.

If you got too much ink on the point it made a blotch, and after every line we needed to use an ink blotter to soak up the excess ink. Sometimes there were ink spills in spite of the children's carefulness, with messes happening on examination papers, books, clothing, floor, and fingers. Almost always while writing with a pen and ink, your fingers became stained.

Two days, Thursday and Friday, were taken for examinations. When a pupil finished one subject, he could leave the room until the start of another. If it was the last subject of the day, he could go home. On the second day of exams we were always through early, and everyone had part of the day off.

We never knew our examination grades until we went back to school after the holiday vacation. The manuscripts were saved to be used again for the examination at the end of the school year. We had written our names in the proper place on the front of the thin cardboard cover. After the last exam we took them home.

I remember just one time during my eight years at Bakers Corner School when we had a large pitch-in dinner on the last day of school. Our parents had been invited; the mothers brought the food. Our fathers were mostly farmers and left off planting their fields for a sumptuous dinner and a half day at school with their children and neighbors, a rare chance for them.

Wide boards were placed on trestles in the school-house front yard, forming a table for the bountiful feast. After the dinner was finished and cleared away, everyone crowded into the Big Room to listen to the children recite pieces, give dialogues and exercises, and sing happy songs.

The vacation song I liked best was:

Hip! Hip! Hurrah! for glad vacation
Gladest time of all the year.
Good-bye books and school and all,
We will find you in the fall
But we go to meet vacation
With a cheer.

This we sang lustily to the tune of "Tramp, tramp, tramp, the boys are marching." Everyone loved to sing it, being inspired by the vacation at hand.

The last day of school was not the only time during the school year that the children put on programs for their parents. The Christmas programs were just as exciting. We usually practiced every day for a couple of weeks leading up to it and enjoyed the practice time because then we did not have to spell or cipher.

Writing and penmanship were such important parts of a school day for all the subjects. I was very happy and proud one Christmas morning when I came downstairs and found a fountain pen in the top of my stocking, sticking out from the midst of the peanuts, candy, and a few other small gifts above the orange in the toe. This was before the time of the now common ballpoint pen. I was a fifth grader, and this was my very first fountain pen, made with a rubber bladder inside to hold the ink. I had to pull down a little lever on the side of the pen, put the gold pen point into the ink, and very slowly and carefully bring the lever back up into place, drawing the ink into the rubber bladder.

The first day that school started again after the holidays, I took my new pen to school. I was so proud of it. It was so much handier and neater to use than the old stick pens. I did not get my fingers stained when I used it. A cap screwed over the end where the point was, and it had a clip to attach to my clothing.

Several of the children wanted to see this marvelous item and try it out. As one of the boys in my class played with it, he broke it. I was just about sick over that. I am sure he did not aim to break it, but he did not offer to pay for it. I was feeling pretty blue when I went home. I showed my parents the broken pen. My father told me not to worry over it, that he would buy me another the next time he went to town, which he did.

Halloween and Valentine's Day were special, great fun, too. We did not do much at school about Halloween, but we were excited about plans for Halloween evening, when we put on old clothes, never wearing "bought" costumes, and went around doing tricks but not in those days receiving treats. We began making valentines days and weeks before Valentine's Day came at school. We were so excited, wondering how many valentines we would receive, what kind they would be, and whether there would be any store-bought ones in our bunch. By the day of the party, the valentine box was full, and everyone's eyes were sparkling with excitement.

I still have a few of those valentines, treasuring most the homemade ones. Many of the donors, yes, most of the donors, are gone to another world, and I miss and cherish their memory so very much, both boys and girls.

Sometimes on some other Friday afternoons after the last recess, we had spelling bees or ciphering matches. Everyone looked forward to these special days, appreciating a variation from the regular routine. I remember I liked the spelling bees much better than I did the ciphering. I could do the arithmetic and get it right, but I was rather slow, and some of the students were so much faster than I that I did not like it very well. I was much better in spelling and liked the spelling matches, when I could go ahead of most anybody in those bees. But if the captain was wise in a ciphering match he would not choose me.

When I was in the Big Room, most of the girls wore their hair long. Maggie Baker and I wore ours combed the same way, braided part way down our back with two hair ribbon bows, one each perky at the end of a braid. Our hair was near the same color. We decided one day to braid our hair together just for a little fun. When it was braided together no one could tell one strand from the other or which one a strand belonged to.

I was a seventh or eighth grader when one bright, sunshine day, John Pickett brought a tiny camera to school. Cameras were scarce in those days, but John had one. It took tiny pictures, but they were very clear. He was taking pictures of several of the children on the playground behind the school building when one of the older boys in my class begged me to let John take my picture with him. I did not like him very well and so would not do it.

Nicknames were common, as I suppose they were at all schools. The two Whicker boys, Raymond and Morris, were Big Whick and Little Whick. The two Wise boys, Herman and Ardra, were called

Big Boots and Little Boots, these names given them because through the cold winter months they wore thick, high-top felt boots with heavy one-buckle, rubber arctics worn over them, which they removed in the schoolroom, and left under the lunch bench in the entrance. They were the only boys in the school who wore these rubber galoshes and also probably the only boys in the school with warm feet.

Lawrence Ross was very small for his age and was called Granny; his pal, Maurice Carr, was called Mock. Leland Beard was called Dick, while his little brother was called Puss because he was so fat and had such fat cheeks. Morris Foulke was called Foulkee and Elmer Hammer was Ham. George Baker was Judge, William Weewee was Willie, and John Pickett was Johnnie, while his little brother Hollas was called Hod. Dewain Bolen was Noonie and his older brother Doyle was Peck. Worth Baker was Toothie because of his two big front teeth. Lester Carr was Leek; Conard Grubbs was Coonie. Dudley Wise was called Dud. Lowell Poore was called Bud. Oddly, very few girls were nicknamed.

During the eight years I attended Bakers Corner School, I can remember only one occasion there at night. That was during the winter I was an eighth grader. Electricity had not as yet been installed in the school building. We had decided to have an old-fashioned box supper, which was a public occasion. People of all ages came from all around the neighborhood.

A few years earlier, box suppers were quite popular entertainments, especially for the young people. It was a good way to raise money for the school, since the money from the sale of the boxes went toward special projects for the school. The girls, with the help of their mothers, prepared delicious food suitable to be packed in a box. They wanted it to be as attractive and tasty as possible. It was then packed into a pasteboard box, the right size to hold enough food for two people. Many times two girls would pack a box together to be sold as a double box to two boys or men.

The girls spent much time for a few weeks before the party decorating their boxes with crepe paper of different pretty hues, some bright and gaudy, others delicate and dainty, sometimes using artificial flowers. Crepe paper was stretched into ruffles and flower shapes and tinsel added. Some were very plain but all were pretty.

Whose decorated box was whose was kept secret from the boys and men, so they would not know whose box they were buying. When the boxes were brought to the schoolhouse they were kept covered to continue to keep the men and boys from figuring out who they belonged to. Sometimes a boy wanted to buy a certain girl's box and would try to find out which was hers. Usually he was disappointed and guessed wrong.

When a box was auctioned off, the boy or man who bought it came to the front to get it. The girl who brought it came to the front, too. He then found out whose box he had bought.

My cousin Ruby and I had prepared a box together. At that time Lowell Ross had eyes for our schoolmate Thelma Hammer, and he and Thelma's brother, Elmer bought our box. I know Lowell was disappointed to have to eat with Ruby and me instead of Thelma. When ours was sold that night at the school, the four of us went out to Lowell's car and ate together.

Before the selling of our boxes we all enjoyed a program of contests, cakewalks, and such things, with several delicious cakes given out that night. But the selling of the boxes and the eating of their contents was the main excitement of the evening, especially for us older children. It was a kind of goodbye party in a way. Our grade school days were drawing to a close in this two-room building at the crossroads in Bakers Corner.

Patriotic?

World War I was happening during our time in the two-room school. It was a popular and patriotic thing to buy war bonds.

Some people always want to be the first to do anything and put themselves forward in the limelight to be popular and to be the big "it," so some men rushed to buy bonds. My father was not that kind of man, but was a good patriotic citizen, a healthy farmer, and young enough to have to register for the draft. I remember well the day he registered. Young as I was, I could feel the sadness my mother felt, her fear he would have to leave us and go to war.

My father had not yet bought any war bonds, but had planned to buy some at a little later date when he thought his money would be a little more plentiful. One night, late, after we were all asleep, my parents were awakened by a loud knock on the dining room door. My father hurried into his clothes and down the stairs to open the door. He could see by the dim kerosene oil lamp in the room behind him that there were two masked Ku Klux Klan men standing outside on Grandpa Hodson's porch. He asked them what they wanted, and they told him they had run out of gasoline and wanted to borrow some. He told him he did not have gas, only what was in the Model T Ford. He had not yet begun to farm with a tractor and had no need for keeping gasoline in a drum.

The men told him they had to have gas and forced him to go to his car, get under it, and drain some out for them. While he was under the car, they told him they did not need or want gasoline at all and for him to get out from under the car.

After he was out they said they had come to force him to buy war bonds, that he was unpatriotic, calling him all sorts of names and telling him what they would do to him if he did not buy bonds immediately. Some people had been tarred and feathered by Klan members for not being "patriotic." This is what they threatened to do to him if he did not buy bonds at once.

He promised he would go to the bank the next day and buy war bonds, which he did. It could have been the end of the matter, and in a way it was. But my father did not forget. The men who came thought my father did not know them, but he knew both of them. He said the voice of one of the men he would know anywhere. Both were from Sheridan, one owning and running a merchandise store there; the other in another business. For a long time we did not patronize either business. Finally after many years we did go into these businesses again some. My father felt one of the men was the best of his trade. I do not know if my father ever let them know that he knew. Although I was not very old I held that wicked night against those two men. Even when I was a teenager, having dates with boys, I would not go with a son of one of these men because of what his father had done to my father.

Prohibition

During the period I was an older child the "Prohibition Movement" was in full sway. Grandpa Hodson was a very strong supporter of that movement. My Grandpa Wilson at Scipio, Indiana, was also very much opposed to liquor, all kinds of hard liquor, as was my father.

There were many "Prohi" rallies here and there. My father and Grandpa Hodson went to most of them in the county. A few times, Mama took my brother John William and me, but usually kept us at home.

On one trip when I was allowed to go, the place for the rally was decorated with red, white and blue bunting all around the speaker's stand and high up around the top of the room. Other times, if the rally was on a street, the fronts of the stores were decorated.

They had a big time at these rallies, with singers and speakers, jokes and peppy, rousing songs. Some people had badges with the pictures of the men the Prohibition Party was running for President and vice-president of the United States, worn on the men's coat lapels or on the women's dresses. (Women's slacks were unheard of then.) We had several of these badges to give away in 1916, and several for a few years after.

My father was a singer. He and three other men formed what they called the Gideon Male Quartet. The other men were Frank Griffin from near Arcadia, Ray Morford from Hortonville, and John Macy from near Westfield, whose daughter Frieda Macy Reves played the piano or pump organ for them. They met quite often to practice in one of their homes. Sometimes their families went with them to practice, and we had quite a social time, sometimes popping corn or making homemade ice cream. The men all had a lot of fun singing or otherwise, especially Ray who was the clown of the bunch.

This quartet sang together for five years and in many places and for many different occasions, including these Prohi rallies and conventions. The following are titles of some of the songs they sang at the rallies: "Twin Ballots and One by a Sunday School Man," "I'm a Temperance Man," and "We'll Git There All the Same." Part of it went like this, "We'll git there all the same; Git there, Git there, boys, let prohibition be your aim." Others were "Grandfather Voted That Way," and "Molly and the Baby Don't You Know." There was one I especially liked with the title "The Brewer's Big Hosses."

The Gideon Male Quartet sang at least one Prohi state convention and also at Sheridan, Deming, Bakers Corner, Carmel, Clarksville, Fishers, and Pleasant View on the Springmill Road, as well as Bishop's Park several times. There were not many places in Hamilton County where they did not sing.

My mother belonged to the women's organization against the "Liquor Traffic" called the WCTU, Women's Christian Temperance Union. I believe they met once each month. Their emblem was a small bow made of narrow white baby ribbon, pinned on the lapels of their coats or dresses.

Around that time there was a movie made called *Ten Nights in a Bar Room*, depicting the evils of a life of drinking. This was shown in many places and I am sure did a lot of good.

The following was copied from a microfilm picture of the front page of the *Noblesville Daily Ledger* dated July 21, 1916: "Hanley's Steam Roller Busy, St. Paul, Minnesota, July 21, J. Frank Hanley of Indiana was nominated Prohibition Candidate for President today."

From the *Ledger* dated August 8, 1916: "Dr. Ira Landrith nominated for Vice President on the Prohibition ticket." The party was very small; there was no chance of their men getting elected, but it was a chance for the people to make a stand for what they believed in. Although the Prohi Party never won any offices, they did eventually get the prohibition law passed. The Prohibition or Eighteenth Amendment went into effect January 16, 1920, but was repealed in November 1933.

I found through the microfilm pictures of an old *Ledger* in the April 18, 1914 issue that John Hodson, my grandfather, was a delegate-at-large at the State Prohibition convention. In the same paper it was noted that my father was elected county chairman of the Prohibition Party.

In 1920 I was in the eighth grade at Bakers Corner School. In the fall just before election time, Mr. Jesse Hodson, our teacher, decided to take a vote among the children in his room, fifth, sixth, seventh, and eighth grades. There was only one Prohi ballot cast. Mr. Hodson embarrassed me by saying, "Well, I guess we know who that one is."

That same year the Gideon Male Quartet had their picture taken together at a photographer's, an early publicity photo for a group that took a stand.

Music Lessons

My father, who had such a strong talent in music, singing in the quartet and playing his guitar so skillfully, wanted to encourage me along that line too. While we were yet living at Grandpa Hodson's place, he wanted to start me taking music lessons on the old pump organ that sat in the northeast corner of our living room. This organ was played like a piano, except it had to have air pumped into it to make the sound. I can well remember how that organ looked, a pretty piece of furniture, light colored, tall with an oval-shaped mirror near the top with fancy gingerbread trim. On each side of the keyboard were round, flat pieces on which to set a kerosene lamp. It had two foot pedals to pump air and a cast-iron footed stool that turned round and round to adjust the height of the seat for whoever was playing.

My father engaged a young woman named Phoebe White who lived at Deming to start me on organ lessons. During the summertime she came to our house once each week in a buggy to give me a half hour lesson.

I was not naturally musically inclined and had little or no talent for it. My mother did not have a talent for music, and it seemed that I took after her. She knew the words to many church songs, but she knew only one tune, "What a Friend We Have in Jesus." When she sang to herself around the house, all words fit into that tune. I remember when my brothers were babies she rocked and sang them to sleep, singing all church songs to that same tune.

My father, on the other hand, had a wonderful talent for music, which he likely inherited from his own father. He never had a music lesson in his life and taught himself to read music. He gave music lessons for many years of his life, making his living by tuning and repairing pianos in addition to farming. My father led the singing at the Bakers Corner Church for many years and the Gideon Quartet I've just described was one of the most important parts of his life.

How I hated those organ lessons, and how I hated to practice, which I was supposed to do one hour each day. My father would go to the barn to do chores while I was in practicing; I'd hit a wrong note, and his voice would shout, "B flat!" I am sure I was quite a worry to my mother, who could hardly get me to sit down there on that stool and practice. I was a worry to my father, too, because he wanted so much for me to learn. There were too many other things I would rather do than practice the organ. Sometimes neighbor children came to play; I could hear them outside and wanted to be out there with them. On and on the moments dragged. It was as bad as when I had to churn in the cellar with the old wooden dasher churn, wishing the butter would come with the next hundred strokes, then the next hundred.

Naturally, not being interested, I did not make much progress. I never had a good lesson and sometimes cried during the time my teacher was there. The summer wore on. Finally the teacher told my parents that I had just as well stop. They were wasting their money; maybe when I got a little older I would do better. I had begun to very much dislike my teacher, but I was thankful she told my parents that. I was really happy to quit the lessons and took no more that summer.

When I was eleven and we left Grandpa's and moved to the Alvin Foulke place, my father bought a piano. I do not know what became of the old organ. I suppose he sold it, because we had it no more. I was very happy to have a piano, which I liked better than the organ. Still, that piano did not improve my talent for music.

Once again my father, who was so musically talented, wanted me to learn to play—this time the piano. So he hired a young colored woman from the Roberts Chapel colored settlement to come and give me lessons. Her name was Eva Cunningham, and she drove a Model T, a very nice lady whom I liked.

I took more interest in my lessons than I had before, but still these lessons were a burden to me as was practicing, because there were so many other things I would rather do. I would even rather clean the house than practice my music lesson.

However, I did try and progressed some, although very slowly. I still took music lessons only during the few summer months when we had vacation from school. Very few children then took music lessons during the school term; their parents thought it was too much for them. My teacher was paid fifty cents for each lesson, which lasted around a half hour.

After taking lessons from Eva for probably two summers, I began to take them from Mrs. Melissa Kirk, a widow who lived at Sheridan with her mother and young son.

To go to take my lesson, I was old enough by now to drive a horse with a closed buggy. I should say that I did not want to take our Model T, although my father had taught me to drive the car when I was quite young. I did not want to learn to drive, but he said that was one thing I had to learn, because it would be necessary for me to know when I was older. I dreaded for Sunday afternoon to come because I was afraid my father would want us to take a "Sunday afternoon drive" and would tell me to drive. This often happened. But to please him once in a long while I would drive our Model T Ford touring car to take my music lesson.

Usually I took the horse and I liked that better. Sometimes our parents would have me go uptown in Sheridan to buy something that was needed at home, such as groceries or dry goods, or maybe to the bank. I would drive into town and hitch my horse to the hitchrack, usually along the north side of what later became the Ben Franklin store.

I remember well one time when my father sent me to get something, probably from the hardware store. He did not have the cash on hand to pay for it. So he gave me a blank check with his signature on it to pay for the article. I knew the importance of being careful to not lose a signed blank check; he had certainly impressed it on my mind.

I believe my friend Elizabeth Hodson was with me that day. We had gone several miles in the closed buggy, but because it was summertime, we had the doors on each side open and the window in front fastened up. Suddenly I missed the tiny coin purse in which I had placed the signed blank check. I was so terribly worried.

We searched and searched everywhere in that buggy in our clothing, among our songbooks and music, but it was nowhere to be found. How could we have lost it? But we surely had. What a worry! Someone might find it and use it for all the money my father had in the bank. What was I going to do? What could I do?

Certainly my parents must have had great confidence in me and trusted me. If they did not fully trust me or worried about me driving to town, they never did let me know it.

There was only one thing I could do: turn the horse and buggy around and head back toward home and look for it. We would be late for our two music lessons, but I had to retrace my steps. I had to find that tiny black coin purse.

We both kept our eyes glued to the road, looking from side to side and along the edge of the cement. There were not many cars or trucks, and the traffic did not bother us. We kept to our side of the road.

We had gone quite a distance when all of a sudden I spied a small black object in the road, three or four feet from the edge, on the cement. Anyone not looking closely would have thought it was a piece of horse manure, which was common on the road then. It was about that size. I am sure I squealed for joy when I was close enough to see it was really the coin purse.

I was not long jumping out of the buggy and picking it up. You may guess I kept close watch on it from there on. Turning around again we went on to Mrs. Kirk's for our lessons and were not very late. I bought the item at the store and happily returned home with it, so very thankful I had had the check to pay for it.

Music lessons or not, Elizabeth and I always had a lot of fun riding along in the buggy. We were like all other kids, curious about everything. There was an old road that ran off to the south from the road to Sheridan, seldom traveled. It went through from Sheridan Road south to State Road 38, which was then called the Lafayette road. Often when we passed it we would wonder what was down there. So one day on our way home after our piano lessons we decided we would find out.

We guided our horse in that direction. Of course there was nothing there but bushes, trees, and old fences with deep matted grass all around, hard deep ruts that had been made when it was very muddy. With so much in our way we had to let the horse walk, and it took us quite a while to reach the other road and made us late getting home. But what did we care? We had our curiosity satisfied. No one seemed to notice we were late.

Our piano lessons were always in the forenoon. We were late for the big noon meal, and on music lesson days I ate leftovers by myself, but that was a small matter. There was an excitement in going to town on our own with the horse or car.

The road from Sheridan was cemented out east of town to the Wilson Reagan farm, about three miles; the rest of the way home was gravel road. One day, driving the buggy, we had come through Bakers Corner on our way home from music lessons. I had let Elizabeth out at her home, the first house east of the store on the north side of the road at Bakers Corner. The range line road had not yet been cemented. What they called "Charlie McConnell's hill" west of the range line road on the Cicero-Sheridan road was much steeper and higher than it is now and the rangeline road was much lower. Construction crews raised and widened it in the 1920s and 1950s when laying out State Road 1 and later U.S. 31.

As I was going east toward the range line road, I met a truck that was coming up the hill. Naturally the top of that truck was seen first. Covering the top of the truck was a loose canvas. I was by myself. Usually my horse did not frighten easily. But he became frightened at the flopping thing coming up toward him, and he began to back up. Luckily there was no ditch at the side of the road. He backed the buggy against a bank. There was nothing I could do. Two men were in the truck, and one of them got out and held the bridle of my horse while the other man drove the truck past us. After the truck had gone, the horse behaved normally.

Although I never accomplished much in music, I enjoyed taking lessons from Mrs. Kirk, and the trip to Sheridan one day each week during the summer months was something to look forward to. I had lots of fun with whoever went with me.

Mrs. Kirk knew my parents wanted me to learn to play church music, so she had me bring my own church songbook. I always had one or two church songs for my lesson as well as some pieces in my lesson book. Then sometimes I would get a new piece of easy sheet music. The pieces she gave me always sounded so pretty when she played them through for me, but it took quite a while to conquer them.

I finally did learn to play these easy church songs and several pieces of sheet music. I especially remember one, "When You Wore a Tulip, A Big Yellow Tulip, and I Wore a Big Red Rose." Sometimes when some young people would come to our house of an evening and we gathered around the piano, I played that song and some others, and we had a great time singing.

I had enough teaching and training in music that I should have been able to be the church pianist, but due to the lack of talent, maybe also the lack of persistence, I never became the church pianist. It did give me pleasure to know that I could play the pieces well enough to play with my father as he played his violin, from a book for piano that had a matching one for the violin.

It was hard for me to imagine how anyone could care about music as much as my father did. He loved to watch lightning; sometimes he played his guitar as he watched the sky light up with electricity. When the weather was warm, after a hard day's work on the farm, evening chores finished and supper over, if there was lightning in the north or northwest, maybe a storm coming up, he would take his guitar and a feather cushion to the front porch. The porch had no railing around it, and its floor was made of narrow wooden boards. He would lay his head on the pillow and on his guitar play the most beautiful melodies while he watched the lightning for an hour or more. It didn't even take lightning to send him out to the front porch; he was often out there anyway.

But on nights of the lightning flashes, it was relaxing and restful to him and the rest of the family to hear him strum that guitar.

High School Memories

Finally I left the schoolhouse of my childhood, there at the crossroads at Bakers Corner.

In those days eighth graders were not promoted to the ninth grade but had to pass a special examination to go from grade school into the freshman year of high school. The eighth graders at Bakers Corner were sent to Boxley High School for this examination. If we passed, we graduated from eighth grade.

The day I took this exam was a beautiful warm spring day in 1921. I rode the five miles with my cousin, Ruby Wilson, in a buggy behind Old Babe, her pony. She was living about six miles east of us at Cicero, and this good friend wanted to spend the night with me and take me the next day for this exciting adventure. One of the boys in my class, Dewain Bolen (Nooney), needed transportation there, too, so he rode along with us. Ruby took us just for fun. After she moved to Cicero from being our neighbor out in the country, she and I found every excuse we could to be together. Having her spend the night and take me the next day was a practical plan because it saved my father from taking time from his farming to transport me for the exam.

It was rather frightening that day to go to a strange school where we did not know many people and to a strange supervising teacher. We could, maybe, have made better grades at our own school with our own teacher.

By the last day of school our papers had been graded and our eighth grade diplomas were given to us by our teacher. I cannot remember if he had a word of congratulation for us or not. Some of the schools had eighth-grade commencements, but we did not. We just moved on to the big high school building next fall.

Naturally I was looking forward to high school with great anticipation, but there were other, mixed feelings. Since I was six years old, I had always attended school at the little country two-room brick schoolhouse at Bakers Corner, two rooms, two teachers. When I was there, with always a lady teacher in the little room and a man teacher with the four older grades, around twenty-five to thirty pupils in each room, it was all so comfortable.

I knew wherever I went to high school there would be many more rooms, teachers, and pupils. I also knew most of them would be strangers to me. There would be new rules and regulations and new studies such as Latin and algebra, about which I knew nothing. There was some dread connected with it all.

During the summer months between my grade school and high school times my parents had not decided where I would attend high school. I had originally been transferred by the Jackson Township trustee to Bakers Corner grade school in Adams Township, and that was my school although I didn't always live in Adams Township. I could go to Boxley High School, also in Adams Township, if my parents wished it. But I really wanted to go to high school at Cicero for only one reason, because my cousin Ruby Wilson lived in Cicero and went to school there. She was one year older than I, and therefore one grade ahead of me in school. She was my best chum.

Most of the other boys and girls in my eighth-grade class were going to high school at Boxley because they lived in Adams Township, and my parents would rather I chose Boxley. Perhaps it was a little closer.

At that time there were not many school hacks or busses, and those few that operated did not haul high school students. If we wanted to go to high school, we had to furnish our own transportation, which was mostly by horse and buggy, unless you lived close enough to walk. A few of the country boys drove automobiles but not many.

My parents felt that six miles was a long way for their fourteen-year-old daughter to drive a horse and buggy five days a week, especially through our Indiana winter weather with school not out of an evening until four o'clock. For about a year before time for me to start high school, my parents began looking for a farm for sale closer to a high school. They looked far and near, even as far as Pendleton.

With all their looking and worry, when the first day of my freshman year came, we were still living on that Alvin Foulke farm, still six miles west of Cicero. It was a good improved farm where they wanted to live after their three children were through high school.

They wanted to stay. Then the problem was solved another way.

My cousin Luther Moore lived a little over a mile south on the range line road. He was a year ahead of me in school and drove an old sorrel horse called Doc hitched to an open buggy. I walked three-fourths of a mile to catch a ride with him; thus I did not have the responsibility of a horse or buggy. I had to walk a few blocks from the livery barn in Cicero to the school building after we had driven the six miles, but that was fine when the weather was good.

I well remember my first day of high school, a very rainy day. My father decided to drive me and my girl friend, Josephine Poore, a neighbor and also a freshman, to school that day in his Model T Ford with side curtains. Since it was raining there was nothing urgent on the farm for him to do, and we would not have to stay very long at school the first day. We did not get wet because he always kept the side curtains in good repair.

When I reached home that day I told my mother that I had met one girl whom I thought I would like really well, and her name was Gladys Crooks. She was a freshman and we became chums, and have remained so for more than seventy years.

The rooms in the old high school building were large. We got together of a morning for assemblies. A few days after school began the rows of seats in the assembly room were changed from east and west to north and south, making two rooms into one. We were seated there in alphabetical order. I soon learned where all my classes were in the basement of the school building. Since the assembly room was on the second floor and all the freshman classes were in the basement, four times each and every day the freshman class was found marching for classes down the several flights of stairs from top to bottom.

At the close of the day for four years we descended the stairs for a final time with a march played on a small piano in the downstairs hallway, usually played by one of the grade school teachers, Mary Kepner or her friend, Pauline Buzan.

The first three and a half years of high school we had no inside restrooms. Behind our large brick school building were two wooden outdoor toilets, boys or girls on each side with six or eight holes in each. These we patronized rain or shine, cold or hot, it made no difference, that was it. In the girl's toilet were two rows of seats, To get water we pumped the long handled old iron pump that stood a short distance from the school building. I carried my own folding aluminum drinking cup.

One year it was a fad among the girls to wear bright purple sateen bloomers. A few of the girls had American Beauty rose color or bright Kelly green ones. If you didn't have a pair you were out of style. Too bad. My mother brought home from town a piece of purple sateen with thread to match. Bloomers! I liked to sew and was happy to be like the other girls.

All freshmen took the same subjects: we had no choices that year. Our freshman year our teachers were: Mr. John Kreag, principal; Mr. Frank Hiatt (I did not have any classes under him that year); Pauline Edwards, first year Latin; and Virgile Osborn, freshman English. We were disappointed in the spring when Miss Edwards planned to get married and announced she would not be back when fall came. Miss Osborn did not return in the fall either.

Mr. Kreag taught us biology one semester, general science the other. One of our classmates was Nolan Timmons. He went to high school only that freshman year. One day in general science class, Mr. Kreag told us to ask our parents how far a pitcher pump would lift water and tell him in class the next day. The next day when Mr. Kreag asked how many remembered the assignment, Nolan's hand was the only one that went up. He was so excited to have been the only one in the class to remember. With a big smile on his face, he raised his hand as high as he could and shook it excitedly, eager to be called upon. When Mr. Kreag said, "All right, Nolan, tell us what you found out," Nolan answered, "I asked my mom and she didn't know."

Another time in general science class, Mr. Kreag said, "A pound of feathers weighs exactly the same as a pound of lead." It seemed perfectly logical the way he explained the simple reasoning. Near the end of the class Nolan again raised his hand and said, "I still can't see how a pound of feathers can weigh as much as a pound of lead." There's one in every class.

The freshman English teacher, Virgile Osborn, required each of us to memorize all forty-eight lines of the poem "Lochinvar," written by Sir Walter Scott. One day just before class started, a friend Alice and I were sitting side by side. One of us jokingly said to the other, "When you get up to say 'Lochinvar' you will say, 'With a tear on her lips and a smile in her eye' when you should say, 'With a smile on her lips and a tear in her eye.'" The other answered, "And you will say, 'There was racing and chasing on Annabel Lee' when you should say, 'Cannobie Lee.'" We were so sure we would not, but we each did.

It would have been inconvenient and unwise for me to ride with Luther the second semester of my freshman year because Luther was on the basketball team and would be practicing many evenings after school. It would be too late, much after dark, when we reached the place that I met him, too late and too dark for me to walk alone three-fourths of a mile, mostly on the range line road.

I rode with him only through the first semester, which ended at Christmas time. By the time school started after the holidays, our parents had made arrangements for me and my neighbor friend, Josephine Poore, to room with an old lady we knew who was living in Cicero, not far from the school building. We took our own bedding, cooking utensils, and food, when needed. Grandma Collins, as we called her, gave us a shelf in her pantry for our utensils and food. We did our own cooking on the coal range, which she also used. She let us sleep in her spare bedroom, her front room, which was not heated. Of evenings we sat with her in her living room, which was heated by a base burner.

From Grandma Collins's we walked the few blocks to the school, which was no farther than walking from the livery barn. My father brought us to Cicero on Monday morning in his Model T and came after us on Friday evening after school. This seemed to be a very good arrangement. The telephone from Cicero to Bakers Corner was not long distance then, so I could telephone home.

We had been rooming there only a week or two when Josephine took very ill with a sore throat. Her parents brought her home and took her to the doctor. It turned out to be scarlet fever. At that time anyone with scarlet fever had to be quarantined. She was not allowed to come back to school for six weeks, which ruined her school year. In some of her classes it was impossible to catch up to make a passing grade. In order for her to graduate, she had to go an extra semester after our commencement, although she was allowed to go through the commencement with the class.

When some of the parents found out about her illness and that I had slept in the same bed with her when she was taking the disease, they were afraid for me to mingle with their children for fear I would take it and expose them. They complained to Dr. Tomlinson, the health officer, and he had me miss two or three days of school. He told us it was only to satisfy the parents because by that time all danger of my taking it was past.

In six weeks Josephine was back in school and staying at Grandma Collins's with me again.

I roomed with Grandma Collins for twelve weeks. By that time it was the latter part of March, the worst of the winter weather was over and we were looking forward to spring. Our parents decided Josephine and I could drive to school together.

My father had bought a good driving horse and a closed buggy with a sliding door on each side, a window in each door, and a large window in the front that had an open slot below the glass for the lines to go through. Snow, rain, sleet, or wind could not touch us inside; we were quite cozy most of the time.

Josephine's parents also had a closed buggy similar to ours. Her father owned a tiny grocery store on the range line road and had a huckster wagon that he drove around over the country certain days of each week. Sometimes, on days he did not run his route, Josephine took their horse and buggy. Most of the time we used my father's.

We put our horse up a few blocks from school at the livery barn operated by old Mr. Lowe and his son. When we reached the livery barn we left the horse for them to unhitch and put in the stall. At noon they fed it the corn and gunny sack of hay we had brought for that purpose. We did just fine driving that spring of the freshman year.

I cannot remember ever missing a day of school because of bad weather. One beautiful evening the spring of my freshman year, we were driving Josephine's horse with my father's buggy. Just before we entered the covered bridge over Cicero Creek, we picked up Ralph

Beck, a freshman classmate who lived about a mile out of town in our direction. Ralph was walking home. Josephine was driving because it was her father's horse, but it was not one of the old gray huckster wagon horses.

We were on our side of the bridge, headed west, almost through the bridge, when a car came into the bridge meeting us. They were not on their side as they should have been, and to make matters worse, they were too busy talking and came into the bridge taking their half out of the middle. They ran into our buggy, with one of the shafts of our buggy running through the running board of their car. The front wheels were jerked off the buggy with the axle standing straight up, then the horse jerked the lines out of Josephine's hands and broke loose from the buggy. Someone caught him around the bend by the cemetery.

No one was hurt except Josephine's fingers a little when the lines were jerked away from her. She went home and went to bed. I was fine; I went home and raked in the chicken yard for spring cleaning. The buggy was so torn up it could not be repaired. My father bought another closed buggy for me at an auction sale.

The boys in the car who hit us were a couple of sophomores, Worth Hiatt and Ernest Carson. Worth was driving. They had started home, forgotten something, and were on their way back to get it when they hit us. Worth picked us up and took us to school a few days until my father could replace the buggy. I rode through the old red Cicero covered bridge twice each day for most of my four years of high school, but that was the only time I ever had a mishap there.

In the early fall of my freshman year, the school had what was called "Freshman Initiation," a wiener roast on a warm evening in a woods across the road from where Erma Bardooner, a senior, lived. All the high school was invited. I spent the night with my cousin Ruby. And I do remember walking along in the dark in the woods when I stepped into a deep hole full of water. It must have been a post hole. It did not hurt me, but I had a wet foot the rest of the evening. I felt I had been really initiated. The freshmen were served sandwiches with soap in them.

One day the spring of our freshman or sophomore year we

were driving the Poores' old gray mare hitched to their heavy closed buggy. That particular day, Edna Bowman was riding with us. Edna was a year ahead of us in school and lived a short distance from both Josephine and me. It was still daylight, a sunny evening. When we reached our next neighbor's, Sallie's, she and her daughter Violet, three years younger than I, were starting to walk to our house carrying a bucket full of eggs.

Josephine and Edna bantered me to ride the old gray mare and let Violet ride in the buggy with them. I had ridden the farm horses all of my life and thought nothing of it, and I crawled out of the buggy onto the horse. We started out okay as Violet took my place in the buggy. The girls took the bucket of eggs on their lap. Sallie said she would walk along behind us. Josephine was driving; it was their horse.

Edna, Josephine, and Violet were cutting up, laughing and hollering. It must have frightened the old horse. She began to run. Who would have thought the old gray slowpoke could have run that fast? We could hardly keep her trotting hitched to the buggy. But she really ran. Josephine became so frightened and excited she threw the lines out of the buggy where no one could reach them, and I was being bounced so hard I could not let loose to grab either the lines or the reins. I think I was hoping to be able to stay on her until I reached Poores'. I didn't think she would stop as she passed our house. I knew that when a horse started to run they headed for home. She was going so fast, I wondered if she would turn the buggy over when she turned the sharp corner at the end of our road and the range line road.

We were in sight of our house. My parents and two brothers were eating supper, and my mother, seated at the west end of the table, could see down the road east. She said, "Archie! There comes Mary Elizabeth on the horse's back and that horse is running away." My father went to the road knowing that when the horse reached him he could just reach out and catch her, which he did.

But twenty-five or thirty feet before she reached him, her harness turned and dumped me off her back down in front of the buggy wheels. The buggy wheels ran over me, bump, bump. The eggs bounced in the bucket. The girls and my mother were very frightened. I believe I was the most calm of anyone except my father.

I tightened into a knot when I fell. I was not hurt at all, I suppose, because I was so tense. I can say I had never before seen a horse's feet look so large, and I saw and heard the buggy wheel rim scrape my glasses frames. That was just a little too close to be fun.

I jumped up and ran toward my mother, who was following my father. I saw the look on her face and said, "Mom! Don't look like that; I'm not hurt." I was not hurt at all, just shaky from the excitement.

During the year and a half that Josephine and I drove a horse to school, we used two different animals of theirs, including one of the old gray huckster wagon horses. At one time for a short time my father owned an albino horse, with pink eyes and pink skin, and hair pure white all over his body. I liked to feel his warm, soft pink nose. The short hair over the pink skin of that nose looked and felt like soft pink velvet. I drove him to school some while my father owned him.

One of my father's driving horses had been trained on a racetrack and did not prove good enough for racing. He was sold as a driving horse. I could race with the boys on the way home from school with him. The boys always won because they had a light open buggy, whereas I had a heavy enclosed one. I will always believe if my buggy had been as light in weight as theirs, my horse would have proven to have been the fastest of all of them.

When fall came and school started again, we drove again but put up our horse in the barn of my great-uncle, Clark Wilson, who now lived at the west end of Cicero. There we had to unhitch and put our horse in the barn ourselves before walking all the way through town to the school building. In the evening, it was walk back through town, hitch up our horse, and drive the six miles home. Uncle Clark fed our horse at noon with the corn and hay we had brought from home. By cold weather our sophomore year my parents decided it was better to put up our horse closer to school. We began to leave it at the livery barn again.

I never stayed of a morning to help Mr. Lowe unhitch my horse, but many times of an evening I would help him hitch up the ones ahead of us so we could get ours sooner.

We drove all winter that second year of high school and did not miss a day because of bad weather.

We were well taken care of. Old Sam Cade had a blacksmith shop between our house and Cicero. After Christmas when it began to get icy, snowy, and slick, my father made arrangements with him to reshoe our horse with rough shoes that would not slip on the ice like regular horseshoes.

The morning we were to have the horseshoes changed, Josephine and I would leave home long before daylight. We would reach Sam's, near Cicero, still before daylight. Sam's wife would invite us in to sit with her by the fire while Sam put the new shoes on our horse. When he finished we drove on to school, arriving at about usual time. In the spring when danger of ice was over, it was the same deal again, changing back to regular horseshoes.

Our sophomore year, the year we drove the horse all winter, the weather was cold, very cold. We placed a heavy bed comforter over the back of the buggy seat, letting the bottom of it reach the floor, to keep the cold air from coming in around our legs from the back. When we were seated, we pulled the top corners in around our shoulders. All night long, bricks and sadirons were heating on our coal and woodstoves. In the morning, we wrapped them in old blankets and placed them on the floor of the buggy around our feet. Another heavy bed comforter was placed over our laps. Our parents helped us get organized, ready to drive the six miles through the severe cold. When we reached Cicero we left our irons and bricks with my great aunt Jane, who kept them hot for us to use going home.

Bed comforters, hot bricks, and sadirons were not all that kept us warm. We each wore long knit underwear with long sleeves, and long legs. How we hated the long legs on the underwear. The long sleeves did not worry us nearly as much as the long legs because we wore long-sleeved dresses that covered the long underwear sleeves. But there was nothing, not even long woolen stockings, that would hide the legs in our long knit union suits. How we hated them, and how happy we were when it became warm enough in the spring to quit wearing the ugly things! Some of the other girls wore them too, but I don't believe all of them did. I will have to confess they did much to help keep us warm. We also wore high-top, laced-up shoes and galoshes.

Early every spring and late each fall of that early part of high school there was a man driving a horse hitched to a hack who camped at the old Sumner schoolhouse which we passed twice each day. Josephine and I were afraid of him. I am sure now we need not have been. One frosty morning while we were still using the heated sad-irons and bricks, we saw him there. I was driving and speeded up the horse. Josephine grabbed one of the sadirons and was ready for him if he had shown any signs of trying to stop us. I don't think the man ever noticed us as we passed.

One Friday evening during my freshman or sophomore year during the warmer weather, I was going to get my horse at Uncle Clark Wilson's. As I walked past the post office, which was at that time on the south side of the street, to get my horse, Shad Young, the postmaster, was waiting for me just outside the open post office door. He told me to tell my father to have our mail box moved by Monday morning from the range line road to the roadside in front of our house. The mail carrier was going to start passing our house.

Our road was a short one mile road ending at the range line road at the west end, and the first north and south road at the east. The last quarter mile at the east end had never been graveled, but was just an old dirt, mud road that was hard to travel on in muddy weather or winter time. But now it would have mail delivery. Times were changing!

One thing that never changed during my four years of high school, was our music teacher, Mr. Charles Carter. He had been my music teacher through grade school at Bakers Corner. I believe everyone liked him and was glad when the music period came. He seated all of us in the front end of the old assembly, two in each seat, leading us, as always, with his violin. We sang all sorts of songs, some old, some new to me, some spiritual, some catchy, slow ones and fast ones and rounds. He had a sharp ear. The first time he came in the fall he seated us by going up and down the aisle asking each one his or her name. He knew instantly by the pitch of our voice what part we could sing best and where to seat us. He could make that fiddle of his talk.

I was always full of ideas, some bad, some good, as I've said before. As long as I was in high school the interurban went through Cicero, as well as the Nickel Plate Railroad. One evening I went home with Lucy, a classmate, to spend the night and come back to school with her the next morning. She had a dental appointment with a dentist at Noblesville after school that evening. We rode the interurban to Noblesville and walked to the dentist's office. I told her dentist I would like to have my teeth examined. Why not? It didn't cost anything to have them examined at that time.

He thought it a good idea, too. He found a small cavity, so he told me. Of course I would not make an appointment; he was not our family dentist. When I reached home the next evening I told my parents. They took me to our family dentist. He could find no cavity at all; there was none there. It seemed to me that Lucy's dentist was hunting a job. It would have been bad for him to drill into one of my good teeth.

Sometimes in high school we had opening exercises first thing of a Monday morning. A few times during the year, Reverend Taylor, pastor of the Methodist church, came and gave us a ten-or-fifteen minute talk, probably ending with a short prayer. This would not be allowed in a school in more modern times, but I don't think it hurt any of us. One thing I remember Reverend Taylor saying was the last part of the twenty-sixth verse of the eleventh chapter of Acts: "And the disciples were called Christians first in Antioch." I do not know why that impressed me, but I never forgot it. A few times each year we had a session of singing for opening exercises. During our senior year, Esther Hiatt read a chapter from Booth Tarkington's book *Seventeen* aloud to us until she finished the book.

The first semester of our sophomore year we studied algebra, the third semester we'd had of it in high school. After Christmas we took plane geometry. Until then we had no choice. I had never liked mathematics. Arithmetic, it was called in grade school, and how I hated it. I told my mother before I entered high school that I planned to take only enough math to graduate. I was required to take three semesters of algebra. I was told I was required to take plane geometry beginning second semester of the sophomore year, and I'd better get ready for it as soon as Christmas was over.

I had started in the plane geometry class when I took the flu and had to miss a week or more of school. When I went back, I was so far behind the class in memorizing the terms that Mr. Kreag took me into the tiny office that was built over the top flight of stairs, and advised me to quit the geometry class and start anew the next fall. I immediately called my mother and told her what Mr. Kreag said. She told me she did not want me to quit the class; she was sure I could catch up and make the grade.

I agreed with Mr. Kreag. I was staying in Cicero that week recuperating from the flu I had the week before because my parents did not want me to ride so far in the cold in a buggy for a few more days. I was sure that when I got home I could convince my mother to let me quit geometry until the next fall. There was no changing her mind. She was so certain I could make it. She said, "Take your geometry book in the other room where it is quiet, no one to bother you, and memorize all the axioms and definitions just like you were memorizing a recitation." Really, I had memorized many poems and recitations, and she knew I could do it if I would try. I tried and I did memorize the geometric terms.

When I went back to school on Monday morning, I was prepared for the geometry class. I went along in it and made as good grades as I would have if I had not missed any school. Mr. Kreag never mentioned my quitting geometry again. He knew my mother would not let me quit, and I knew I couldn't quit. The strange thing about it was that in spite of its being mathematics, I liked it. The next fall Mr. Hiatt said if there were enough of us who wanted it, he would give us a class in solid geometry. Believe it or not, I wanted it and took it along with six others, liked it, and made good grades in it.

Our second year of Latin we studied Caesar, taught to us by a beautiful, tall young woman by the name of Dorothy Hoover. She came to us from Selma, Indiana, near the Ohio line. Her cheeks were pink and as soft looking as rose petals, her eyes a beautiful soft brown. Her hair was very red with a slight soft wave, and she arranged it attractively. She also knew her Caesar well. I liked her and never heard of anyone who didn't. One year there and she too left. It seemed to be a pattern.

Junior year was an important milestone in my young life. In the winter I began going with Lee Stewart, a local farmer who attended our church in Bakers Corner. Lee was a WWI veteran, ten years my senior, who had lost his wife in childbirth in 1923. At first my parents were upset about our courtship because he was older and had been married. But he was a good Christian man and they came to love him.

I remember one Sunday when we were going together, Lee came home with us after Sunday morning service for dinner. When we were seated ready to eat, my father asked Lee to give the blessing. He did not say his prayer very loudly. My little brother Myron was not yet five years old. As soon as Lee finished, Myron looked up and said, "Why didn't you say it louder?" This was quite embarrassing to the rest of us, but my mother had presence of mind and said, "He was not talking to you."

I needed to finish my two years of high school. As long as I was in high school, each spring there was a Junior-Senior Banquet put on with everything furnished by the junior class, feeding and entertaining both senior and junior classes.

The year I was a junior, this banquet was held in the basement of the Christian church in Cicero. In order to do all the planning our class had many class meetings with many discussions. One thing to be decided besides when and where to have the banquet and who to have to do the cooking was the problem of entertainment. Someone suggested that my father, Archie Wilson, entertain singing with his guitar. Some in the class knew what he could do. Others said they had never heard any pretty guitar music; all they had ever heard had been chording, which is not very entertaining. But they had never heard my father play.

I was at the church in the afternoon before the banquet, helping prepare the tables and with the many things there were to do. While we were placing the name cards, one of the girls asked, "Whom shall we place by Mr. Wilson?" I immediately spoke up and said, "Me! I want to sit by my father!" She said, "You want to sit by your father? I would not want to sit by my father. He would be the last one I would want to sit by." I was shocked. I could not think of anyone feeling like that about their father when I loved mine so dearly and would rather sit by him than anyone else there.

A few days before the Junior-Senior Banquet my junior year, my father took me to Noblesville and bought me a new pair of slippers to wear to the party. We went to a store on the south side of the square, and he bought me black suede, one-strap slippers trimmed in patent leather. He paid the enormous price of six dollars for them. But he was proud to do it; I was his only daughter and he wanted me to have nice things. I thought they were the prettiest shoes I had ever seen. I made my own banquet dress from a piece of a pretty shade of blue knit crepe. I was proud that banquet evening of my dress, my shoes, and my father, who entertained so well.

So the junior year passed. Our senior year when we went back to school after the Christmas holidays, we moved into the new addition to the school building. Everyone seemed happy; it had a nice new large assembly room, replacing the old one with the two rooms opened together. There was an office room instead of a tiny place built over an open stairs. We had a room where we could perform experiments in our physics class and there were more classrooms. Probably the most appreciated part of the new construction was the gymnasium. Our boys had had no place to practice basketball or play their games, except over Gordon's drugstore or Cash Scherer's old skating rink, which we called the Coliseum. Now they had a real gym.

The new gym was also a great place for our school class plays and other entertainments. Our class would be the first to use the new gym for our Junior-Senior Banquet, and plans for that were underway. Also we would be the first to use it for our graduation exercises, baccalaureate and commencement. The Class of 1925.

One morning before I left home for school, my mother gave me a one dollar bill to buy something at Lively's General Store to bring home to her that evening. When school was out in the evening, I needed to call home about something. I called from the new school office. I had the money in a small purse, which I laid down while I used the telephone. When I left the office I forgot to pick up the purse. The janitor was working just outside the office door. I had not gotten far down the hall when I missed the purse, turned around, and went back for it. Just before I got to the door I heard my purse fastener click. As I entered I got a glimpse of the janitor leaving through the other door. My heart began to pound. I thought, "He wouldn't do that?" But he did. I opened my purse and the one dollar bill was gone.

As quickly as I could I found Mr. Hiatt. When I told him about my suspicion, he had a strange look on his face and he ran to the office with coattails flying. I followed. When I reached the office he was looking in a place where they kept some school money. It was still there. He said something very low, I cannot remember his exact words, something about we cannot leave money laying around where he, meaning the janitor, could find it. I knew then that my ordeal had not been the first for the school.

Just as it is still somewhat customary for seniors to have their picture taken by a professional photographer to give to relatives and class friends at commencement time, our senior class had ours taken individually. Josephine and I rode to Noblesville to the photographer with our friend and classmate, a boy named Shirley Whisman. I do not remember the make or year of Shirley's father's car. It was a larger, heavier car than a Ford, and I was impressed.

The road between Cicero and Noblesville had not yet been paved; it was just an old country gravel road, and it was not crowded with automobiles as it would later be. When anyone spoke of traveling a mile a minute it sounded almost unreasonable. Well! Shirley watched his speedometer closely and brought it up to sixty miles an hour. Josephine and I were hanging onto our seats almost scared to pieces, as they say. It was the first time in our lives either of us had ever ridden at that rate of speed and we knew it. Shirley did not keep it that fast very long. I think he was a little shaky too.

Senior classes who had graduated before us at Cicero High School had left a memory gift to the school as a remembrance of their class. Our gift was a large painting of a blue heron. I had never seen a blue heron and never did see one until March of 1977, when I was a widow and spent the month in North Fort Myers, Florida. The blue heron are plentiful there and I saw many of them. I don't think I saw a single one without thinking of the picture that hung on the south wall of the new assembly room at Cicero High School and wondering what became of it when the building was torn down. I never knew.

Our senior year the Junior-Senior Banquet was furnished as always by the class following us, the juniors. The new gym was a perfect place for a banquet. It looked so pretty that evening, a wonderful evening. We were allowed to bring a guest. I had been going with Lee for a year, and we were engaged to be married in June, after graduation. I took him as my guest.

We seniors were looking forward to baccalaureate and commencement which were soon to follow. This year spring class meetings were held to plan the graduation exercises. My father had told me that Reverend Francis Eddy, who was a wonderful speaker in our denomination, the Wesleyan Methodist Church, would make a fine speaker for our baccalaureate sermon. He had been pastor of the Bakers Corner church where we attended several years earlier. He was the one who always called for soda cake when he visited us.

I suggested his name in one of our class meetings. It went over well with some in the class who knew him. Also Mr. Hiatt, our class sponsor, knew him and thought we couldn't find anyone better. Reverend Eddy accepted our invitation.

He knew I was planning to be married soon after commencement. Near the beginning of his speech he made a remark that "before the snow flew this fall some in the class would have entered the state of matrimony." I knew and so did some others that he was talking about me. I may have gotten red in the face, I don't know. Reverend Eddy spent the night of our baccalaureate at my parents' home. For our commencement speaker we had a man named Oswald Ryan, who gave us a political commencement address.

Our baccalaureate and commencement, the first ones held in the new gym, were crowded, testing the ability of the new facilities. We all fit in nicely. We were the second class in the history of Cicero

High School to wear caps and gowns at our graduation exercises, and the robes were made of beautiful soft gray wool, but were very warm to wear.

At both the baccalaureate and commencement we marched into the gym from the back and down the center aisle in twos, starting with the tallest boy and girl in the class. Leonard Thompson was the tallest boy and I the tallest girl, so I led.

The evening of our commencement, before the class began to assemble (we had not yet donned our caps and gowns), I was standing on the steps just inside the outside door watching a few early arrivals coming in when my uncle Clyde Wilson, my father's brother who was very special to me, came in. He was a high school teacher living in southern Indiana. I had not known that he was coming and I ran to him. While we were standing there talking he slipped his hand into his pocket and brought out two small coins. He said, "Here are a couple of pennies for your graduation. One is from Grandpa and Grandma Wilson and the other from me."

I looked at them and knew instantly they were five-dollar gold pieces. I was so proud to get them. Grandpa and Grandma seldom came to Hamilton County, afraid he would be needed at home, and the gift would mean even more to me since they couldn't attend.

I wanted to use the gold pieces for something special, so it was even more memorable. So I used one of them to pay for a small, gray suede-back picture album to put individual senior class pictures in. It cost exactly five dollars. The other gold piece I used to purchase a frame for the oil painting I had painted in art class the last semester of my senior year with Beryl Eaks as our art teacher. Lucy Bowman and I were the only two people who ever took oil painting in the history of Cicero High School. We painted a copy of the same picture, *The Birches*, from an original painted by DeVoe, the artist.

Many years have passed, much has happened, good times and bad, joyful and sad, since our class graduated from good old Cicero High School. The building is gone, and many who spent many happy hours there, including some of our classmates, have gone, too. But many are the memories that linger. Sometimes I enjoy dwelling on these memories for a while.

Fears

As I look back on the years I was growing up as Hamilton County grew from a rural area to one with at least some modern conveniences, I know there were some things I was afraid of. Fear was a part of life, just as celebration and family life and learning were. I did not want to go into a pen with an old sow and her little pigs or into a field where there was a bull. I became afraid if lightning got too close and the thunder snapped too loudly. I did not like the looks of a worm, except a wooly worm, which I liked to play with, wrapping them in a doll blanket and playing they were my children. And a big green tomato worm would give me the creeps.

But that was not real fear. The three things I really feared were mad dogs, old tramps, and gypsies. Any of them were terribly frightening to me.

A mad dog I would dream of, over and over again, the same dream. I believe they were more than dreams; they were nightmares, because I was unable to move or scream. In these dreams I would be standing in the middle of a gravel road. It was always a large, light brown, long-haired dog, two or three rods from me, coming slowly toward me with his head and tail hanging low. His head was swinging from side to side with white foam dripping from his lolling tongue, his eyes drooping, looking at nothing. But this terrifying beast was coming slowly, straight toward me.

I could do nothing, not even move to step out of his direct path nor stoop to pick up a stone to throw at him. I could not call for help; I was totally paralyzed. I always awakened just before he reached me. I do not remember that I had ever seen a mad dog, but I had heard stories about them since earliest childhood.

The fear of an old tramp was bad, too, but I did not dream about them. Tramps really came, and I saw them, more commonly along main traveled highways and railroads. A tramp liked to hop a freight train, not knowing or caring where he was going. So we were always told.

And people told tales of how tramps lived. Sometimes the tramp would get caught bumming a ride, asleep in the corner of an empty freight car. Usually the train man just let him sleep on. When he got hungry and the car stopped he would get off, most likely in the country where he could go to a farmhouse and ask for a handout. Sometimes this hobo would get some good food. If it was something he did not care for, he would throw it away along the roadside and go on to the next house hoping for something more tasty. If the farmer's wife saw him coming and did not want to feed him or was afraid of him, she would lock her doors and hide. After a time he would go on down the road to another house.

There was a code among tramps, so the stories went. If a tramp got good food at a house, he made a sign on a fence post, so for the next tramp who came, or if he returned, the sign told him the food was good or the food was bad or he could not get any there.

The one I recall in my own experience was later when I was married. When we were living on our forty-acre farm near Johnson schoolhouse, two and one half miles northeast of Bakers Corner, a tramp came to our door. Our daughter Mary Lee and I were there alone, she was only around nine or ten years old. As they always do, the tramp asked for food. I gave him a good-sized bowl of plum pudding with milk over it. He sat on the back steps and ate it, gave the bowl back to me, thanked me, and went on his way.

It was said of my grandmother Hodson that she never turned anyone away from her door hungry. There were many more tramps and gypsies in her day than in mine. I am pretty sure she never turned any of those people away without asking them about their soul and pointing them to God.

But I had another tramp experience myself. I remember only one time I refused to go to the door when a tramp knocked. We were living in a log house around two and one-half miles east of Bakers Corner in 1945. Son Eugene and his wife Mary were living on our forty acres. Lee had been gone that afternoon, chore time had come. I had sent the girls, Mary Lee, sixteen, and Margaret Ann, five, to the barn to get hay down to feed the cows.

They were romping, having a good time jumping and playing in the hay, hollering and squealing. Our white Spitz dog, Peggy, whom I had never known to be afraid of anything, began to bark. She was so afraid she had crawled under the house. I could not understand why she had hid herself there.

I looked out the east kitchen window. There at the far corner of the garden, along the roadside, stood the ugliest piece of humanity I had ever seen, dirty, ragged, with long straggling gray hair and beard. His front teeth protruded like white hooks or tusks. I could understand then why Peggy was under the house, barking.

I locked all the doors and decided if he did not go toward the barn or the girls did not come toward the house, I would stay hidden. He came on toward the house, the dog kept barking, and the girls kept noisily playing. He tapped lightly on the kitchen door. I stayed hid, too afraid to open the door. If he did not bother the girls, I would keep my eyes on him and on the barn. He pumped and pumped water, got a drink, and pumped more water. He pumped until he filled a large old iron kettle where we watered the cows. Then he went on his way down the road west.

The first house west was empty. I watched him as he went into the back door of this empty house; then I called a neighbor who lived in the other direction. He had been watching him, too, and said he did not want him to spend the night there. He went down and sent the tramp on west.

In a few days I heard he had spent the night in the church at Bakers Corner. At that time Hester Foust, who was our church organist, came out from Sheridan often of an evening to practice on the church organ. She said that particular evening she heard some noises in the church and was sure someone besides herself was in there. She left in a hurry and never came out to practice after dark by herself again.

Although I feared mad dogs and old tramps, neither frightened me like the gypsies. To me they were the worst thing there ever was. I believe the reason for this was something that had happened in Henry County. The tale was often told by people around Bakers Corner. When I was small, a little girl, maybe a little older than I, named Kathleen Winters, disappeared. The mystery of her disappearance was never solved. It was feared that gypsies had kidnapped her. So I was always afraid the same thing would happen to me.

Gypsies traveled in groups or maybe large families. They were a nomadic people, descendants of the people of India or Egypt and were supposed to be musically talented, especially loving the violin and dancing. Some were craftsmen and made jewelry to sell as they traveled. They were horse traders, sometimes with several extra horses following along with them. If you traded with them, we were told, you were sure to be the one who got skinned. They really knew horses.

As we learned about them as children, we knew they were never too clean, had lots of children and dressed in bright colors which went well with their dark complexions and black hair. Some of their girls and young women were very pretty. The women's dresses were made very full, both blouses and skirts, as well as the sleeves. Some were great pick-pockets and could take anything loose right in front of your eyes and you would not see them take it. This was a reason for their full dresses, which were a wonderful place to hide their loot. The women always wanted to tell your fortune, for which you were to give them money. After they had told your fortune, likely your watch or billfold was gone.

Uncle Alvin Baker hauled raw milk in eight-and-ten-gallon milk cans in a truck to the Wilson Condensery at Sheridan for several years. One time he was on the Cicero-Sheridan road going toward Sheridan, stopped for traffic at the range line road, when a gypsy woman stepped up on the running board of his truck and begged to tell his fortune. He thought, "Why not, there's no harm in it." He had a ten-dollar bill in his shirt pocket. He thought he would keep his mind on it and watch it so close she could not get it but when she was gone so was the ten-dollar bill. They were too sharp at that trade for ordinary people.

Outside of the horse trading and the small amount they made from crafts, it seemed the women made the most of their money from fortune telling and stealing. Some said they were rich.

They also said that most of their food came from their begging and stealing from the farmers. They would make camp in the yard of an abandoned schoolhouse or an old deserted house or the roadside at the edge of a woods. The gypsies would go to a farm house and beg for an old hen, eggs, or milk. They did not mind visiting a chicken roost at night when you were fast asleep to satisfy their hunger for an old fat hen; neither did they mind visiting your hen house for eggs in the daytime, or your garden for vegetables when you were gone or they thought you were not looking. They gathered corn from fields along the road to keep their horses fat and slick. They would go to your pasture and milk a cow in the morning before you were awake.

They lived and traveled in covered wagons drawn by a team of horses, fine ones, but you would learn they did not trade their best. Their wagons were made differently from those of the pioneers, more like huckster wagons, a large rectangular box, some with rounded top and carried on four wheels. They had a door on each end; some had a door on each side with a window in front like a Klondike. There were many different styles, some rather fancy. In later years they began traveling in automobiles. After changing to cars, they chose fine expensive ones. The modern house trailer or mobile home would be fine for them now.

One day when I was about five or six years old, we were living on the range line road, I and John, Dortha, and Ruby Wilson and Katheryn Hasket, all neighbor children a little older than I, were playing down the road below our house, under what we called "Mary Jane's bridge." We were fishing or thought we were, with bent pins, carpet chain, and ironweeds for poles. Minnows and very small silver-sides were the only fish to be found in that shallow ditch, but it was fun to wade in the crystal-clear warm water. The bridge was high enough we could stand upright under it.

The sun was shining brightly that late afternoon when someone noticed a pack of gypsies had stopped. I do not know if anyone else was frightened, but I was "almost scared to death." John was the oldest of the group and the only boy. He was around twelve years old and was not at all afraid of the gypsies. He told me he would take me home safely. I don't remember crying. He took hold of my hand and led me past all the wagons, which were several, probably ten or twelve wagons all together, all the way to my home. There was very little traffic then on the range line road. Seldom was there an automobile. These gypsies had stopped their horses and wagons in the middle of the road.

I remember particularly passing a wagon that was not as large as the others. There seemed to be only one person in it, a very fat old man sitting in the doorway of his wagon on a low straight chair. He was dressed in bib overalls, dark blue with narrow stripes about an inch apart. I do remember his very fat round belly like Santa Claus with those striped overalls stretched over it. A large blue and white motley enameled dishpan hung on the wall behind him.

When I reached home I kept myself hidden for a while unless I was with my father or mother. Some of the gypsy women came to our house at milking time. They wanted to tell my parents' fortune, but my father and mother did not believe in anything like that. These gypsies begged for an old hen, eggs, and milk. My father gave them milk in their little bucket. I do not remember if they gave them anything else.

My first two years of high school, when I was driving the horse hitched to a closed buggy, I had an experience I thought was with gypsies. One evening after the weather had gotten rather cold, a man and a boy, supposedly his son, stopped to camp at the old abandoned Sumner schoolhouse we always passed. The next morning, Josephine Poore and I approached the spot. I knew "the gypsies" would still be there when we had to pass. We were afraid of them.

We knew the man and boy would still be there. Just before reaching the school house we speeded our horse up to a merry gait. Josephine picked up one of the old sadirons in her mittened hand and said if they started to bother us she would throw it at them. They had a campfire going and were cooking their breakfast over it and did not look up at us. Such useless worry. They were not gypsies. It was a big laugh later.

For several years, gypsies, this time real ones, camped there at the old Sumner schoolhouse a few days during the week of the Cicero Fall Festival. So they did not vanish with the disappearance of those odd wagons.

I have never seen a mad dog. I have not seen a tramp nor any gypsies for many years. I still do not want any of them to come to my door.

Smallpox Vaccinations

Gypsies and mad dogs weren't the only things to be concerned about in our village area. One year during the cold winter weather, probably in February, a smallpox scare shook our community. All the children in the school and many grownups were getting vaccinated against that deadly disease.

I believe I was still in the Little Room, probably in the fourth grade when the time came for me to be vaccinated. I walked every day to the school in Bakers Corner when the weather was suitable. Other days my father or a neighbor would take us in the morning or get us in the evening, usually in a buggy. On wintry days my father would come in the Klondike or the bobsled.

My father had made arrangements for me to go from school that day across the road and up the long outdoor iron stairway to the telephone office which was above C. B. Jones's general store. Here Doctor George Warren Teter from Boxley was to meet us and give us our vaccinations.

My father's first cousin, Fern Wilson, who was working at the telephone office as one of the regular operators, was to be vaccinated, too, as were her sisters, Ruby and Dortha, who were also in school at Bakers Corner. So that family was there with my father and me. Fern fainted, then quickly came to herself, and it was my turn.

As a smallpox vaccination is supposed to do, mine took and formed a thick, dark red scab. It seemed it would never get well because I kept getting it knocked off. It would bleed and form a new scab.

It kept a scab on it until along in the hot summertime, I was sitting beside my mother at church one Sunday morning during preaching service, in the third or fourth pew from the front in the middle section at the Bakers Corner church.

Nora Slater was sitting in the next seat behind us. The big dark red scab on my arm, looked at through the thin dress sleeve, seemed to her like a big black beetle. She was afraid it might bite or pinch me, so she reached over and picked it off my arm.

My! Did that hurt! I cried, and of course she was really surprised and so sorry she did it.

We were told that our vaccination would keep us from having smallpox for seven years, but we would need to have vaccinations in later years just to be sure.

Flu

Flu! Flu! Flu! Why don't you "flu" away and let people alone? The dreaded flu has been a menace to the human race for thousands of years. There were and are so many "Flu brothers," and I hate every one of them.

The first time I ever heard of "flu," which is a nickname for influenza, was the winter of 1918-19. Before that we called it "grippe." That winter many soldiers who were serving in World War I died from it. Also many people in our area and other communities grew very ill and died. Many times flu went into pneumonia. In 1918 many drugs that are used now for flu and its symptoms had never been heard of. Influenza spread into other countries. American soldiers died in England from it. Okley Eller, my husband Lee's cousin, did.

I found out when I married a World War I veteran that Lee was in an army camp in northern Indiana during that time. One morning when he looked at the bulletin board his name was up there to nurse those who were sick with the flu. It was hard to go in those barracks, among so many so sick and dying, knowing there was not much one could do for them except try to make them more comfortable. He dreaded so much maybe finding one who had died. He found only one corpse.

One of my close girl friends in grade school at Bakers Corner lost her mother to flu. Denzal Cross was the oldest of four daughters left behind, the youngest being an infant. Denzal's mother's funeral was in their home and my father sang for it. After that Denzal took on many women's responsibilities in their home and was respected for it.

In the day before funeral homes, funerals were held either in the church or the home. Mama always worried when my father went into a home to sing where there was flu that he might contract it, but he never did.

No matter how busy or how urgent the job he was doing, my father never turned down any family who wanted him to sing at a funeral. He would leave his planting or harvesting long enough to accommodate them. For many years he sang at most of the funerals near Bakers Corner, and during flu time he was called upon more than usual.

It was Christmas 1918 when I was twelve and our home was very solemn and quiet. Usually on Christmas Day our family went to our Hodson family Christmas dinner. As long as Grandpa lived the family Christmas Day dinner was at his home. After his death his children, my mother with her brothers and sisters, took turns having the annual dinner. It was always a joyous day when Mama's brothers and sisters gathered together for that holiday time. Gifts were not often exchanged, but oh, the fun we children had, the good food, and the music. I never will forget "Red Wing," "Turkey in the Straw," and "Yankee Doodle." My father would play his fiddle or guitar with his French harp or the mandolin, Uncle Burnie Moore plucking his jews harp, while Floyd Moore chorded on the piano or organ.

But the 1918 Christmas was different. We were at home, not at Hodson's. The reason for the solemnity in our home this Christmas Day was that my mother was seriously ill with the flu. Old Doctor Teter was coming twice a day to see her, and everyone was afraid she was not going to live through this bout. One reason for so much concern for my mother was that she was pregnant with my younger brother, Myron.

I was not allowed to go in my mother's sick room, the flu was so very contagious. One day soon after the doctor left, I was hovering close to the wood-saver stove which we were using in our living room. My father looked at me and said, "You have the flu." I did not realize I was sick, chilling, or hot with fever, but he could see it.

He brought in a narrow folding cot, set it up along the north side of the living room, placed some bedding on it, and got me into it very quickly. How sad that I was twelve years old and it was Christmas holidays and I was down sick. While I was still lying weak and ill on this cot my father peeled an apple and gave me a piece. I took one bite and did not like it. My taster was upset and the apple tasted like butter.

So at that Christmas season there were two of us down. My father had a quarter of beef hanging frozen in the smokehouse, and he would go out there, saw off a large chunk, several pounds of bone and meat, and cook it in Mama's large heavy enameled kettle on top of the wood and coal Majestic Range. We ate the meat and broth with crackers. This was easy for him to prepare and a very good dish for sick folks.

Through the years since 1918-19 I have had the flu a few times but was never as sick as I was then. My mother had it often during the winter months as long as she lived. That winter Old Doctor Teter told my father, "You watch, in a few years there will be lots of heart trouble because this flu is affecting people's hearts." That did prove true for my mother, along with lots of other later complications.

About fifteen years after that my mother died suddenly with an attack of heart asthma. I never did learn for certain if her having the flu so many times had caused this disease, but it seems likely.

One winter after I had left home, my mother, father, and both brothers had flu at the same time. Some of the neighbors or my husband Lee did their outside chores.

A Reverend Stevenson of the Church of God was staying with neighbors Charlie and Sallie Pierce. He was a very good help in time of sickness. He went and stayed with them and helped them through that time.

In times of widespread sickness neighbor helped neighbor with farm chores, bringing groceries from town or anything they could do, especially when they did not have to go into the sick room. They did that too, though, when it was necessary. Likely soon they might be the one needing help.

As I remember there were more deaths caused by flu and complications that winter, 1918-19 than any winter since. Very few people escaped.

Those who escaped it that winter likely never had it again in their lifetime, at least that kind of flu!

My Mother

I should pause to consider and write about my mother, Minnie Hodson Wilson, a sincere, devout Christian, a generous, unselfish and conscientious person.

She never missed church unless it was really necessary. and it was one of the centers of her life.

My mother was even tempered, and I do not remember ever seeing her angry. I had seen her hurt, disgusted, and worried but never heard her say a hateful word to anyone. She was a charming woman with many friends.

Mama loved to have neighbors and family over on Saturday night, often to make and enjoy ice cream. Charlie and Sallie Pierce and their daughter Violet probably came more often than anyone else.

One Saturday evening in June when the strawberries were ripe and plentiful, my mother used fresh strawberries in her ice cream. It was quite a delicacy.

One amusing incident happened the night of the strawberry ice cream. There was an elderly widow, a cousin of my grandpa Wilson, who lived a quarter of a mile from us on the range line road.

Mary Jane Trueblood was deaf and used a hearing trumpet, and she was afraid to stay at home alone at night. She stayed with my parents some at night, so she was there that evening as well as some other company.

She used glasses for reading; she probably couldn't see well either. She said to my mother, "Minnie, I guess I can't eat my ice cream. It has red ants in it."

My mother told Mary Jane it was all right, it only had strawberries along with the cream.

Mary Jane

Mary Jane! As far back as I can remember, this old deaf neighbor lady who lived on the range line road was in our life, and when I think of Mama I think sometimes of her.

Mary Jane was born in North Carolina, the only child of my great-grandfather Wilson's sister. In 1851, when several of the Wilson family came to Indiana in a covered wagon caravan train, moving their families from North Carolina to Henry County, Indiana, Mary Jane was a small girl. Her father had died some time before. Uncle Eli Stanley, the wagon master, was himself a widower with three small children. He and Mary Jane's mother, Aunt Hamie, agreed that if she took care of Uncle Eli's children on the trip, she and Mary Jane could come to Indiana free of charge. The Wilsons later came to Hamilton County in 1865.

And so she was our relative, and when she grew older and was alone, my parents helped care for her. Mary Jane's house on the range line road was a small, rustic unpainted house with wide poplar weather boarding running straight up and down its sides. A low rambling porch ran across its front, with only one small step up to its floor. Under the porch roof, the wall of the house was whitewashed, giving it a cheerful, inviting look.

A narrow footpath led straight from the low front porch down the slope, through the narrow gate and down two stone steps to the roadside. Along each side of the dirt path grew a wide row of early dark blue iris. Intermingled among the iris were blooming, old-fashioned wild red columbine. Along the front fence grew several bushes of rosecolored, sweet-scented peonies and red velvet old fashioned roses.

With an apple orchard behind the house and tall persimmon trees beside it, altogether this homestead made a beautiful old-time scene.

When I was a child, my cousin Ruby and I visited Mary Jane quite often. I picked bouquets of white violets, which grew and bloomed in the tall grass under the apple trees in the shady orchard.

After Mary Jane's husband Isaac died, Mary Jane was afraid to stay at home alone at night. Uncle Clark and Aunt Jane Wilson, who lived nearby, gave her a room at their house to sleep in. It was a very small room with a small, white iron bed with feather tick piled high on it and one of Aunt Jane's pretty quilts as a spread. There was a door on the east side of the room that opened onto the long front porch and another door on the south side of the room that opened into the backyard near the windmill pump and toward the barn, shoe-shop and cave. Everyone went through this tiny room to go from the dining room to the outside. It was called the tank room or Mary Jane's room.

Each evening, just at dusk, you could see Mary Jane trudging her way up the range line road about a quarter of a mile to Uncle Clark's to spend the night. The next day at daylight she slowly walked home.

In late summer 1919 Uncle Clark moved his family to Cicero and Mary Jane had no place to go to spend her nights. My mother finally gave in and let her come to spend the nights on a sanitary cot in our dining room. She wanted to bring her own bedding, but my mother said "no." Mary Jane had bedbugs, and Mama did not want them brought to our house. She did allow her to bring one feather pillow without a slip on it. When not being used it stayed out on the iron railing cellar banister on our back porch. My mother examined it often.

My mother was probably the closest friend Mary Jane had and she cared for her, as she did for everyone.

Mama was a devoted Christian. We always had a family altar at our house. Every night before we went to bed, either my father or mother read a chapter from the Bible, then we all knelt and prayed. My brothers started out with a little prayer, "Jesus make me a good boy." As far back as I can remember, I said, "Now I lay me down to sleep, I pray thee Lord my soul to keep, if I should die before I wake, I ask thee Lord my soul to take, for Jesus sake, Amen." As the boys grew older they learned it, too. I remember often my mother closed her prayer with "and home us all in heaven, for Christ's sake, Amen." She seldom prayed in public except at prayer meeting. There too she always had a testimony of praise.

The Bakers Corner Wesleyan Methodist Church was only about three fourths of a mile from where she grew up, and she devotedly attended it all her life. Her own mother, Mary Elizabeth Bates Hodson, had been a wonderful Christian woman who took the family regularly to church services, although her husband, my grandpa John Hodson did not attend when the children were small. He started regularly around 1900.

After my father and mother were married, they attended the Bakers Corner Wesleyan Methodist Church except for about two or three years when they attended West Grove Friends Church. During that time my younger brother Myron was born on June 11, 1919. This gave him a birthright in the Friends Church.

She taught a Sunday School class of small children most of her life, as her mother had done before her and as I did after she was gone. Mama had a strong belief that children should obey their parents. She kept a peach sprout on top of the kitchen cabinet, which she used when it was needed. Another form of punishment she used was to set us on a chair until she told us we could get down. We could not get down until we promised her we would behave. If we did not, we were put back on the chair.

She had great faith in prayer. I remember well one night at a revival meeting at Bakers Corner church when Erdie Spear came, a neighbor of ours who was probably in his sixties. He did not attend church often, and when he did he went to West Grove Friends

Church. It was very unusual for him to come to Bakers Corner to a revival. When he came in the church door my mother felt led to pray for him right then, that he might be saved and give his heart to Christ that night. When the altar call was made he went to the altar, prayed through, and lived as a Christian the rest of his life. He threw his pipe and tobacco away.

Mama was born on June 30, 1883, and raised about three-quarters of a mile south of Bakers Corner on Grandpa's wonderful farm, where we all later lived. Once a week during the summer when she was not in school and after she was old enough, it was her task to deliver the cream from the farm to Hortonville to sell. The milk was kept in the cellar until the cream raised on it, then it was skimmed to be used for cottage cheese, with the surplus fed to the chickens or hogs.

They used enough of the cream to churn all the butter they needed. All extra was put into cans and kept in the cool cellar until the day came for Mama to deliver it. She drove one horse to a buggy or a one-seated hack without a top the three or four miles to Hortonville. She made this trip each week alone as quite a young girl.

Mama was the youngest of seven children. I believe my mother was very close to both of her parents. She called them Ma and Pa, the custom at that time. Maybe her parents had more time for her since she was the youngest. She may have been spoiled, although I cannot think so. When she and her brother, Ernest, who was next to her, were both at home, they had a billy goat, just as I did later.

I believe she must have been something of a tomboy. Her main playmates were her brother Ernest, two years older than she, and a first cousin Marvin Foulke, who lived just a short distance north of her and was also older. Naturally she played the games the boys liked to play. Although she played mostly with boys, she had her dolls she loved. She had a small china doll that I now treasure, along with a small black cast-iron toy iron. She was close to all her brothers and sisters, visiting them quite often and talking often to them on the telephone, especially the sisters, since none of her brothers or sisters was a long-distance call.

She attended all eight grades of school at Bakers Corner, near her home; then she went two years to high school at Boxley, riding the five or six miles in the buggy with her brother Ernest, who graduated the spring she ended her second year. His graduation may be the reason she did not attend any longer because she would have to drive alone. Girls were not particularly encouraged to graduate at that time anyway.

I do not remember her ever telling how or when she met my father. I doubt if she would remember, because they both lived in the same community when they were small. He moved away but was back with his grandmother Wilson quite a bit now and then. He attended Boxley High School from there and was in the same grade with Mama.

I remember a lady telling me several years ago that when they were going together, my father and mother were the most beautiful, handsome couple she had ever seen. She said my mother always wore a ribbon in her hair.

Minnie Hodson married my father, Archie Wilson, on February 22, 1905, in a beautiful wedding with several guests in her father's farm home, where we later lived. Home weddings were the style then. T. P. Baker officiated.

My mother was a pretty woman, about five feet six inches tall and 130 to 135 pounds in her later days, though in her younger days she was quite thin. Her eyes were dark brown, her hair very fine, like soft silk threads dark brown, long and straight. She parted it in the middle, combed it back on each side, and usually pulled it up into a knot on top of her head. Sometimes she made the knot on the back of her head into a figure eight. The sides above her ears were combed up not too tight, and she wore side combs, one on each side. When she died at fifty years of age she had scarcely a gray hair on her head. As I remember she had all her teeth, at least almost all of them, when she died. Her feet were very narrow; she wore a size 6aa shoe. Her hands were small with long slender fingers.

When she was growing up she did not seem very rugged but was frail, fine featured, and delicate with a beautiful cameo face. She had told me about riding a bicycle and falling off it, breaking her arm. She took a tonic that helped to keep her going, overcoming the frailty after she was married.

The winter of 1918 and 1919, the bad influenza winter, my mother was expecting my brother Myron, who would be born in June. Over Christmas my mother was so very ill with flu that the doctor came every day, sometimes twice. It seemed to me she was never strong after that. It took so much rest and sleep to keep her going, and she slept quite often in the daytime. Because her resistance was low, it seemed she took colds and flu easily.

Still, she laughed lots, especially when she was with old friends. I remember sometimes her cousin, Laura Baker Coffin from Indianapolis, would come and stay overnight. I loved to listen to them talk and laugh, staying up very late and reminiscing and having such a good time.

She also loved to read, but when she was young she felt condemned for reading novels, so she never read them when I knew her.

Mama was no hand to joke, but she could take a joke. Sometimes Grandpa Wilson would cause her to blush with some of his jokes. He liked to make her blush. During the time we lived with Grandpa Hodson, her father could tease her, too. He had really encouraged her to take the old nag Dolly into town, and he probably was intending that pressure partly as a joke. She certainly didn't think it was funny when Dolly fell down in the road and someone had to help hitch her up again, so she was late and returned home after dark.

Mama was a good seamstress and made most of our clothes until I was old enough; then she gladly turned the sewing over to me. She liked to do fancy work, to crochet and embroider, but she did not knit. Most of the time there was some patching to be done or something to make over or make larger or longer for three growing children. Along with all her other work there was not much time left for fancy work.

My mother liked pretty, neat clothes but not too fancy. She always dressed decently and becomingly, usually in homemade clothes. The dress she had on when she died is the only ready-made dress I can remember her ever having, a pretty black silk with tiny tucks and embroidery trim. Doctor Havens slit the front of it open in his haste to put a hypodermic into her heart when she died of heart asthma in his office in Cicero. I still have that dress. She died on March 19, 1934.

Mama did not wear any jewelry. She thought it made one look proud, but she did not object to me wearing a little, though she did not want me to overdo it and look gaudy. She might have worn a wristwatch if she had one, but not many people owned a watch, although my parents bought me one for graduation from high school. It was quite a gift then, and they had sent to Sears Roebuck or Montgomery Ward for it. It cost just under fourteen dollars and was white gold with a black ribbon wristband. That watch ran for thirty-seven years, and I expect Mama would have considered it useful.

Mama was a good cook and enjoyed having company. When she was in her prime our revival meetings usually lasted two weeks, over three Sundays. She always expected to have the evangelist and the pastor and family come home with them for dinner one of these revival Sundays.

She was a good neighbor, helping whenever she could in sickness or other needs. I remember when a neighbor lady was very ill and passed away. Mama was there at the time. When she realized it would not be long, she telephoned for me to come. I was a young teenager, and I believe she thought the experience would be good for me. I had never been so near death before.

One warm summer afternoon when I was sixteen years old, I walked to visit some friends who lived near a mile from us, the Demarees. The mother was having trouble making the younger daughter, Florence, a dress. To me it looked so easy, I finished it for her that afternoon. Mrs. Demaree was so appreciative she gave me fifty cents. I took it home and showed my mother. She told me I should not have taken it, that I should do that much for a neighbor without pay. She had me take the fifty cents back and give it to Mrs. Demaree.

She was a hard worker, willing to plant and hoe in the garden some, although my father did much of the garden work with us children helping. The fruits and vegetables from our farm were canned, great quantities of them. Then fruit was plentiful; most people had plenty of their own. We had apples ripe in July, and began our season with the yellow transparents, good for pies and sauces.

She made gallons of apple butter, usually cooking the cider apple butter out of doors in the front barn lot in a large copper kettle. This kettle, which belonged to Mama and her brothers and sisters, probably held twenty-five gallons or more. It had been Grandpa Hodson's and was very black with smoke and soot on the outside from so many years of use, but the inside was bright copper. It was so large it had to be stored in the barn or a shed.

Usually next-door neighbor Sallie Pierce and Mama made the cider apple butter together at our house. The apples were picked up and the cider made the day before. Early next morning a fire was built under the large copper kettle; it was filled with gallons of fresh cider. The fire was kept going with cornstalks and sticks that the boys picked up. Every one helped that day. While the cider was boiling down to one third its original amount, every one peeled or cored apples. Sometimes we used an apple peeler. When we did, someone ran the peeler while others quartered and cored them. The apples were fun to work with, so pretty, red-striped, big, and perfect. We peeled and cored them by the bucketsful, even using a clean washtub and large dishpans to put them in. Then they went into the pot.

Sometimes she dried corn and apples from the garden and truck patch, and there were always tomatoes and corn to can. It took many quarts of canned green beans to keep her family. We picked these mostly from the cornfield. In the spring when the corn began to show its tiny green tips over the fields, it was time to plant the cornfield beans. We planted mostly Kentucky wonders, Missouri wonders, and cut-shorts for green beans and vining soup beans for dry beans. We used jobbers to plant them with; one was automatic, but with the other we had to drop the beans in each hill. This was much faster than using a hoe.

After using and canning all the beans she wanted green, the rest were left to dry, to be picked in the fall and shelled for cooking in the winter. The tough-hulled ones could be put in a gunny sack and be beaten or tramped out of their shell, but the ones raised for green beans and let dry had to be shelled by hand, a nice winter evening's job.

Each year she canned fifty quarts of cucumber pickles besides mustard pickles and some other kinds, which she put away in earthen jars. She also stuffed mangoes with a cabbage filling using vinegar. Then there were two or three large earthen jars of sauerkraut to be made and also a jar of green tomato pickles.

I remember well for several years my parents had a large strawberry patch. After using all they wanted fresh and to do up, they sold them for fifty cents a gallon. We did not have wooden or plastic boxes to pick in then but used pans and kettles. Mama measured them in a half gallon tin, piling them so high the buyers got almost two for the price of one. Sometimes people picked "on the shares." While the berries were thick the picker got one quart out of every four he picked. Later in the season when the berries were fewer, she gave them more. Mama made strawberry shortcake for dinner and supper every day during the three weeks of strawberry season. We did not need much else but ate at those shortcake meals a lot of wilted lettuce, radishes, and green onions, which were always ready to use at strawberry-picking time.

If there was a surplus of any fruits or vegetables, she usually found someone to use them. She did not want anything wasted.

Mama made and used homemade soap almost all of the time for laundry and dishes. She bought toilet soap for use in the bath and the kitchen sink. I've told earlier how she made the soap from lye and fat, a soft soap which I liked for laundry but not dishes.

Mama had a skin disease on her hands called tetter, which was a form of eczema. Her fingers got very sore, and they would crack and bleed. She had a medicine that helped them, but there was no cure. She wore rubber gloves some. I feel sure the homemade lye soap was more harmful to them than some other soap would have been.

In September 1933 she took very ill and grew unconscious at a reception for our new pastor at the parsonage at Boxley. My father stayed with her overnight there, and the doctor diagnosed her ailment as encephalitis, sleeping sickness. She did not know anything and was not in her right mind for about nine days. From then on until she died, the nineteenth of the next March 1934, she was never quite the same and had a strange look in her eyes. I would catch her staring at herself in the mirror. I believe she saw herself looking this odd way, but we never said anything to her about it. She expressed saying to my father a few times that she was afraid she would lose her mind. God took her before that happened.

Mama led such a good Christian life that my father's aunt, Aunt Jane Wilson, when she herself knew she could not live long with cancer, said, "It is easier now for me to go since Minnie is over there." I remember when Mama died her sisters said, "Minnie is the best one of all of us. Why did she have to go first and so young?" She was fifty years of age.

Known as the Alvin Foulke farm, this farm was purchased by Archie Wilson in 1918, and the family lived there until shortly after Minnie Wilson's death in 1934. Archie remarried in 1935 and moved to Noblesville, and later in 1944 moved to Arcadia, California, where he died in 1964. (Evelyn Wilson)

Bakers Corner Domestic Science class 1919-1920. L to R: Mary Elizabeth Wilson, Denzel Cross, Lela Cherry, Josephine Poore, and Alice Fremire. Mary Elizabeth was in the seventh grade.

Upon C.B. Jones's death in 1921, David Clyde (D.C.) Sowers (left) and Wayvern "Casey" Jones purchased the operation. They ran the store as partners until about 1928 when Casey purchased D.C.'s share. (Evelyn Wilson)

Casey Jones shown here in the Bakers Corner store, a community landmark from 1893 until 1978, when Casey retired. The store was razed in 1992.

The New Binder

Archie Wilson shown here with his team. (Evelyn Wilson)

The Gideon Male Quartet August 30, 1920. L to R: John Macy, Ray Morford, Archie Wilson, Frank Griffin and Freida Macy Reves, accompanist.

Mary Elizabeth and brother Myron Wilson on the farm, about 1924. (Evelyn Wilson)

John William Wilson and friends, about 1924. (Evelyn Wilson)

Mary Elizabeth Wilson, Cicero High School graduate, 1925.

Charlie and Sallie Pierce, long-time friends and neighbors of the Archie Wilson family.

John Hodson family about 1892. Front L to R: Ernest, John (father), Minnie, Mary Elizabeth (mother). Back L to R: Anna, Mima, Harley, and Myrtie.

Archie and Minnie Hodson Wilson wedding photograph February 22, 1905.

Minnie Hodson Wilson (1883-1934) as a young girl.

Myron, Mary Elizabeth, and John William Wilson about 1923. (Evelyn Wilson)

Lee Stewart in his WWI uniform, about 1918.

Cicero High School, built in 1910 and expanded in 1924 to include more classroom space and a combination gym and auditorium. (Hamilton County Museum)

In 1913 Robert Warren Pickett began producing and selling sorghum. His family continued the operation until the factory burned on July 24, 2009.

Pickett's sorghum, the best in the country! (Ronnie and Janice Pickett)

180

Part Four

Young Married Life
and Beyond

Do you remember, O cousin mine. . .

Eleven Egg White Wedding Angel Food Cake

Whites of 11 eggs
1 ½ cups granulated sugar
2 tablespoons cornstarch
One cup less 2 tablespoonsful of flour
½ teaspoonful cream of tartar
1 ½ teaspoonsful almond extract or vanilla
1 level teaspoonful baking powder

Measure cornstarch into cup and finish filling with flour. Mix with baking powder and sift 7 times. Add to this the sugar which has been sifted several times. Next beat the white of eggs for a short time, being certain no speck of yolk gets in. Next add the flavoring extract and cream of tartar and finish beating until eggs are stiff. Lightly fold the flour mixture into the beaten egg whites. Bake in ungreased pan in slow oven 1 ¼ hours or better until the cake begins to shrink from the edges of the pan. Turn pan upside down and wait until almost cold before removing from the pan.

From Bakers Corner Liberty Wesleyan Methodist Church Cookbook c. 1920.

Johnny's Sorghum Cookies

1 cup sorghum molasses
1 egg
1 heaping teaspoonful ginger
1 cup lard
1 rounding teaspoonful soda
Dissolve soda in water, add enough flour to make a soft dough.
Roll this, sprinkle with granulated sugar, cut out and bake in quick oven.

Mrs. T. C. Wilson, [Aunt Jane mentioned earlier]
From Bakers Corner Liberty Wesleyan Methodist Church Cookbook. 1914.`

Getting Married and Going to Housekeeping

Let's move forward again. Lee and I were married on the evening of June 17, 1925. As I've said, we began seeing each other when I was a junior in high school and he was twenty-six. My parents had come to accept that Lee and I loved each other and should be married

On the day of the wedding, my father took Lee and me to Noblesville to get our marriage license. It rained all the way there and all the way back home. Luckily, the side curtains on my father's old Model T were in good repair.

The ceremony was in my parents' home, just as my mother's wedding had been in her parents' home twenty years before. I wanted my wedding to be as much like my mother's as I could have it. We both were married on a Wednesday evening in June without attendants. Lee and I came down the stairs together, just as my parents had at Grandpa Hodson's home in 1905. I had made my dress myself out of orchid colored crepe-de-chine with much white silk lace. My father ordered two-layer brick ice cream, one layer white and the other lavender, to match my dress, from the Pulliam ice cream factory at Sheridan. My friend Josephine Poore and her mother Katie made angel food cakes to go with the ice cream for our seventy-five guests. Plain angel food cakes, eleven egg whites each, without icing always in those days, and a really delicious wedding treat.

Reverend Walter Morris, our pastor, performed the wedding ceremony. It was the longest one I have ever heard. Everyone said that as long as it was the marriage should last! It did.

Our honeymoon didn't happen. We had to go to housekeeping right away.

The next day after we were married, Lee and my father picked several milk buckets full of the luscious, big, juicy, dark red cherries from the tops of the old cherry trees behind the hen house.

In the afternoon Lee and I took my mother and went shopping for some new furniture. We went to old George Shoemaker's furniture store at Cicero. There my mother bought an oak buffet for us as a wedding gift from my family.

A few evenings after our wedding, Josephine Poore had a miscellaneous shower for us at their house. She invited our two Sunday school classes, the young married people's class and the one for the young people. At the close of the shower the group and some others had a chivari on us. There was lots of fun for everyone and several nice gifts for us.

The realities of farm life soon took hold. We needed money; I needed to get busy making some. It wasn't hard. I'd always known how to work. When I was growing up, for a few summers I had raised baby chickens. Late in the summer Mama would let me set a few old Rhode Island red hens, the kind that made very good mothers. I set each one of them on fifteen eggs. I had to tend them, give them feed and water each day, and keep watch that they were on their nests most of the time.

We set them at a time that after they hatched in three weeks it would be roasting ear-stage, for the field corn. I started these little chicks on soft corn. Twice each day I went to the corn field where I had put the chicken coops with a mother hen in each coop. Usually there were two coops. Each mother hen could take care of about twenty-five little chickens.

For the first few days the mothers were kept in the coops with a small opening where the little ones could run in and out and the mother could stick her head out. Close enough for her to reach, I placed a shallow pan of water, which had to be kept filled at all times for the mother and her chicks.

Morning and evening I would take a sharp knife and break off a few ears of the new corn. Then with the sharp knife I would slice off the soft grains and feed to the little biddies. The mother hens were fed old dried shelled corn. When the new corn developed and became too hard to cut from the ear, the little ones were fed cracked corn, which they liked and thrived on.

After two or three weeks the mothers could be turned out of the coops and let run with their chicks. The little ones would stay close to their mothers, wandering around through the tall green corn catching and eating bugs and worms. On their rich diet of insects and corn they grew very fast. The mother hen knew her way back to the coop when evening came or a storm came up. If she could not beat a storm, she hovered with the little ones under her wings. It was not many weeks until they were ready to sell as friers.

So I raised chickens from childhood on, and I could do it now as a newly married woman. Later, when hard times hit, we raised Rhode Island reds so they could not be seen, and perhaps stolen, from the road.

I also had made a little money helping my Aunt Mima and Aunt Myrtie (my mother's sisters) do some spring housecleaning after school was out, and I could take in washing when the time came.

Money was not plentiful then as now. I was taught to be very saving with any little bit I earned, giving one tenth to the church, spending a little for something I really wanted, and carefully putting the rest away to be kept for something very, very important some day.

And by the time I was married I had saved a few dollars. I felt that a few pieces of new furniture were important. My parents had bought the buffet. Lee put enough money with what I had to buy six leather-bottom oak dining chairs and a round pedestal oak table to go with the buffet. It had enough leaves to extend it to make a twelve-foot table.

That big day we also bought an oak dresser to go with an oak bed that Lee had. This new furniture we did not have to move because the furniture store man, Mr. Shoemaker, delivered it to the house where we were going to housekeeping.

The next morning after buying the new furniture, Lee backed up his little Ford roadster truck at my parents' home for me to bring out my personal things. I did not have much furniture, but there were a few pieces. During the winter my father and Lee had been to a public auction. There my father bought for me an old cupboard that had the bottom cut off and the two little drawers turned to the top. It made a nice piece of furniture with glass doors to show my pretty dishes.

When my father bought this cupboard, inside it there was a beautiful, small glass basket vase. It was the right size for a bouquet of violets or lily-of-the-valley in season. Lee had found it and put it in one of the large pockets of the overcoat he was wearing. Before they had the cupboard loaded, after the sale, the lady who had the sale went around checking into everything to see if she had missed anything. Lee did not tell her about the vase. He said it belonged to my father because it was in the cupboard when it was sold. When he came calling that evening he gave it to me.

Besides the cupboard I had my little rocking chair that had been given to me on my first Christmas by my grandpa and grandma Hodson, the davenport from that much-loved playhouse from my childhood, and my dollies, clothes, dishes, quilts and hope chest.

When we moved my things away from my parents' home, my mother said that a certain oil painting that I'd done was the only thing among my possessions that she hated to see go. It was the one we copied in high school art, from the only painting class the high school had ever given. My mother did not live many years after that, and I have always wished that I had left it for her to enjoy as long as she lived.

Moving and Moving Some More

We stayed in that first house, Molly Owens's little farm on the Cicero-Sheridan Road, for a year and a half and went into several other houses after that.

Our first child was born there: Lloyd Eugene, on May 13, 1926. During this time, Lee had a very sick spell. His appendix ruptured, and we almost lost him. Sadly, he never really had a well day after that.

We had rented the Owens's farm and were also farming Uncle Clark Wilson's fields across the road. Lee had taken sick and was hospitalized at this very time and did not yet have his corn planted.

My father, Lee's father, some of Lee's brothers, and some of our neighbors came in with their farming equipment and planted our corn for us. There were several men there for dinner. My mother, Lee's mother, and his sister Ruth came to cook dinner for the men.

Ruth's son Robert was still a toddler. Someone had wrapped Eugene in a blanket and laid him on a cot across the room from me.

I had just turned my head when I heard a thump.

Ruth and both mothers came running. Little Robert had pulled Eugene off the cot onto the floor! Of course he cried but was not hurt at all.

In 1929 we bought and moved to a forty-acre farm in Jackson Township, a little over two and one-half miles northeast of Bakers Corner, the first house north of the old Johnson schoolhouse, the old school which my grandpa Wilson had attended. The old building was beyond ever having school there again.

Here is how we were able to have that house. It was the winter of 1928–29 when that Cecil McCarty farm of forty acres was put up at auction. My father heard about it and told us. My parents wanted us to get something of our own near them. This was only about one and one-half miles from them. Since Lee's health was poor, the men could work together.

The day of the auction, our little Eugene and I stayed with my mother while the men went to the sale. When they returned they brought the news that Lee had bid it off at fifty-three dollars an acre, an unbelievable price nowadays. The farm was surveyed and measured and it over-run some. The total price was, the best I remember, $2,383. One cannot imagine a price like that now. It was enough then. The ground and buildings were both run down, but it gave us a place to call our own, although it took a long time with prices as they were then to get it paid for.

This farm home was not a very pretty scene when we went to move in. The house needed a new roof, and its yellow paint was mostly washed away. The trees that had been set out by a previous owner were still very small. I don't know the history of the old leaning shack of a barn nor the old log house where Lee used his feed grinder and stored oats. I remember one time Claude Goff, president of the American State Bank at Sheridan, told us that he was born in the old log house. I don't know where it stood at that time. It had been at one time an old store building and had been moved there from Boxley. Its doors and windows did not fit tight. Its two back rooms, kitchen and bedroom, were merely sealed with wide boards that let in much, much cold air. The ceilings in these two rooms were ten feet high and sealed with three-inch boards with no insulation above them.

The soil was poor and run down, the house decrepit, but we were young and relatively energetic. This "almost a shack house" made a home for us. We knew it would take lots of time, energy, and money to build up the farm, but we looked forward to it and eventually we made a nice place out of it.

We built up the soil with clover, re-roofed, repaired, and remodeled and painted that house and built a new barn. Our second child, Mary Lee (named for both of us), was born on November 2, 1929, on our forty-acre farm. Although we moved around quite a bit, our youngest child, Margaret Ann, was also born on our forty-acre farm on May 16, 1940.

The thirties were lean years, but we were happy. One fall during this time, Lee's brother Ross was out of work. We were poor as Job's turkeys but lived on a farm, so could grow our own food. Lee needed help with corn husking, so Ross and his wife Mildred brought their boys and came to stay at our house a few days. We had planted rows and rows of cornfield beans and vining soup beans, too. Mildred and I, along with some of our neighbors, spent a lot of time picking them. We put the soup beans in gunnysacks and beat or trampled them out of their pods. The others had to be shelled by hand. There were plenty of beans to last all of us through the winter.

During this time, while living on our forty-acre farm, we worked closely with our neighbors to get in the crops. Making hay and cutting wheat and oats required several men to do the job. Loose hay was put into the haymow; wheat and oats were cut with a binder and the sheaves tied with binder twine and stacked in shocks by hand to be threshed later with a threshing machine.

Neighbors helped neighbors, trading work back and forth. Usually some of their wives went along to help with the cooking, a neighborly thing to do. Everyone knew each other and worked together.

Bakers Corner Wesleyan Methodist Church: Part of Life

Lee and I continued to attend the Bakers Corner Wesleyan Methodist Church (which became Bakers Corner Wesleyan Church in 1968) after our marriage and throughout our lives. I belonged to the women's mission group, taught Sunday school, and served as church board secretary. The church came together on projects and activities through the year.

The Bakers Corner Church was known as Liberty in the conference and was founded February 21, 1870. Shortly afterward it went on a circuit with various churches. When the brick church was built in 1916-17 as Grandpa Hodson was in his last months, we were still on the Boxley circuit which was comprised of four area Wesleyan churches that shared a pastor. These were: Liberty, Boxley, Deming, and Roberts Chapel, a colored congregation northeast of Bakers Corner. I think it's interesting that Roberts Settlement was one of a small number of historically free negro communities established in the early nineteenth century, and they were an active and accepted part of our community. The settlement was well situated since most of the white settlers in the area in the 1830s–1850s were Quaker and later Wesleyan abolitionists. In 1843 the Wesleyan Methodist Church had separated from the Methodists to form their own denomination as they felt the larger church was not standing strongly enough against slavery. And that's the affiliation we had at Bakers Corner, including a colored church. We would attend services at various of these churches Sunday nights. The Roberts Chapel church was lit by gas lamps.

The four churches on the Boxley Circuit each hosted one quarterly meeting at their home church, which all four congregations attended. These events included an evangelist, a business meeting, a Sunday morning love feast (testimony meeting) and communion, and usually a Sunday fellowship dinner. All four congregations closely worked and worshipped together regardless of race. In 1931 the circuit dissolved. Liberty church hired a full time pastor. Boxley had gone under. Roberts Chapel left the denomination and relied on supply pastors. And Deming I don't know about.

I remember in the spring of 1938 our church hosted a three-day ministerial convention for pastors of the Indiana Conference of our Wesleyan Methodist Church.

The women of the Bakers Corner Church gathered several of their kerosene oil stoves and work tables, pots and pans, dishes and cutlery, and made a kitchen in the long east Sunday school room downstairs in the church. I believe Aunt Pearl Pickett was in charge of the cooking and the people of the church donated the food, which was raised on our farms and in our gardens. Many of us had our own chickens, eggs, and milk and also meat, both beef and canned and cured pork. Much of the baking was done at our homes and brought to the church the day it was needed.

Each fall Marion College, our church school in Marion, Indiana, had what was called "Harvest Day." For a few years Charles Pickett, a poultry dealer who attended our church, furnished barbequed chicken for all the students and guests on campus. He took his equipment and enough dressed fryer chickens to feed everyone. Some of the ladies from Bakers Corner helped him with the barbeque. All guests were to bring in covered dishes of food. That was the day home-canned food was delivered. It was a great and wonderful day for everyone.

In addition to teaching the children's class at Sunday school, I also served as superintendent of the Y.M.W.B., Young Missionary Workers Band, and was in charge of the Children's Day program. At that time we had no speaker system, and some of the children's voices were not very strong and could not be understood. During practice, we urged them again and again to "speak louder, speak louder."

On the night of the program, my youngest brother Myron rose up to give his recitation. He had a good, strong voice and had memorized a rather lengthy recitation. He gave his reading, every word of it, very, very *loudly*. If he had wanted to embarrass me, he certainly did. But, it did show that the children could speak loud enough to be understood if they would try.

The Coldest Weather Ever

During much of this time I've been describing, we were living on our forty-acre farm. Although we had worked hard on that house, by January of 1936, we still had much to do.

The weather that year was really frigid, and that house was particularly cold. We had a good wood and coal range in the kitchen, but in zero weather it did little toward heating the room. In the living room we burned an old-fashioned wood saver in the spring and fall but burned coal in a Florence hot blast, which was a good heating stove, during the cold months.

The winter of 1935 and 1936 we had two children in school. Eugene was in the fourth grade and Mary Lee was a first grader. It was at that time that we had an experience we never forgot with the coldest weather we'd ever encountered. It all started with a quilting bee.

I had made a beautiful wedding ring quilt top joined with apricot-colored broadcloth. I'd quilted it on my grandma Hodson's quilting frames, the frames on which all of my mother's quilts and those of her sisters had been quilted. I used a pretty shade of light blue broadcloth for the lining and had sent to the Sears Roebuck mail order catalog for the broadcloth. The quilt was filled with cotton batting.

I had planned to have a group of friends and neighborhood ladies to come for an old-fashioned all day quilting bee on January 22, 1936.

That morning the weather was cold, very cold, but we decided it was not too bad to have the quilting bee. The school bus came, and the children went to school as usual. A few of the ladies decided to brave the cold and did travel to our house. We began to quilt together.

I had cooked an old hen, planning to make dumplings for our dinner, which I did although the kitchen was so cold I could hardly stay in it. A few minutes before twelve o'clock I noticed my husband putting on his blanket-lined denim waist, buttoning it up to his chin. I said, "What are you going to do?" He said, "I'm going after those kids." Just at that time the school bus drove in with them. We were really happy for them to be home.

The weather was getting continually worse. I was busy and had not realized how really awful the weather had turned; it was much colder and much more snow had fallen. It had turned into a real blizzard.

We hurried and ate our noon meal. As soon as we were through eating, Lee said he was going to take the ladies home. He was afraid it would not be long before the roads would be impassable.

Alice Ehman, who lived in the first house north, said, "He won't need to take me, I can make it on foot." It was almost one-fourth of a mile. We watched her to be sure she made it home.

Lee started with Grace Wright, Sallie Pierce, and Esther Stewart, my cousin and sister-in-law. Grace lived one-half mile east of the crossroads where the Johnson schoolhouse sat. He got her home without any trouble. When they got back to the schoolhouse, the south road which he would have normally taken was drifted so high he knew he could not get through. They went on west a mile to the range line road. Soon after turning south there were tracks that showed everyone who came along had slid off the road. Fred Hiatt was there with his team of horses pulling people out. Lee tried to not slide off as the others had done but slid anyway. Fred pulled them out, and they went on about a mile to his brother John's.

Now he had Esther home, but he still had Sallie, who lived another quarter mile down the road. When he started to go on with her something broke in the car motor and it would not start. His brother John took Sallie home.

Lee called me at home telling me that he could not get home that evening. He of course had a good, warm place to stay and was welcome overnight at his brother's house.

My older brother, John William, was living with us at that time. He saw that our cows were milked and other farm chores were taken care of that evening and the next morning. After the ladies left we took the quilting frames out because our living room was very tiny. We had a kerosene three-burner stove to cook on in extremely hot weather in the summertime, and we moved it into our living room along with our drop-leaf kitchen table. I cooked and we ate in the living room.

We brought probably one hundred fifty to three hundred quart cans of home-canned fruits and vegetables, which we kept upstairs, down to the living room, lining them on the top of the piano. We closed the top over the keyboard and filled all of this with canned goods, plus the part where the songbooks and sheet music rested. Because this was not enough space, we placed the rest of the cans on the floor in the corner behind the living room stove. The next morning a quart glass can of gooseberries in the corner behind the stove had frozen and burst.

Our chimney was in the corner of the room. When we put up the coal stove we placed the door toward the corner. This way more heat would be thrown into the room. Our davenport opened into a full-sized bed. This is where the children and I tried to sleep. The end of the stairs was open into the living room. We tacked a heavy comforter over it to try to hold the heat in the living room.

John William went to sleep upstairs, but he could not get warm enough to doze off. About every hour or so he came downstairs, got himself warmed up, wrapped himself in a heavy comforter, and went back to bed. Again he could not get to sleep before he was cold and came back down to get warm again. He kept this up all night and so did not get any rest.

I tried to sleep some, but by the time I was settled the room was cold again. I would get up, put some coal in the stove, open it up and let the side get red hot, close it up and crawl back into bed. Soon it was cold in there again. I would go through the same procedure again. I did not dare lay down until I could shut the stove. I was afraid I would go to sleep and the red-hot stove would burn down the house.

The next morning when daylight came my brother went to the barn to care for the stock. Some of the feeder shoats had piled up to get warm, and a few others had smothered to death underneath.

By the next afternoon the wind had subsided, the snow had stopped, and the sun came out. The world was white and bright but still bitter cold. We looked out our south living room window and saw

Lee plodding home through impassable drifts in the south road.

The temperature that night was the coldest I had ever remembered, I believe—28 or 27 degrees below zero. I don't think that Indianapolis recorded it that low.

None of the houses we lived in those early days could be called at all comfortable when we got them, but we made them so. One of my favorite times on our forty-acre farm was when we would have a dark, dreary, chilly, rainy day. Our wood or coal heating stove had been taken down for the summer and had not yet been put back up for the winter. On these early fall days we cooked mostly on a wood and coal range. It was a wonderful day to stay in the kitchen, keeping the outside door and those to the other rooms all closed to keep the kitchen warm and cozy, with a good roaring fire in the range. How good a little warmth felt!

These days were great for making a four-or-five gallon earthen jar of sauerkraut or grape jelly or maybe shelling some lima beans or a few gunnysacks of dry cornfield beans.

Around four o'clock in the evening we could expect our two school children to arrive home from school. After chores and supper were over, there were likely some school lessons to prepare for the next day. Sometimes we popped corn or ate apples, or maybe played a game or listened to a favorite radio program on our battery radio set. Bedtime arrived early in those happy, gloomy, rainy, chilly, fall days with kerosene lamps at night. A happy season! A happy family!

Bedbugs

There were bumps in the road, of course, and lots of odd things happened, as they do in life. One odd thing folks battled was bedbugs. One day, probably a couple of years after I was married, my mother and I went to a sale, a public auction. It was in an old log house where no one ever lived in after that sale, soon torn down.

The bidding was going on outside, and my mother and I were inside the old log house. I had my baby son in my arms when I felt something creeping on the back of my neck. Naturally I reached my hand back to rub my neck. I felt a bug, picked it off, mashed it between my fingers, and threw it away, not thinking what kind of a bug it might be. I had never seen a bedbug.

In a few minutes I got my hand close enough to my nose to smell a terrible odor. I told my mother, and she said it had been a bedbug which had dropped down from the ceiling on me.

Bedbugs are a small flat bug, the dictionary says, "a small, wingless, biting insect with a broad, flat, reddish brown body and an unpleasant odor; it infests beds, upholstered furniture, etc. It is about three sixteenths of an inch long." I remember they had narrow faint stripes cross-ways of their body. My mother had told me they always had a terrible odor. Since that time an elderly lady told me that one of the bedbugs' habits was to drop from the ceiling onto a person.

When motels began to be popular, before you rented a room, you needed to examine the bed for bedbugs. Later guests would likely not find any in any motel or hotel room because there are so many things to use to get rid of them.

Like fleas and mosquitoes, some people are more susceptible to these nuisance insects than others, but they will bite arms and legs, leaving a red itching place. It is also thought that bedbugs carry diseases.

When Mary Lee was around three years old in 1931, we rented the old Meehan farm which was a little over a mile northwest of where we were living on our own forty acres. Like some of our other homes, the house there was old and not very good. There was no electricity or bathroom. It had been a rented place for many years.

We had lived there less than two weeks when one evening Mary Lee went to sleep on a cot in the living room. When I picked her up to put her to bed I saw a dark-colored bug run from her head across the white pillowcase. I caught it and mashed and killed it. From the odor I was almost sure it was a bedbug. I placed it on a saucer and kept it to show to my mother. It had been so long since she had seen one of these things and she had never seen very many that she was not sure. Since it had a bad odor we were suspicious.

The following Sunday while I was getting dinner Lee went into the dining room, the only room downstairs that had not been repapered just before we moved in except a large wash room across the back of the house. He took the point of a sharp knife and began to pry the old wallpaper loose, turning it back.

We had moved into this house in April, the spring of the year, when new life was appearing in everything. Under the edge of the wallpaper were rows and clusters, tiny new baby bedbugs about the size of chicken lice. I am sure there were hundreds, maybe thousands of them, in that room, enough to grow and infest the whole house.

Monday morning we got busy—really busy. We tore off all the wallpaper in that room and burned it along with all the big bedbugs, little bedbugs, bedbug eggs and filth. We painted every inch of wood-work and plastered walls and floor in that room with coal oil (kerosene).

Along the west wall there had at one time been a fireplace. It was closed then, but on each side from floor to ceiling were cupboards, called presses in the early days. Each one of these we painted inside and out with kerosene. We took a sprayer that we had used to spray the cows for flies and sprayed kerosene into every crack and crevice in the wood-work, plastered ceiling, side wall, and the floor. At that time kerosene or gasoline was the best thing available to rid things of bedbugs.

We also painted all three rooms, woodwork, plaster, and floors upstairs with kerosene. We really fought the dirty little bugs hard. I had seen at least one bedbug in every room in the downstairs except the wash room.

After we had lived there two months I never saw another bedbug, but I was always on the lookout for them. We had a tall wooden bed that we had not moved before we discovered the bedbugs. We never did move it there.

When we moved to this particular bedbug farm we had left our own forty-acre farm we had bought in 1929. The corner of it came to the northeast corner of the crossroads at Johnson schoolhouse.

While living on the farm we rented our house on our forty acres to an elderly couple. They were moving in the next day because their house had burned. I told my mother the names of the couple who was moving there, and she told me she would be very much surprised if they did not have bedbugs.

We certainly did not want to get them started in our rental house. The side walls and ceiling of the two back rooms were sealed with boards. Once bedbugs got in the cracks, crevices, and behind those boards, it would be almost an endless job to get rid of them.

Lee was doing custom plowing for a man a mile or so away. I went to him very upset, and told him what my mother had said. He left his plowing and went with me to our house. He told the would-be renter he had decided he could not rent the house to him. They had already moved one load of their things and I had gone into the house and inspected the tall wooden bed that was leaning against the board wall in the bedroom with its back side toward the room. The cracks in the head of that bed were lined with rows of bedbugs.

It made the man very angry because Lee had told him that he could not have the house, and he would have to get all his possessions out before dark. He argued with Lee until Lee told him why he could not rent it to him. This made him angrier than ever.

The man said, "No, no, we do not have bedbugs; whenever we get them, my wife gets rid of them." That was telling us they had had them in the past. And we knew they still had them.

Although he was so very angry, he got everything out before dark and I painted with kerosene all the walls and floor where anything of theirs had touched. So we did not get any bedbugs in our house. Saved by the skin of our teeth.

Doing the Laundry

Life continued as it had in all these places we lived—hard work and few comforts through the twenties and thirties. One of the chores which had to be done every week was washing clothes. I'd been doing laundry all my life. When I was a little girl living in Pegville, I watched my mother do the clothes—a hard, hand-work job.

The wash water was pumped by hand by the pitcher pump, which stood in the backyard near the new back porch that my father had built, then carried by bucketsful into the kitchen, enough to fill a large wash boiler on the small wood or coal cast-iron cook stove.

A small amount of lye was added to the water to break it, in other words, to soften it. If a little too much lye was added, it ate the skin off a woman's hands. When the water was hot, not boiling, a scum of white lime and yellow or brown iron rust foam would rise to the top of the water, and this had to be skimmed off, leaving the water very soft and clear. All of this was a process women had been using in this exact way for hundreds of years; Aunt Louva talked about our Wilson great grandmother using it before the turn of the century. This was in the days before any such places had or ever thought they would have the conveniences of electricity. The homemade lye soap was thinly sliced into the water or melted in a pan with water, making a strong, liquid soap.

The hot clear water was dipped out of the boiler and carried by bucketsful to the old Rocky-by washing-machine on our long back porch, where more soap was added. This Rocky-by washer was actually better than what Great Grandmother Wilson had used; she just had a washboard.

The boiler was then again filled with water from the pump in the yard and the process repeated, because Mama always washed the clothes through two hot suds. I think Grandmother Wilson used only one hot suds. Mama was a stickler for cleanliness, and that Rocky-by was a "modern improvement" anyway, which made things easier. With this contraption, the handle of the washer was then pushed back and forth, back and forth counting the strokes, up to one hundred— two hundred, more or less, depending on how soiled the clothes were. And it had a lever-operated wringer also operated by hand. So it was still hard but better. It must have been awful to scrub every piece of a family's clothing on that washboard as our grandmother did.

I'll describe the washing process from the beginning, with the machine now filled with very hot water. Mama sorted the clothes, mainly in order of the lightness and darkness of their color, but partly according to how much they were soiled, into washer-size loads. The white, least soiled load was put into the washer of very hot water first. Using the white ones first saved the sort-of clean water for more clothes.

After the whites had been scrubbed in the machine long enough until they looked clean, they were run through the rubber-rollered wringer operated by turning a crank and feeding the clothes into it, but not until they were examined for dirty spots on shirt collars and cuffs. If they had not come clean, these spots were rubbed clean on a washboard after extra soap had been added.

When the whitest load had all been run through the wringer, the second lightest in color went into the same hot suds in the washer and were taken through the same process as the first. After all the batches had been through the first water, the dirty water was carried out in bucketsful and emptied into the drive or some place where the somewhat cooled suds would not kill the grass.

The first load of white clothes now was being put into the wash boiler with the remaining hot water with soap added. The fire was built up and the boiler full of white clothes was brought to a boil and boiled for a few minutes. They were pushed down into the boiling suds now and then with a clothes stick, a three-foot length of broom handle.

After they had boiled long enough, the now very white clothes were lifted from the boiling water with the clothes stick into milk buckets and again put into the Rocky-by into the hot suds and scrubbed with the lever handle a few times, but not as many as the first time. Again they were wrung out through the wringer into a clothes basket to wait to be rinsed, while the rest were taken through the same routine. The prints and colored clothes were never boiled.

After all the clothes had been taken through the second hot suds, the washer was again emptied. This time it was filled with cold water from the well. Sometimes my mother poured a tea kettle of boiling water into the cold rinse water, she said, "just to take off the chill." I believe they were afraid the cold water would set some of the suds in the material, causing a yellowish tint.

A few balls of ball bluing, long since gone from the market, were tied in a scrap of clothes. This was placed in the rinse water in the washer and squeezed a few times causing the rinse water to become slightly blue. Then the bag of ball bluing was removed from the rinse water. This small amount of bluing kept the white clothes sparkling white, removing all traces of iron rust from the clothes.

This final rinsing process was detailed. Starting with the white clothes first, a few at a time were put into the rinse water, rubbed a little with the Rocky-by, rinsed one piece at a time, up and down in the blue water, then run between the rubber rollers with the crank, squeezing most of the water out of them. They went from the wringer into clothes baskets, ready to be hung on the line, except those which were to be starched. Those to be starched were sorted out and set to one side until there was time to make the starch. Usually the clothes that did not require starch were hung on the line first.

Then starch was made. My mother bought Argo lump starch in a blue box at the grocery store. She mixed some starch with a small amount of water, stirring it to dissolve the lumps. Then into this she poured boiling water from the tea kettle to thicken and cook it. It was then thinned and mixed with enough water in which to dip the clothing that needed starching. The excess was wrung out by hand, sometimes with the wringer. They too were then hung on the clothesline with wooden clothespins to dry.

The white clothes were hung in the sun to keep them white, the colored ones in the shade to keep the sun from bleaching and fading them. How good the washing looked and smelled that had been dried in the fresh air, sun and breeze! Some women thought they had to wash on Monday every week regardless of the weather. Others desired to wait until a sunny day.

And this was the process, Rocky-by and many loads, all done by hand, when I was first married and into the thirties. I did it all just as my mother and grandmother had.

Most of the things we washed had to be ironed. An old saying was, "If it is worth washing, it is worth ironing." Some ironed their Turkish towels. I always thought they were softer and fluffier after drying on the line in the breeze and not ironed. I liked to fold them and put them away without ironing.

When I was a child and for a long time after I was keeping a house of my own, we did not have electricity. The ironing was quite a task. My mother had two kinds of irons, both with a detachable handle fastened onto the hot iron when it was taken off the stove. As soon as the iron cooled it was exchanged for another, hotter one. The handle was taken off the first and fastened to the next one.

The irons I used when we first went to housekeeping were more old fashioned than my mother's. Their handles were permanent. Of course their handles became very hot and had to be held with a very heavy cloth pad. When the weather was cool and during the long cold winter months, we used the wood-or-coal-fed cook stoves or ranges to heat the irons, but during the hot summer days our three-burner kerosene stoves were used to heat them.

We usually used two burners and six irons per burner. A heavy iron skillet was turned upside down over each burner to carry the heat to the irons. Ironing was a tiresome job and took many hours.

Some women helped their living expenses by taking in washings and ironing each week. I was one of these women in later years when I had an electric automatic washer, dryer, and iron, which were unheard of in the early part of the century.

Those were the years I needed to make the living of our household. Lee was not strong, and his condition, which we discovered was muscular dystrophy, was progressing. Part of that time I spent in a factory. Then I was needed at home all of the time. I still needed to make the living. Washing and ironing was one way to help.

During the time I was doing Burtons' laundry and some for other people, it seemed my ironing board was up from Monday until Saturday. With their ironing and our own, including the elderly people I took into our home to care for in later years, each week I spent many tiresome hours at the ironing board.

Happy was the day in the fall of 1939 when electricity came to our farm home. The house had been wired by a trained electrician, poles had been set, and wires had been run to our house. We had been told the day the juice would be turned on, and believe me, I was prepared. I had bought a new electric iron and had a basket of clean clothes dampened, ready and waiting for the new iron. On it went and out my iron came. What an improvement, beyond words!

I often think of my mother. If only she could have had such wonderful conveniences. She did not live long enough to ever have and know the luxury of electricity.

Wallpapering

Less burdensome as a household task than washing was papering the walls. In my married life time I wallpapered several rooms. Certainly I had to put up bright papers when Lee and I furnished our homes. It was the way to add freshness to an otherwise dingy and dirty old room. I was experienced by that time because I had watched my Aunt Jane Wilson, the Bakers Corner wallpaper lady, do lots of papering of rooms.

When I was thirteen years old in 1920 my mother hired Aunt Jane to paper a room. I had wanted my mother to let me paper it, but she was afraid I would not do it right and hired Aunt Jane.

Our next-door neighbor Sallie Pierce said, though, "I'll let her paper a room." My mother allowed me to try. Sallie got the wallpaper and moved the furniture out of an upstairs room. Violet, her daughter who was three years younger than I, was to paste for me.

All went well until around ten o'clock, when some friends of the family came to pay them an all day, unexpected visit, which took Sallie and Violet away from helping me.

I then had it all to do by myself. I could do it and did not mind too much, but it made me quite a bit slower. When evening came Sallie had a nice, new, freshly papered bedroom, which she was proud of, and so was I. I thought it looked as nice as if Aunt Jane had papered it herself. I think my mother thought so, too. From then on I papered a room now and then when some relative or friend needed it.

I believe I did as good a job at age thirteen as Aunt Jane, but not nearly as fast.

Quilts

Quilting had always been part of my life, and that cold, cold night when we almost froze after a quilting bee was only one of the many times neighborhood women quilted together. I took six quilts with me when I married, as was the custom. And I certainly needed quilts that cold night—as every night in winter.

I have always liked to sew and do any kind of fancy work, including quilts. I can't remember when I did not sew doll dresses on the sewing machine. I can't remember learning to use the sewing machine—I must have been too young. Neither can I remember my mother ever trying to keep me from using it. I guess I have always had a talent for such things.

We were living on Grandpa Hodson's farm when I began making my everyday underthings, such as panties or bloomers or slips, from feed and flour sacks. I also made some gingham butterfly aprons (dresses) trimmed in red rickrack. It was while living there I started piecing my first quilt.

My mother had cut me a pattern for a Flying Star quilt block and showed me how to put the light and dark triangles together to make the block. She also gave me some pretty scraps left from some of the cotton dresses she had made.

I started cutting, placing, and sewing the triangles together on the sewing machine, but I was not quite as particular in putting them together as my Aunt Mima Briles, my mother's sister, wanted me to be. She said I was too careless and showed me how to place the centers together and sew from the middle each time. From then on my blocks were much more perfect.

I stuck with making the blocks, making a few now and then, just when I wanted to, keeping them in an old shoe box, stored in the old press on my shelf with some toys, paper dolls, and other things I wanted to keep. Eventually I had the seventy-two that it took to make a quilt top.

I had collected scraps from my aunts and Grandma Wilson. My grandma at that time made my grandpa's shirts, since Doctor Wilson was a very large man and particular about how his shirts fit. Most of them were made from some kind of print. Light colored calico was a material very much used in those days and many of his shirts were made of calico. I remember particularly some scraps she gave me that were brown percale with a fancy white stripe. She had made Grandpa a shirt from that material.

By having such a large collection of scraps I had pretty, finished quilt blocks. I kept them stored in the old shoe box until I was beginning to make quilts, preparing to get married. Then I joined those

Flying Star quilt blocks with a yellow printed calico and lined it with plain rose-colored gingham, making a pretty quilt. The imperfections did not show nearly as much after it was quilted. My mother and her neighbor Sallie Pierce quilted it.

When I was quite small, just a baby, an old lady who lived on the range line road, a short distance north of the Lafayette road, gave to my mother some quilt blocks to make a baby quilt for me. I can faintly remember going in a buggy one time to visit her. My parents liked to visit her although she was not related to us. The quilt blocks she gave to my mother were called a Sixteen Patch, made up of two inch squares, with four squares each way. All the squares were cut from dark-colored cotton material and were pieced together by hand.

When I began to make quilts, preparing to go to housekeeping, my mother had that old deaf lady, my father's distant cousin Mary Jane Trueblood Pearson, who lived about a quarter of a mile down the road, slept in others' houses, and thought ants were on her ice cream, piece enough similar blocks to make a full-size quilt top. This one I joined with a tiny dark blue gingham plaid making a very dark quilt, good for everyday use. This one also was quilted by my mother and Sallie Pierce.

Before my mother was married she made a Charm quilt of four inch squares, joined to each other with no joining material. No two pieces were cut from the same material. When I was a young teenager I decided I wanted to make a charm quilt too, so I collected scraps. Finally I had enough different kinds of squares for a full-size quilt top. Spreading them on the floor to distribute the colors evenly, I sewed them together in rows to comlete another quilt top.

I did not put a border on it, although my Aunt Mima told me that a quilt without a border is like a rooster without a tail—not very pretty. Now I think it would have been much prettier with a border. I lined it with unbleached muslin. It was not nearly as pretty as a designed block quilt, but Mama and Sallie quilted it anyway.

Another quilt that I pieced and joined before I was married was a nine-patch. Each square was about four inches in size, which made a very large block. It was pieced entirely of scraps from my cotton dresses. This I joined with a light blue striped gingham, making the stripes all run the same direction. It did not have a border and was lined with unbleached muslin and was not as pretty as some others I had done.

I made a Four-Patch pattern, with squares about three and one-half inches in size. It was just a common everyday quilt, lined with unbleached muslin, joined with pretty rose-colored tiny print calico. It also was like a rooster without a tail; it had no border. My mother and Sallie quilted all of these quilts for me while I was in school, my senior year of high school and getting ready to be married, because I needed "six quilts to go to housekeeping."

When my mother, Minnie Hodson Wilson, died March 19, 1934, she and I had been each piecing Flower Garden quilt blocks. A few of our blocks were made from the same material. She was piecing hers by hand but I was using the sewing machine for mine. At the time of her death she had fourteen blocks pieced. I put hers with mine and finished the still-needed blocks and joined them together with white muslin. For the lining of this quilt, I used the Sears Roebuck mercerized broadcloth but this time a pretty lavender shade.

I had never quilted a quilt all by myself. I knew it would take me a very long time to quilt this special one because I wanted it quilted on each side of most of the seams. I did not want the large quilting frames taking up space in our tiny living room for so long a time, so I sent to Sears Roebuck and bought a set of large round quilting hoops. These could be put away out of sight when not in use.

Finally, after many months, I finished the quilting. Then came the binding. I did not trim off the tiny points, but bound around each one of them. I sewed the bias binding, cut from the lavender broadcloth, onto the quilt with the sewing machine but whipped every stitch of it down by hand. Flower Garden quilts are always beautiful and this one had special memories.

Before my mother's death she had bought several yards of a pretty shade of medium light green quilt material. My neighbor, Alice Ehman, said if I would get something to go with it she would piece and do a quilt for me. I bought a pretty shade of pale yellow to go with it and some white and chose the Ocean Wave pattern.

Alice could make the tiniest stitches of any quilter I ever knew.

She measured every piece very exactly. That quilt was the most perfect of any I have ever seen. All the stitches are small and perfect.

For many years Cicero had a Fall Festival, similar to a miniature state fair. Many prizes and ribbons were given to the country people who brought in their wares of farm and garden produce and all kinds of crafts, art, and hand work. I took this beautiful quilt to two of these festivals, each time winning the blue ribbon for quilts. The last time with the blue ribbon was a note asking me to never again bring that quilt because no one else had a chance against such fine quilting.

More Moves and Making a Living

The years went along; World War II came and was drawing to an end. After several moves, wedding quilts and all (we always seemed to move a lot; farmers in that time did that) in the spring of 1944, Lee rented a farm one mile south of Kirklin. Mr. and Mrs. Stern, owners of the farm, moved into Kirklin. This move was the farthest we had ever moved. It was about sixteen or seventeen miles from our little forty-acre farm. The buildings were in Clinton County but part of the farmland lay in Boone County. We moved there about the first of March. Still, the old days when you moved with horses and wagons into dirty old sometimes bug-ridden places with kerosene lamps were over.

We had taken Sallie and Violet with us to help clean the house. Mrs. Stern was a good housekeeper and had left the house in good shape, but we went over it good anyway. They had left a decent linoleum on the kitchen floor, and we put our one rug on the living room floor. They had left window shades, and with the curtains we put up, the house looked very nice to move into the next day.

This move we could not move everything at one time. Eugene and Mary Lee were going to stay at the forty-acre farm and finish the school year at Jackson Central High School at Arcadia. Eugene was a senior and would be graduating, Mary Lee a freshman who would rather not change schools during the year. The things necessary for them to get along for a few weeks were to be left in our farm house.

We had Margaret Ann with us, of course.

Several neighbors wanted to help us move. I guess they were curious to see where we were going. On the moving day we were up early. This time, partly because of his failing health and because of the distance, Lee engaged a mover to take our household goods. Mr. Clark a mover from Noblesville came early. His van and the neighbors' cars as well as ours were filled. The van and neighbors had gone. Lee and I were in our car ready to pull out when we saw Lee's brother John and his wife Esther coming to help. Lee told me to stay and help them load the smokehouse things into their trailer, and come with them. He needed to go on to be there when the van was there.

By the time John and Esther and I got there the van was unloaded and gone. Most of the neighbors' cars had also been unloaded. The heating stove and coal range were both up, with good hot fires going in them. The furniture had been set in place, the table set, and the food I had sent on with the women was hot on the stove ready to eat.

That was one of our easiest moves, although it was the farthest. That evening almost everything was in place. The lights were all on. The ladies had unpacked the dishes and they were sitting bright and shiny on the cupboard shelves. We soon made the beds, the clothing had been hung up, and we were at home. That evening after supper Lee sat in a rocking chair and read the newspaper as if he had lived there for a year. Things had certainly changed for us, as they had for our neighborhood.

That spring while we were living near Kirklin, Eugene graduated from high school. We moved the rest of the furniture and stock. Margaret Ann celebrated her fourth birthday, and Lee finally retired from farming in midsummer. Mary Lee had the mumps but neither of the other children took them. Mary Lee started her sophomore year at Kirklin High School. While we were living in that house, Eugene and Mary King were married on October 18, 1944.

We loved living on that modern Kirklin farm. It was an easy place to keep, even the house was easy to keep clean. But Mrs. Stern, who owned the farm, had lived there all of her life until they moved into Kirklin. She became homesick and wanted to move back to the farm. That meant we had to move again. Eugene and Mary had been living with us after their marriage. We both needed places to go.

We still owned our little forty-acre farm. We rented a farm on the Cicero-Sheridan road and moved there. Eugene and Mary then moved onto our farm.

As I have mentioned, my husband Lee developed muscular dystrophy and was forced to retire in 1944. After a year there we felt it was unsafe for Lee to be around the cows and to milk them because of his falling so often and being unable to get up by himself. Someone had to make a family living; we still had a daughter at home and in school. So I went to work at Lament's Glove Factory in Noblesville to help make the living. I was riding to work with a cousin of mine, Herbert Foulke. We then moved into half a house of my Aunt Myrtie Coffin in Westfield.

During the year and three months we lived there Mary Lee went her senior year and graduated from Westfield High School, and Margaret Ann started first grade. Our first grandchild, a little girl, Kathie Jean, was born to Eugene and Mary on Christmas Day, December 25, 1946.

I changed jobs from the glove factory at Noblesville to Biddle's Screw Machine Products at Sheridan. I worked for Biddle's Screw Machine Products for eight years. I was the third woman hired in the factory part after the factory opened in Sheridan. It was interesting to me in both these places to be off the farm and in a group of men and women who were working together, getting paid, and getting to know each other maybe better than they wanted to. Sometimes shenanigans went on, too, as they will in a work place.

The two women already working there were Ethel Waitt, who was about ten years older than I, and Thesia Rockey, who was only a year older. Thesia was a maiden lady. After she had worked with us a few years she married a Kansas farmer and moved out there to live. Ethel was still working there when I quit and for many years after.

While Rockey, as we often called Thesia, was still working there, an old man we called Old Rick came there to work. He was not very clean and was given the job of clean-up man. Also he was to carry buckets of "milk," a white oil solution, to the second operation machines when needed. This was where we three women worked.

By this time a few more women had been hired into second operation, one by the name of Hilda Robinson. One day Old Rick as we sometimes called the clean-up man, asked Hilda if she would ask that maiden lady Miss Rockey for a date with him. Hilda, laughing inside, told him she would. Of course we women in the restroom had a lot of laughs about it. It was so unreasonable to think that a nice clean, respectable woman like Thesia would even think about having a date with Old Rick. But we laughingly teased her anyway. She took the teasing good naturedly. Finally the word got out over the shop that Old Rick wanted to date Miss Rockey. She was amused but was becoming disgusted and would not even ask the old man to bring oil for her machine. She would go after it herself to avoid him.

I did not like to get near the smelly old man but did not hesitate to ask him to bring oil to my machine when I needed it. When he brought oil he always liked to stay and chat a few minutes with me. I would talk to him as much as the others, which wasn't very much. I did not particularly like the way he looked and smiled at me but passed it off. What was he up to?

It soon turned out that Old Rick was mixed up in who was Miss Rockey. Rick thought I was the one who encouraged him. Did I ever get a shock! I could hardly believe it. I could understand then why he looked at me like he did and liked to talk to me. He thought I was sweet on him. This was a relief to Thesia; she did not have to avoid him any longer.

The word soon spread over the shop, but no one wanted to tell Old Rick that he was wrong. It was too much fun to let it go as it was. After a few days, Fred Fox, one of the younger fellows working there, told Rick he was mistaken, that I was married to a great big, husky fellow, and if he ever found it out he would beat the tar out of Rick.

Rick was pretty careful after that about coming around me and gave up getting a date with Miss Rockey. These doings kept things fairly interesting at Biddle's.

A Permanent Home, Thank Goodness

One Sunday morning in 1946 or 1947 we came as usual to Bakers Corner to Sunday school. We parked the car on the west side of the church near the road. Lee pointed to the little square white house across the road and said, "That right there is what I would like to have." I looked and just said, "I would, too." No more was said at that time. I went to work as usual that week and thought nothing at all about the little white house.

One evening when I came home from work, Lee met me and said, "You can have what you want if you are willing to pay the price." "What do you mean?" I wondered. "Amba has the house at Bakers Corner for sale," he told me. Amba Simmonds, a cousin, lived directly across the road from the church in Bakers Corner.

Lee had already been to see Amba's brother, Marvin Foulke, who was selling it for her, about buying the house. Marvin already had a bid on it. Marvin had told the other folks that if he got another bid on it he would be back, and he had to keep his promise. Lee raised the bid. When Marvin went back the other people raised the bid, too, but Marvin did not promise to go back again.

That evening after I had gotten home from work, Marvin called Lee on the telephone. He told Lee that the other people had raised their bid. I am sure Marvin and Amba wanted us to have the house. Marvin said, "Lee, if you will raise that bid just fifty dollars, it is yours." Lee turned around to me and said, "What shall I do?" I said, "Do as you please." Lee turned back to the telephone and said, "I'll take it."

There! We had bargained for it and had never been there to look at it. But it was wonderful! With Lee in his condition it was likely he would come to be in a wheelchair eventually. By living in this house, he would get to church so much easier and more often. Buying that meant another move, but it would likely be more permanent. Thank goodness!

A few weeks went by, and the people living there moved out. We were free to go see the inside of the house. It was tiny, but a very nice solid house. A lady from Horton came and repapered all of the rooms, we cleaned them, and we were ready to move in. Since Mary Lee was graduating, we waited until after the high school commencement to move.

On May 29, 1947, Mr. Clark, the mover from Noblesville, brought his moving van to Westfield and loaded us up again. The day was dark, chilly with snow flurries in the air. This was a happy move for us. We were again in a home of our own, a little white house in Bakers Corner, from which we hoped we would never move again. We were very crowded in the space but happy.

That fall, on her eighteenth birthday, November 2, 1947, Mary Lee married Delbert Jones and left the little white nest. The summer of 1952, following Lee's ideas, we remodeled and enlarged the little house. We added two large bedrooms downstairs and one upstairs. We also made the small bedroom into a bathroom and removed the partition from between the living room and the original larger bedroom, turning them into a large living room. This made a beautiful home and we loved it. Surely we would never want to move away from this home.

Lee's health continued to fail. It was harder for him to get around, and he fell more often. It was getting so he could hardly get up alone when he fell, so it became necessary for me to quit my job to stay at home to care for him. Someone still had to work; someone still had to make the living. Margaret Ann, our youngest, was still in high school. To make our living I had worked in a factory for almost nine years—nine months at Lament's Glove Factory at Noblesville, and then eight years at Biddle's Screw Machine Products at Sheridan. In 1954 I was needed at home so badly that I quit the factory.

I had to make a living in some way. How? I decided to start by caring for some elderly people in our home. I kept from one to four elderly folks, mostly women, in our home for seventeen years.

During those seventeen years of caring for them, some things happened with which I do not care to connect names. One of my old ladies would not, simply would not, clean herself good enough to get rid of a horrible odor. Can you take a bath with your shoes and stockings on? She could—so she said.

While I was on a trip to California, another of my elderly ladies sat down on the toilet stool with the seat up and stuck fast. She could not get up by herself. Mary tried to help her, but the two of them could not get her up. Mary had to get Eugene to get her off that seat. This was embarrassing to both of them.

That was the August 1960 trip I took to California with my brother John William and his wife Evelyn and daughter Jeanie to visit our father Archie. My father had remarried in 1935, and after living in Noblesville for several years, he and his wife Charlotte moved to California in 1944. We did not get to see them often, although we kept in touch through letters. On this visit we convinced him to come back with us to Indiana for an extended visit. We were so fortunate that he was able to stay through January 1961 for Margaret Ann's wedding to Kenneth Stewart. He returned to California, where he died in 1964 from complications of Parkinson's disease.

The caring for the elderly went along well for many years. Then Lee became very ill with a heart attack. After being critical for two weeks he was taken to the veteran's hospital at Indianapolis with a very serious illness with his heart and complications. During the six weeks he was in the hospital, it seemed there was not much chance for his improvement. But one day they sent him home. He was better.

In a day or two he told me that he said to himself while in the hospital that if he lived to get home, he was going to build a new house on our vacant lot beside the other house. I thought this was one of the most foolish things I had ever heard. I was afraid Lee would not live a month, maybe not even a week, after he came home. He had been taken off the critical list and sent home, but he was not well.

I talked to our children about it. They said, "If Daddy wants a new house, build it." I was ashamed for anyone to know about it, it looked so foolish. I did not tell many people about it. That winter Eugene took us around to decide on a plan. We decided on one to be built by Capitol Lumber Company at Indianapolis.

The next-door house was started on April 6, 1964. On August 15, 1964, we would be moving again, this time into a brand-new house of our own. For a long time I had been calling this house "Invalid House" because it had been planned to care for an invalid and for an invalid to live in, with low windows so he could see out and a large bathroom with a wide door into it. We planned a wider hall than most newer houses, and there was no partition between living room and kitchen and very few steps. The garage was to be heated for loading and unloading him. All of this made it more convenient for a wheelchair.

The house was finished in the middle of July. It had only two coats of finish on the woodwork, and I wanted four. Lee said I had better put the other two on before moving in because it would be very hard to do after we had moved in. I did and the house was ready. All of our family, children, grandchildren, in-laws, and even grand-daughter Kathie's boyfriend helped us move. In order for everyone to help we needed to move on Saturday, so Saturday, August 15, 1964, was set for moving day.

And so I was moving again, after I said I hoped we never would. But this was just next door. Nothing needed to be packed. The dishes could be placed in baskets and carried over. Other things would be picked up and carried over and put in place. Lee did not need to be put in the car, just pushed over in the wheelchair. I have often wondered but never asked who pushed him over.

Early that morning everyone came, as the saying goes, "rarin' to go." Everyone but me. I had gotten up early, but before the helpers came, I was taken down with a very severe migraine headache. In those days a migraine put me out for the rest of the day, sometimes longer. I went to the back room, pulled the window shades and the door curtain, and piled down on the floor on a heavy comforter. I was very fortunate I could go to sleep, the only cure for a migraine.

At noon, when they awakened me to go to the new house for dinner, most of the things had been carried over. "Many hands make light work," is an old saying; how true it is. The furniture was in place, and many things had been put away.

I still needed to add some more shelves in the pantry, closets, and garage before I could completely straighten everything.

We were moved, at least things from the house; the things in the barn could be taken care of later. And so it was our last move as a couple, married all those years. For Lee that did not include his trips to the hospital. There he passed away on February 1, 1975.

I was lonely lots of times and missed Lee so very much, but I tried to overcome it, knowing that he was so much better off and that he had wanted so much to leave this old earth for his heavenly home. I was doing well as a widow, I thought. My son was helping me with business, and he and his wife saw that I needed nothing. I was never of a disposition to be lonesome as much as many women.

One summer day in 1977, a man named Myron Robbins came to my front door to ask if I could help him with Baker genealogy. I was not directly related to the Bakers but Aunt Louva had given me a small book about them, so I invited him in. It seemed that God had a hand in this meeting. Years ago, when Lee had been critically ill, my Aunt Louva said she hoped that if Lee did not get better, that some day I would find a husband that was able bodied and liked the same things I did. Aunt Louva had died in 1976, so she never knew that little book on Baker genealogy started us on our courtship.

Myron and I became good friends, fell in love, and were married in less than a year on February 12, 1978. We enjoyed the same things: travel, history, and genealogy. Over our twenty-five-year marriage, we took many wonderful trips across the country to visit family and friends, enjoyed several church tours to historic and family places, and worked together on our genealogy and church projects. I believe our marriage was a true plan of God. "God works in mysterious ways His wonders to perform."

I did not have to leave our little brick house. He moved into it with me. We both hoped we could stay here as long as we lived.

There had been so much leaving of houses and going into different ones. But always as we moved, we went up, if only a little. And always there was that sense of a good home. I could sense the bonds of our family around our dinner tables, when everybody seemed to feel loved and welcome, and we sometimes laughed until we cried at a good joke. There's something satisfying about living near the same place all your life, and not everybody gets to do that. I could reminisce that I had started in Bakers Corner and now here I was for good, living about two hundred yards from the corner where the schoolhouse stood and twenty steps from the church that was so important to me all my life. A circle of living, and most of it good.

Reflections on Life

One time my uncle said to me, "Don't dwell on the past; look forward to the future." That is fine for the young and middle aged, but since I have gotten older, although I have had my share of sadness and sorrow, ups and downs, sometimes I like to think back over my eighty-five years to the many happy hours of childhood; school days; my happy life that followed; my two wonderful husbands; my three lovely children; five good-to-me, stepchildren, grandchildren and great grandchildren; and many, many friends. Could anyone ask for more?

There are of course advantages and disadvantages to growing older. One of the advantages is length of days, which may give a little wisdom or at least perspective. I lived long enough to see what the word "inflation" means. At one point, when I was a grandmother, we received through the mail "Dr. Leonard's Health-care catalog." There were a few things we were rather interested in. I looked through the catalog and came across a small can of White Cloverine Salve. It looked so familiar it brought back some childhood memories.

I was still in grade school in Bakers Corner, probably in the fifth or sixth grade. There was an ad in a farm magazine for one to send for twelve cans of White Cloverine Salve to sell to neighbors and friends for twenty-five cents each. With each can the customer received their choice of a picture suitable for framing: the picture was around twelve by fifteen inches in size.

My parents allowed me to answer the ad and I sent for the salve. I walked around to our country neighbors to sell them. In those days twenty-five cents was not as easy to come by as now and a quarter was spent less freely.

Nevertheless I sold most of them, maybe a couple never got sold but were around home to be used for a long time. There was a percentage of money I received. I was happy to get it. I had earned it myself.

I still have a can of the White Cloverine Salve that I bought in a drugstore several years after I had sold it. There is still a small amount of salve in it. It keeps well. I do not remember what it cost, but I do remember it was much more than twenty-five cents.

Then there is that recent one I saw in the catalog. The clover blossom design on the lid of the tin box was the same on both of these last boxes. The ingredients are listed the same. On the can from the drugstore it says it was manufactured in New York, N.Y. The one in the catalog says it is manufactured in Jackson, Wyoming. The one from the drug store says "Since 1895," it also says "Fine Original."

The one from the catalogue shows it costs almost six dollars. Surely, surely they cannot charge $5.99 for one small one ounce, twenty-five cent tin box of White Cloverine Salve? Who would pay that much? Then I thought, "That is not all, there is postage, which has inflated, too." I looked to see and could hardly believe it would cost $2.49 to handle and ship a small article like a one-ounce can of White Cloverine Salve.

Then my husband spoke up and said, "It will cost twenty-nine cents for a stamp to mail your order, and this company charges sales tax, which would be thirty cents."

This makes a total of $9.07 for one tiny, one-ounce, twenty-five-cent can of White Cloverine Salve. Inflation!

Or maybe I have just lived a long time. I knew that already!

The old saying is: If it rains on the wedding day, the bride will reap a life of tears. We always hope not…

It rained on my first wedding day, all morning. My father took Lee and me to Noblesville in the forenoon to get our marriage license. It was June 17, 1925, and the weather was warm, but there was that continual rain all the way there and all the way back.

I had heard the saying about rain on the wedding day. I hoped my life would not be a life of tears. As I look back over the fifty years we lived together, it was a happy fifty years. Of course there were tears, but there is no life without tears. My tears and burdens of those fifty years were caused mainly because of the failure of Lee's health.

In the darkest moments of old age, I might sometimes feel I have outlived my time and am not needed any more. I suppose all people who reach advanced old age do. I could see myself as just an old woman named "Grandma" with only a few old friends left. The littlest family members don't know me. They hide behind their mothers' skirts when they see me and wonder, "Who is that silly old woman?" Will I be missed, I sometimes wonder.

But as I have been writing these stories so many, many memories flood my mind. So many happy ones. If I could write them all, what an enormous book it would make. Most of the time I am glad and thank God that I have been privileged to live such a happy life in a country where we can worship God as we please and look forward to a home in heaven with Jesus and loved ones.

There is a story about "I've Pitched My Tent in Beulah." When the brick church was very new, the song was sung with much vigor and zest. At some point in the later years of the church my cousin and friend, Elizabeth Hodson Bevington, who lived in Terre Haute, asked me if I remembered this song and if I had a copy of it. I did not find it in my father's old songbook and decided I did not have it.

Then Miriam, our pastor's wife, asked me for some old songs from the earliest days of the new church to be used at the homecoming. I looked in the piano bench. There were two old songbooks, one "Songs of Mounting Up No. II." I took them to my easy chair, sat down, and relaxed. I wanted to reminisce. I was enjoying myself immensely when suddenly there was "I've Pitched My Tent in Beulah." I was really excited, I had found it, just what Elizabeth wanted. Our pastor, Max Kingsolver, made several copies enough for everyone. It was sung by the congregation. I think everyone enjoyed it, especially the four of us who remembered it from long ago: Elizabeth Hodson Bevington, Susan Baker McDole, Margaret Hodson, and I, Mary Elizabeth Wilson Stewart Robbins. This favorite song of mine is on the next page.

43 I've Pitched My Tent in Beulah.

(Respectfully dedicated to the choir at Hadlow Rock.)

M. J. H.   Mrs. M. J. HARRIS.

1. I long a-go left E-gypt, for the promised land, I trust-ed in my
2. I fol-lowed close be-side Him and the land soon found, I did not halt or
3. I start-ed for the high-lands where the fruits a-bound, I pitched my tent near
4. My heart is so en-rapt-ured as I press a-long, Each day I find new

Sav-ior and to His guiding hand, He led me out to vict'ry through the
tram-ble, for Ca-naan I was bound, My Guide I ful-ly trust-ed and He
He-brea, there grapes of eshcol found, With milk and hon-ey flowing, and new
blessings which fill my heart with song, I'm ev-er marching on-ward to that

great red sea, I sang a song of triumph, and shout-ed I am free.
led me in, I shout-ed hal-le-lu-jah, my heart is free from sin.
wine so free, I have no love for E-gypt, it has no charms for me.
land on high, Some day I'll reach my mansion that's build-ed in the sky.

CHORUS.

You need not look for me, down in E-gypt's sand, For I have pitched my

tent far up in Beu-lah land; You tent far up in Beu-lah land.

Mary Elizabeth and Lee Stewart wedding photograph June 17, 1925.

Mary Elizabeth and her two older children Eugene and Mary Lee 1936. (Evelyn Wilson)

The Lee Stewart family. L to R: Mary Elizabeth, Eugene, Margaret Ann (baby), Mary Lee, and Lee, about 1940.

A Good Dairy Market

*TRY WILSON'S MILK FOR CAKES, ICE
CREAM AND COOKING IN GENERAL*

SELL YOUR MILK TO WILSON

THE DAIRY INDUSTRY is fast increasing
in this State. The dairy cow brings a steady
income and the farmer does not have to take
the risk on the market, that he does with
other classes of farming. The farmer with
good cows and a silo makes the most profits
from the dairy business.
MORAL: A Silo and a Registered Bull on
every farm.

SHERIDAN, INDIANA

*John T. Pickett (1870-1946), brother of Susan Pickett Wilson,
hauled milk for Wilson's Condensed Milk Company for many
years. He is shown here on July 13, 1941.(Jim Pickett)*

*Indiana Condensed Milk Com-
pany, founded about 1900 by W.
N. Wilson, was internationally
known. The business was sold
to Kraft in 1955. This advertisement appeared in the Bakers
Corner church cookbook in the
1920s.*

*Archie Wilson family 1947. Front (L to R): Robert and Ernest Wilson, Margaret Ann
Stewart, and Jean Wilson. Second Row (L to R): Mary Elizabeth Stewart, Mary Lee Stewart,
Roberta Wilson, Mary Stewart, Evelyn Wilson, and Lee Stewart. Back (L to R): Myron Wilson, Gene Stewart holding daughter Kathie, and John William Wilson. (Myron and Roberta's
daughter Mary Mae Wilson was born in 1949.)*

Bakers Corner Wesleyan Methodist Church Mothers Day Sunday, 1951. (Evelyn Schmollinger)

BAKERS CORNER

Wesleyan Methodist Church

HOME COMING

and

GOLDEN ANNIVERSARY *(of the Dedication)*

MAY 4, 5, & 6, 1917 -------- MAY 7, 1967

REV. LLOYD LOUKS, PASTOR

R. R. 2   Sheridan, Indiana 46069

Phone: 758-4168

~ ~ ~ We Welcome You To Our Services Today ~ ~ ~

Bakers Corner Wesleyan Methodist Church was founded in 1870. The congregation built a frame structure shortly thereafter that stood just north of the crossroads. In 1916-1917 they built the current building on 236th street, the main street through the community. (Evelyn Wilson)

Lee and Mary Elizabeth and family lived in this home in Bakers Corner from 1947 to 1964.

Mary Elizabeth married Myron Foulke Robbins (1911-2006) on February 12, 1978. Their twenty-five year marriage was filled with trips, hobbies, and family gatherings.

Mary Elizabeth giving a presentation at a church homecoming in her grandma Hodson's bonnet about 1990.

Mary Elizabeth in her living room in Bakers Corner 1998. Here she wrote stories, peeled potatoes, visited with friends and family who stopped by or relaxed for moment or two. (Carol Longenecker)

Mary Elizabeth Wilson: My Family Ties. . . .

I have always been interested in family history.

I ask myself, how did I, Mary Elizabeth Wilson Stewart Robbins get to where I am? Who went before? What were they like? Realizing that we have eight great grandparents, all of us have over fifty direct ancestors if we go back one hundred and fifty years, to say nothing of relatives on all sides.

I am going to tell some brief stories about only a few of these and go back only two generations. Mostly I want to talk about the lives of two of the especially interesting ancestors: those of my grandfather's. These are the ones whose records I have been able to locate and they show my roots! They also let us glimpse a little of the earliest history in Hamilton County in Indiana

Grandpa John Hodson, my mother's father, was born in Hamilton County, but his parents had been here only a year when he was born. His father and mother came to settle here in the fall of 1838. Hamilton County had not been settled long when they arrived to their homestead just south of what today is Bakers Corner. His father Uri drove a covered wagon from southwestern Ohio; his bride Great Grandmother Mary and possessions were inside.

Great Grandfather Uri had paid a man to put up a log cabin, which was to be ready when the family arrived. The man had grown ill; he could not finish the cabin and thus when the Hodsons arrived on the cold winter evening, they faced a dismal welcome. Their cabin not being finished when they arrived, and had to sleep the night in the covered wagon. When they awoke the next morning, three inches of snow was on the ground. They had to pull up the floor boards in the cabin to build a fire.

The wild deer, bear, and wolves were still roaming this part of the country at that time, as well as wild turkeys and other small game. They formed a good part of our pioneer ancestors' diets.

Uri helped slaves seeking their freedom in the underground railroad. His second wife Anne Baker Bailey helped the colored John Rhodes family when their slave master came to get them. Uri was a signed witness on the will of John Rhodes the colored ex-slave. Uri's children: Aunt Mary Hodson Foulke and Grandpa John Hodson grew up. John Hodson and Mary Elizabeth Bates were married at New London, Howard County, Indiana December 26, 1866. Grandpa was twenty-seven years old.

Grandpa Hodson had bought land, one-hundred sixty acres, of his father, of which only seven acres had been cleared, across the road from his father. John and Mary Elizabeth Hodson set up housekeeping in the old back part of his father's house and lived there until he could get the little four room house built on his own land. It was built in the timber with the trees so close he chopped them and brought the timber in from where it fell.

In 1881 the four room house became the back part of his large ten room home where we eventually lived with him. So many houses in Hamilton County "evolved" like that, from round or hewn logs to milled lumber, sometimes both on top of each other.

But in the beginning Grandpa Hodson set about clearing his land with his own hands. At one time he had five miles of rail fence on his farm. He had split all of the logs himself, from the trees on his own land. He also had a very large bank barn built. He made a beautiful farm of it.

My other grandparents were William and Susan Pickett Wilson. The Wilsons and Picketts were real covered wagon pioneers also. William's father was Howland Embree Wilson, born May 14, 1826 in Guilford County, North Carolina. He was the fifth child among eight sons and three daughters of John and Mary (Osborn) Wilson. It is thought Mary Osborn was an Indian maiden of the same tribe as Pocahontas. The Wilsons were Quakers.

Howland had an incident with the Friends church, there, however. Howland and his brother Nathan took part in a Presbyterian neighbor's wedding. The Quakers were very strict in those days; their members were not allowed to marry outside, or participate in, weddings outside the church. A committee of three men called on the two brothers. Nathan repented and said he was sorry, but Howland said, "I have done nothing wrong, why should I say I am sorry?" Nathan was taken back into the church but Howland was "churched," meaning, put out of the church as a member.

Great Grandmother Ruth H. Stanley, Howland's future wife, had a niece, Ruth Foster who was younger that she. When they were girls they had attended New Garden Boarding School (now called Guilford College) in Guilford County, North Carolina, together.

It was a school rule that the girls must wear the dark gray, plain Quaker garb with a small white cap on their heads. When a girl was interested in a boy she set the little cap jauntily to one side.

One morning a fireplace at the school needed repair. Thomas Wilson was called to work on it. Both Ruths decided to "set" their caps for Uncle Tom. The next morning, Howland, my great-grand-father-to-be, came to finish the job. Ruth Stanley said to the other Ruth, "Thee can have Thomas Wilson. I am setting my cap for Howland." They both got their man.

Howland Embree Wilson and Ruth H. Stanley were married October 15, 1846.

Thomas A. Wilson and Ruth Foster were married September 28, 1853.

Since Great Grandfather Howland had been churched, Ruth Stanley Wilson was also churched, or left out of the church and could not be married there. They were married in Raleigh, North Carolina.

It is thought that it was the summer of 1851 that Great Grandfather Howland with his wife Ruth, and their two children, Jesse Elwood born July 13, 1847 and Mary Ellen born August 19, 1850 came from near Greensboro, Guilford County, North Carolina to Spiceland, Henry County, Indiana.

They came by a train of eleven covered wagons mostly of relatives. It was said that Great Grandmother Ruth Wilson was pregnant for their third child, Thomas Clarkson, Uncle Clark Wilson, on this trip. Howland and Ruth's fifth and last child, a son, William Linden was born July 30, 1860. He was my grandfather.

When young William Wilson was five years old, 1865, the family moved to Hamilton County. They settled near Bakers Corner, one mile north and three fourths of a mile east of what is now 236th Street and State Road 31 intersection. The buildings sat far back from the road on the south side. Although there was at one time a dirt road running north and south past this place, it was probably there when they moved there.

When they moved into the log house that would be their home, there was just one room and an attic called a loft. First Great Grandfather built two rooms on either side of the little house, then three rooms across the back, still later a partially enclosed back porch. In this house, now long gone, they raised their family. Still later he built a new house and barn.

Great Grandfather Howland Wilson was a very, very large man. An opinionated but often jolly man, he did not believe in, and was very opposed to the use of tobacco and strong drink of any kind. He did not even believe in drinking coffee, but drank gallons of rich, whole milk with all the cream left in and ate heavily. Great Grandmother Ruth drank coffee and wanted enough rich cream in it "to make it the color of a new saddle."

During the Civil War Howland, being a Quaker, did not believe in war, fighting or killing and did not go to war, but was a government blacksmith. He shod horses and did many other blacksmith jobs for the Northern army.

Great Grandfather Howland Wilson did barn raising—putting up many of the barns in the community. A man decided to build a barn—got all of his lumber, sills, pegs and everything ready—and a day was set. The neighbors all gathered in, the men to do the building and the women to do the cooking. It was a big neighborhood affair. Great Grandfather did the bossing or the directing, telling each man what to do. At the end of the day—there was a new barn.

My grandfather William Wilson, Howland and Ruth's son, grew up in Hamilton County and became a doctor. He married Susan Pickett from another Hamilton County pioneer family. I have told more of his story, and more of the story of my other grandfather (and the two grandmothers) in this book.

Wilson

Pickett

Hodson

Bates

Howland E Wilson (1826-1889)

Ruth Stanley Wilson (1825-1902)

William Pickett (1824-1897)

Lydia Simcox Pickett (1826-1707)

Uri Hodson (1811-1886)

Mary Thornburgh Hodson (1811-1812)

John Bates (1808-1898)

Jemima Rees Bates (1822-1858)

Mark Hodson (1842-1912)

Elizabeth Hodson (1842-1906)

Susannah Jane Baker (1848-1906)

Phebe (n.d.)

Mary Hodson Fouke (1841-1919)

John Hodson (1839-1917)

Jesse Elwood Wilson (1847-1930)

Mary Ellen Baker (1850-1909)

James Harley Wilson (1847-1915)

Job Wilson (1848-1911)

Sarah Cornell (1851-1823)

Martha Jessup (1853-)

Mary Simmonds (1856-1843)

Rhoda (1857-1859)

Susan Wilson (1860-1891)

Enos (1862-1927)

William (1866-1944)

John T. (1870-1946)

Thomas Clarkson Wilson (1852-1927)

Narcissa Fouke (1855-1877)

William Linden Wilson (1860-1945)

Archie I Wilson (1892-1981)

Lisbon Wilson (1884-)

Clyde I Wilson (1895-1975)

Louva Wilson Baker (1891-1983)

Harley (1867-1958)

Myrtle Coffin (1869-1956)

Alma Brils (1870-1952)

Florence (1873-1873)

Anna Acore (1874-1946)

Ernest (1881-1960)

Minnie Wilson (1883-1934)

Myron Layton Wilson (1919-1998)

John William Wilson (1891-1913)

Mary Elizabeth Wilson (1907-2003)

229

OLD AUNT MARY'S

Wasn't it pleasant, O brother mine,
In those old days of the lost sunshine
Of youth-when the Saturday's chores were through,
And the "Sunday's wood" in the kitchen, too,
And we went visiting, "me and you,"
Out to Old Aunt Mary's?

It all comes back so clear today!
Though I am as bald as you are gray-——
Out by the barn-lot, and down the lane,
We patter along in the dust again,
As light as the tips of the drops of rain,
Out to Old Aunt Mary's!

We cross the pasture, and through the wood
Where the old gray snag of the poplar stood,
Where the hammering "red-heads" hopped awry,
And the buzzard "raised" in the "clearing" sky
And lolled and circled,-as we went by
Out to Old Aunt Mary's.

And then in the dust of the road again;
And the teams we met, and the countrymen;
And the long highway, with sunshine spread
As thick as butter on country bread,
Our cares behind, and our hearts ahead
Out to Old Aunt Mary's.

Why, I see her now in the open door,
Where the little gourds grew up the sides and o'er
The clapboard roof!—And her face—ah, me!
Wasn't it good for a boy to see—
And wasn't it good for a boy to be
Out to Old Aunt Mary's?

The jelly—the jam and the marmalade,
And the cherry and Quince "preserves" she made!
And the sweet sour pickles of peach and pear,
With cinnamon in 'em, and all things rare!—
And the more we ate was the more to spare,
"Out to Old Aunt Mary's!

—By James Whitcomb Riley.
Copied from one of my grade school readers. M.E.R.

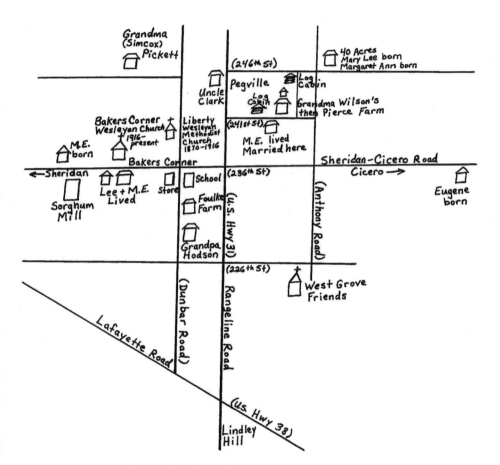

Bakers Corner during Mary Elizabeth's growing-up years.

Index

All towns and counties are in Indiana unless otherwise indicated.

X

Y

Z